Tkinter GUI Application Development Blueprints
Second Edition

Build nine projects by working with widgets, geometry management, event handling, and more

Bhaskar Chaudhary

BIRMINGHAM - MUMBAI

Tkinter GUI Application Development Blueprints
Second Edition

Commissioning Editors: Aaron Lazar
Acquisition Editor: Denim Pinto
Content Development Editors: Lawrence Veigas
Technical Editor: Adhithya Haridas
Copy Editor: Safis Editing
Project Coordinator: Prajakta Naik
Proofreader: Safis Editing
Indexers: Pratik Shirodkar
Graphics: Jisha Chirayil
Production Coordinator: Deepika Naik

First published: November 2015
Second edition: March 2018

Production reference: 1160318

Published by Packt Publishing Ltd.
Livery Place
35 Livery Street
Birmingham
B3 2PB, UK.

ISBN 978-1-78883-746-0

www.packtpub.com

`mapt.io`

Mapt is an online digital library that gives you full access to over 5,000 books and videos, as well as industry leading tools to help you plan your personal development and advance your career. For more information, please visit our website.

Why subscribe?

- Spend less time learning and more time coding with practical eBooks and Videos from over 4,000 industry professionals
- Improve your learning with Skill Plans built especially for you
- Get a free eBook or video every month
- Mapt is fully searchable
- Copy and paste, print, and bookmark content

PacktPub.com

Did you know that Packt offers eBook versions of every book published, with PDF and ePub files available? You can upgrade to the eBook version at `www.PacktPub.com` and as a print book customer, you are entitled to a discount on the eBook copy. Get in touch with us at `service@packtpub.com` for more details.

At `www.PacktPub.com`, you can also read a collection of free technical articles, sign up for a range of free newsletters, and receive exclusive discounts and offers on Packt books and eBooks.

Contributors

About the author

Bhaskar Chaudhary is a professional programmer and information architect.
He has a decade of experience in consulting, contracting, and educating in the field of software development. He has worked with a large set of programming languages on various platforms over the years.
He is an electronics hobbyist and a musician in his free time.

I would like to thank my parents for everything that I am. Thanks to my wife Sangita, son Chaitanya, sisters Priyanki and Shambhavi, niece Akanksha, nephew Praneet, and friend Souvik for being around. Anurag, you are always remembered.

About the reviewer

Erik S. Rapert is a pale, slim programmer and a twin who loves Linux and video games. He lives in Dallas with his wife, who is also a software engineer. Erik has a wide range of experience, which includes creating blinking LEDs using Arduino, building small desktop apps using Python and Tkinter, web development with PHP or Ruby, and developing cutting-edge virtual reality using C++. He has used a very broad range of programming languages, but Python is one of his favorites.

Thank you William C. Slater for teaching me how to write software. Thank you Andrew Closson for being a teacher. Thank you Ashley N. Tharp for being you.

Packt is searching for authors like you

If you're interested in becoming an author for Packt, please visit `authors.packtpub.com` and apply today. We have worked with thousands of developers and tech professionals, just like you, to help them share their insight with the global tech community. You can make a general application, apply for a specific hot topic that we are recruiting an author for, or submit your own idea.

Table of Contents

Preface

Tkinter GUI Application Development Blueprints, *Second Edition* will walk you through the process of developing real-world graphical applications using Python and Tkinter, the built-in GUI module of Python.

This book attempts to highlight the features and capabilities of Tkinter while demonstrating best practices involved in writing GUI programs, irrespective of the library that you choose to build your application with. Here, you will learn how to use Tkinter to develop exciting, fun, and useful GUI applications with Tkinter and Python.

We hope to take you on a fun journey through more than 10 projects from different problem domains. As we develop new applications in each project, the book also builds up a catalog of some commonly used strategies to develop real-world applications.

Who this book is for

Software developers, scientists, researchers, engineers, students, and programming hobbyists with basic familiarity with Python will find this book interesting and informative. A motivated Python newbie with a background in writing programs can fill in the gaps of knowledge with a little outside research.

People familiar with basic programming constructs in other programming languages can also catch up with some brief reading on Python. No GUI programming experience is assumed.

What this book covers

Chapter 1, *Meet Tkinter*, begins from scratch, providing an overview of Tkinter and covering details of how to create root windows, add widgets to a root window, handle layout with geometry managers, and work with events.

Chapter 2, *Making a Text Editor*, develops a text editor using the procedural style of programming. It gives readers their first taste of several features of Tkinter and what it is like to develop a real application.

Chapter 3, *Programmable Drum Machine*, uses object-oriented programming to develop a drum machine that is capable of playing user-composed rhythms. The application can also save compositions and later edit or replay them. Here, you will learn the techniques of designing a GUI application using a model-first philosophy and writing multithreaded GUI applications.

Chapter 4, *Game of Chess*, introduces the key aspects of structuring a GUI application using the model-view-controller (MVC) architecture. It also teaches the art of taking a real-world object (chess) and modeling it in the notations that your program can manipulate. In addition, it introduces readers to the power of the Tkinter Canvas widget.

Chapter 5, *Building an Audio Player*, covers the concepts of working with external libraries while showing you how to work with many different Tkinter widgets. Most importantly, it shows how to make your own Tkinter widgets, thereby extending the capabilities of the Tkinter manifold.

Chapter 6, *Paint Application*, looks at the Tkinter Canvas widget in detail. As you will see, the Canvas widget is truly a highlight of Tkinter. The chapter also introduces the concept of the GUI framework, thereby creating reusable code for all your future programs.

Chapter 7, *Piano Tutor*, demonstrates how to represent the given domain information using JSON and then apply the data thus created to create an interactive application. It also discusses the concept of program responsiveness and how to handle it with Tkinter.

Chapter 8, *Fun with Canvas*, is dedicated to harnessing the powerful visualization capabilities of Tkinter's canvas widget. It looks at examples from several important mathematical domains to build different kinds of useful and beautiful simulations.

Chapter 9, *Multiple Fun Projects*, works through a series of small but functional projects, demonstrating problems from different domains such as animation, network programming, socket programming, database programming, asynchronous programming, and multithreaded programming.

Chapter 10, *Miscellaneous Tips*, discusses some vital aspects of GUI programming that, though not covered in the previous chapters, form a common theme in many GUI programs.

To get the most out of this book

We assume an introductory level familiarity with the basic constructs of Python programming language. We use Python version 3.6 with Tkinter 8.6, and it is recommended to stick to these exact versions to avoid compatibility issues.

The programs discussed in this book have been developed on the Linux Mint platform. However, given the multiplatform abilities of Tkinter, you can easily work on other platforms such as Windows, Mac OS, and other distributions of Linux. The links to download and install other project-specific modules and software are mentioned in the respective chapters.

Download the example code files

You can download the example code files for this book from your account at `www.packtpub.com`. If you purchased this book elsewhere, you can visit `www.packtpub.com/support` and register to have the files emailed directly to you.

You can download the code files by following these steps:

1. Log in or register at `www.packtpub.com`.
2. Select the **SUPPORT** tab.
3. Click on **Code Downloads & Errata**.
4. Enter the name of the book in the **Search** box and follow the onscreen instructions.

Once the file is downloaded, please make sure that you unzip or extract the folder using the latest version of:

- WinRAR/7-Zip for Windows
- Zipeg/iZip/UnRarX for Mac
- 7-Zip/PeaZip for Linux

The code bundle for the book is also hosted on GitHub at `https://github.com/PacktPublishing/Tkinter-GUI-Application-Development-Blueprints-Second-Edition`. We also have other code bundles from our rich catalog of books and videos available at `https://github.com/PacktPublishing/`. Check them out!

Download the color images

We also provide a PDF file that has color images of the screenshots/diagrams used in this book. You can download it here: `https://www.packtpub.com/sites/default/files/downloads/TkinterGUIApplicationDevelopmentBlueprintsSecondEdition_ColorImages.pdf`.

Conventions used

There are a number of text conventions used throughout this book.

`CodeInText`: Indicates code words in text, database table names, folder names, filenames, file extensions, pathnames, dummy URLs, user input, and Twitter handles. Here is an example:

"The `reset_to_initial_locations()` method initializes all the locations to reflect the starting position of the game."

A block of code is set as follows:

```
def toggle_play_button_state(self):
  if self.now_playing:
    self.play_button.config(state="disabled")
  else:
    self.play_button.config(state="normal")
```

When we wish to draw your attention to a particular part of a code block, the relevant lines or items are set in bold:

```
def on_loop_button_toggled(self):
  self.loop = self.to_loop.get()
  self.keep_playing = self.loop
  if self.now_playing:
    self.now_playing = self.loop
  self.toggle_play_button_state()
```

Any command-line input or output is written as follows:

```
>>> import pyglet
>>> help(pyglet.media)
```

Bold: Indicates a new term, an important word, or words that you see onscreen. For example, words in menus or dialog boxes appear in the text like this. Here is an example: "In our example, we will add menu items to the **File**, **Edit**, and **About** menu."

Warnings or important notes appear like this.

 Tips and tricks appear like this.

Get in touch

Feedback from our readers is always welcome.

General feedback: Email `feedback@packtpub.com` and mention the book title in the subject of your message. If you have questions about any aspect of this book, please email us at `questions@packtpub.com`.

Errata: Although we have taken every care to ensure the accuracy of our content, mistakes do happen. If you have found a mistake in this book, we would be grateful if you would report this to us. Please visit `www.packtpub.com/submit-errata`, selecting your book, clicking on the Errata Submission Form link, and entering the details.

Piracy: If you come across any illegal copies of our works in any form on the Internet, we would be grateful if you would provide us with the location address or website name. Please contact us at `copyright@packtpub.com` with a link to the material.

If you are interested in becoming an author: If there is a topic that you have expertise in and you are interested in either writing or contributing to a book, please visit `authors.packtpub.com`.

Reviews

Please leave a review. Once you have read and used this book, why not leave a review on the site that you purchased it from? Potential readers can then see and use your unbiased opinion to make purchase decisions, we at Packt can understand what you think about our products, and our authors can see your feedback on their book. Thank you!

For more information about Packt, please visit `packtpub.com`.

1
Meet Tkinter

Welcome to the exciting world of GUI programming with Tkinter. This chapter aims to get you acquainted with Tkinter, the built-in **Graphical User Interface (GUI)** library for all standard Python distributions.

Tkinter (pronounced tea-kay-inter) is the Python interface to Tk, the GUI toolkit for Tcl/Tk.

Tcl (Tool command language), which is pronounced as tickle, is a popular scripting language in the domains of embedded applications, testing, prototyping, and GUI development. On the other hand, Tk is an open source, multiplatform widget toolkit that is used by many different languages to build GUI programs.

The Tkinter interface is implemented as a Python module— `Tkinter.py` in Python 2.x Versions and `tkinter/__init__.py` in Python 3.x Versions. If you look at the source code, Tkinter is just a wrapper around a C extension that uses the Tcl/Tk libraries.

Tkinter is suitable for a wide variety of areas, ranging from small desktop applications to scientific modeling and research endeavors across various disciplines.

When a person learning Python needs to graduate to GUI programming, Tkinter seems to be the easiest and fastest way to get the work done.

Tkinter is a great tool for the programming of GUI applications in Python. The features that make Tkinter a great choice for GUI programming include the following:

- It is simple to learn (simpler than any other GUI package for Python)
- Relatively little code can produce powerful GUI applications
- Layered design ensures that it is easy to grasp
- It is portable across all operating systems
- It is easily accessible, as it comes pre-installed with the standard Python distribution

None of the other Python GUI toolkits have all of these features at the same time.

The purpose of this chapter is to make you comfortable with Tkinter. It aims to introduce you to the various components of GUI programming with Tkinter.

We believe that the concepts that you will develop in this chapter will enable you to apply and develop GUI applications in your area of interest.

The key aspects that we want you to learn from this chapter include the following:

- Understanding the concept of a root window and the main loop
- Understanding widgets—the building blocks of programs
- Getting acquainted with a list of available widgets
- Developing layouts by using different geometry managers
- Applying events and callbacks to make a program functional
- Styling widgets by using styling options and configuring the root widget

Technical requirements

We assume a basic working knowledge of Python. You must know how to write and run basic programs in Python.

We will develop our application on the Linux Mint platform. However, since Tkinter is multiplatform, you can follow along with the instructions in this book on Windows, Mac, or any other Linux distribution, without making any modifications to the code.

Project overview

By the end of this chapter, you will have developed several partly functional dummy applications, such as the one shown in the following screenshot:

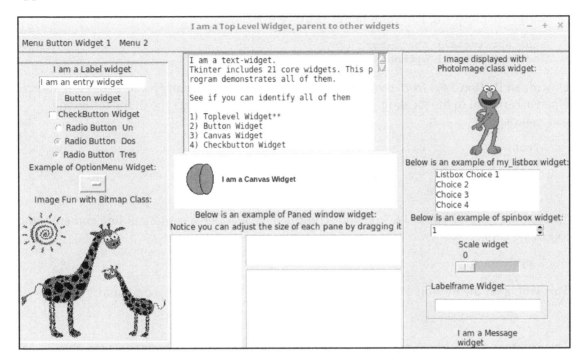

We call these dummy applications because they are neither fully functional nor do they serve any practical purpose other than to show a particular feature of Tkinter.

Getting started

We will write all our projects using Python Version 3.6.3, which is the latest *stable* release of Python at the time of writing.

The Python download package and instructions for downloading for different platforms are available at `https://www.python.org/downloads/release/python-363/`.

The installer binaries for macOS X and the Windows platform are available at the aforementioned link.

If you are following along on Unix, Linux, or BSD, the following procedure will install Python from the source.

First, install `tk8.6-dev` and `python3-tk` packages on your computer using your applicable package manager. For instance, on Debian-based systems such as Ubuntu and Mint, run the following two commands from the Terminal:

```
sudo apt install tk8.6-dev
sudo apt install python3-tk
```

Download Python 3.6.3 from the preceding link and extract it to any location of your choice. Open a Terminal in the location where you extracted Python and type in the following commands:

```
./configure
make
make test
sudo make altinstall
```

This should install Python 3.6.3 on your computer. Now open a command line and enter the following command:

```
$ python3.6
```

This will open the Python 3.6 interactive shell. Type in the following command:

```
>>> import tkinter
```

This command should execute without any errors. If there are no error messages, the Tkinter module is installed on your Python distribution.

When working with examples from this book, we do not support any Python Version except for Python 3.6.3, which comes bundled with Tkinter Tcl/Tk Version 8.6. However, most of the examples should work out-of-the-box on other minor Python 3 Versions.

To check whether you have the correct Tkinter Version on your Python installation, type the following commands in your IDLE or interactive shell:

```
>>> import tkinter
>>> tkinter._test()
```

This should confirm the Tcl/Tk Version as 8.6. We are now ready to build our GUI programs!

The next steps are optional and you may skip them at your discretion. While the preceding steps are sufficient for us to develop our programs, I highly recommend that you use a virtual environment for developing your programs.

Virtual environments provide a secluded environment with no conflicts with system programs, and they can be easily reproduced on any other system.

So now let's set up a virtual environment. First, create a folder where you will keep all projects from this book. Let's call it myTkinterProjects or whatever suits you.

Next, find the location of the Python 3.6 installation on your computer. On my computer, I can find the location of the Python installation by running the following command:

```
$ which python3.6
```

Take a note of the location. For me it is /usr/local/bin/python3.6. Now open a Terminal in your myTkinterProjects folder and run the following command:

```
$ virtualenv -p /location/of /python3.6    myvenv/
```

This will create a new virtual environment in a folder named myvenv inside your project folder.

Lastly, we need to activate this virtual environment. This is done by running the following command:

```
$ source myenv/bin/activate
```

Now if you type the command python, it should pick up Python 3.6.3 from within your virtual environment.

From now onward, every time we have to run a Python script or install a new module, we will first activate the virtual environment using the preceding command and run or install the module within this new virtual environment.

GUI programming – the big picture

As a GUI programmer, you will generally be responsible for deciding the following three aspects of your program:

- Which components should appear on the screen?

  This involves choosing the components that make the user interface. Typical components include things such as buttons, entry fields, checkboxes, radio buttons, and scrollbars. In Tkinter, the components that you add to your GUI are called **widgets**. Widgets (short for window gadgets) are the graphical components that make up your application's frontend.

- Where should the components go?

  This includes deciding the position and the structural layout of various components. In Tkinter, this is referred to as **geometry management**.

- How do components interact and behave?

  This involves adding functionality to each component. Each component or widget does something. For example, a button, when clicked on, does something in response. A scrollbar handles scrolling, and checkboxes and radio buttons enable users to make some choices. In Tkinter, the functionality of various widgets is managed by command binding or **event binding** using **callbacks**.

The following diagram shows the three components of GUI programming:

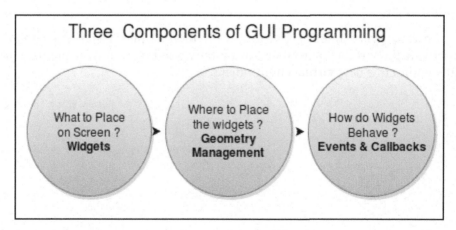

The root window – your drawing board

GUI programming is an art, and like all art you need a drawing board to capture your ideas. The drawing board that you will use is called the **root window**. Our first goal is to get the root window ready.

The following screenshot depicts the root window that we are going to create:

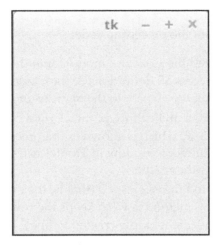

Drawing the root window is easy. You just need the following three lines of code:

```
import tkinter as tk
root = tk.Tk() #line 2
root.mainloop()
```

Save this with the `.py` file extension or check out the code present in the `1.01.py` file. Open it in the IDLE window or run it from within your activated virtual environment using the following command:

```
$ python 1.01.py
```

Running this program should generate a blank root window, as shown in the preceding screenshot. This window is equipped with functional minimize, maximize, and close buttons, and a blank frame.

Downloading the example code

You can download the example code files for all Packt books you have purchased from your account at http://www.packtpub.com. Apart from going to Packt's official website, you can also find the code files for this book at https://github.com/PacktPublishing/Tkinter-GUI-Application-Development-Blueprints-Second-Edition. If you purchased this book elsewhere, you can visit http://www.packtpub.com/support and register to have the files emailed directly to you.

The following is a description of the preceding code:

- The first line imported the tkinter module into the namespace with tk as its alias. Now we can access all definitions of the classes, attributes, and methods of Tkinter by appending the alias tk to the name as in tk.Tk().
- The second line created an instance of the tkinter.Tk class. This created what is called the **root window**, which is shown in the preceding screenshot. According to the conventions, the root window in Tkinter is usually called **root**, but you are free to call it by any other name.
- The third line executed the mainloop (that is, the event loop) method of the root object. The mainloop method is what keeps the root window visible. If you remove the third line, the window created in line 2 will disappear immediately as soon as the script stops running. This will happen so fast that you will not even see the window appearing on your screen. Keeping the mainloop method running also lets you keep the program running until you press the **Close** button, which exits mainloop.
- Tkinter also exposed the mainloop method as tkinter.mainloop(). So, you can even call mainloop() directly instead of calling root.mainloop().

Congratulations! You have completed your first objective, which was to draw the root window. You have now prepared your drawing board (root window). Now, get ready to paint it with your imagination!

Commit the three lines of code (shown in code 1.01.py) to memory. These three lines generate your root window, which will accommodate all the other graphical components. These lines form the skeleton of any GUI application that you will develop in Tkinter. The entire code that will make your GUI application functional will go between line 2 (new object creation) and line 3 (mainloop) of this code.

Widgets – the building blocks of GUI programs

Now that we have our top level or the root window ready, it is time to think over the question: which components should appear in the window? In Tkinter jargon, these components are called **widgets**.

The syntax that is used to add a widget is as follows:

```
my_widget = tk.Widget-name (its container window, ** its configuration
options)
```

In the following example (1.02.py), we will add two widgets, a label and a button, to the root container. Also, note how all the widgets are added between the skeleton code that we defined in the first example:

```
import tkinter as tk
root = tk.Tk()
label = tk.Label(root, text="I am a label widget")
button = tk.Button(root, text="I am a button")
label.pack()
button.pack()
root.mainloop()
```

Running the preceding code(1.02.py) will generate a window with a label and a button widget, as shown in the following screenshot:

The following is a description of the preceding code:

- This code added a new instance named `label` for the label widget. The first parameter defined root as its parent or container. The second parameter configured its text option to read `I am a label widget`.
- Similarly, we defined an instance of a Button widget. This is also bound to the root window as its parent.
- We used the `pack()` method, which is essentially required to position the label and button widgets within the window. We will discuss the `pack()` method and several other related concepts when exploring the geometry management task. However, you must note that some sort of geometry specification is essential for the widgets to be displayed.

Some important widget features

Note the following few important features that are common to all widgets:

- All widgets are actually objects derived from their respective widget classes. So, a statement such as `button = Button(its_parent)` actually creates a button instance from the `Button` class.
- Each widget has a set of options that decides its behavior and appearance. This includes attributes such as text labels, colors, and font size. For example, the Button widget has attributes to manage its label, control its size, change its foreground and background colors, change the size of the border, and more.
- To set these attributes, you can set the values directly at the time of creating the widget, as demonstrated in the preceding example. Alternatively, you can later set or change the options of the widget by using the `.config()` or `.configure()` method. Note that the `.config()` or `.configure()` methods are interchangeable and provide the same functionality. In fact, the `.config()` method is simply an alias of the `.configure()` method.

Ways to create widgets

There are two ways to create widgets in Tkinter.

The first way involves creating a widget in one line and then adding the `pack()` method (or other geometry managers) in the next line, as follows:

```
my_label = tk.Label(root, text="I am a label widget")
my_label.pack()
```

Alternatively, you can write both the lines together, as follows:

```
tk.Label(root, text="I am a label widget").pack()
```

You can either save a reference to the widget created (`my_label`, as in the first example), or create a widget without keeping any reference to it (as demonstrated in the second example).

You should ideally keep a reference to the widget in case the widget has to be accessed later on in the program. For instance, this is useful in case you need to call one of its internal methods or for its content modification. If the widget state is supposed to remain static after its creation, you need not keep a reference to the widget.

Note that calls to `pack()` (or other geometry managers) always return `None`. So, consider a situation where you create a widget, and add a geometry manager (say, `pack()`) on the same line, as follows: `my_label = tk.Label(...).pack()`. In this case, you are not creating a reference to the widget. Instead, you are creating a `None` type object for the `my_label` variable. So, when you later try to modify the widget through the reference, you get an error because you are actually trying to work on a `None` type object. If you need a reference to a widget, you must create it on one line and then specify its geometry (like `pack()`) on the second line, as follows:
`my_label = tk.Label(...)`
`my_label.pack()`
This is one of the most common mistakes committed by beginners.

Getting to know the core Tkinter widgets

Now you will get to know all the core Tkinter widgets. You have already seen two of them in the previous example—the Label and Button widgets. Now, let's explore all the other core Tkinter widgets.

Tkinter includes 21 core widgets, which are as follows:

Top-level	Label	Button
Canvas	Checkbutton	Entry
Frame	LabelFrame	Listbox
Menu	Menubutton	Message
OptionMenu	PanedWindow	Radiobutton
Scale	Scrollbar	Spinbox
Text	Bitmap	Image

Let's write a program to display all of these widgets in the root window.

Adding widgets to a parent window

The format used to add widgets is the same as the one that we discussed in the previous task. To give you an idea about how it's done, here's some sample code that adds some common widgets:

```
Label(parent, text="Enter your Password:")
Button(parent, text="Search")
Checkbutton(parent, text="Remember Me", variable=v, value=True)
Entry(parent, width=30)
Radiobutton(parent, text="Male", variable=v, value=1)
Radiobutton(parent, text="Female", variable=v, value=2)
OptionMenu(parent, var, "Select Country", "USA", "UK", "India","Others")
Scrollbar(parent, orient=VERTICAL, command= text.yview)
```

Can you spot the pattern that is common to each widget? Can you spot the differences?

As a reminder, the syntax for adding a widget is as follows:

```
Widget-name(its_parent, **its_configuration_options)
```

Using the same pattern, let's add all the 21 core Tkinter widgets into a dummy application (1.03.py). We do not reproduce the entire code here. A summarized code description for 1.03.py is as follows:

1. We create a top-level window and a `mainloop`, as shown in the earlier examples.

2. We add a frame widget and name it `menu_bar`. Note that frame widgets are just holder widgets that hold other widgets. Frame widgets are great for grouping widgets together. The syntax for adding a frame is the same as that for all the other widgets:

   ```
   frame = Frame(root)
   frame.pack()
   ```

3. Keeping the `menu_bar` frame as the container, we add two widgets to it:
   - Menubutton
   - Menu

4. We create another frame widget and name it `frame`. Keeping `frame` as the container/parent widget, we add the following seven widgets to it:
   - Label
   - Entry
   - Button
   - Checkbutton
   - Radiobutton
   - OptionMenu
   - `Bitmap` Class

5. We then proceed to create another frame widget. We add six more widgets to the frame:
   - `Image` Class
   - Listbox
   - Spinbox
   - Scale
   - LabelFrame
   - Message

6. We then create another frame widget. We add two more widgets to the frame:
   - Text
   - Scrollbar

7. We create another frame widget and add two more widgets to it:
   - Canvas
   - PanedWindow

These constitute the 21 core widgets of Tkinter. Now that you have had a glimpse of all the widgets, let's discuss how to specify the location of these widgets using geometry managers.

The Tkinter geometry manager

You may recall that we used the pack() method to add widgets to the dummy application that we developed in the previous section. The pack() method is an example of geometry management in Tkinter.

The pack() method is not the only way of managing the geometry in your interface. In fact, there are three geometry managers in Tkinter that let you specify the position of widgets inside a top-level or parent window.

The three geometry managers are as follows:

- **pack**: This is the one that we have used so far. It is simple to use for simpler layouts, but it may get very complex for slightly complex layouts.
- **grid**: This is the most commonly used geometry manager, and provides a table-like layout of management features for easy layout management.
- **place**: This is the least popular, but it provides the best control for the absolute positioning of widgets.

Now, let's have a look at some examples of all the three geometry managers in action.

The pack geometry manager

The pack manager can be a bit tricky to explain in words, and it can best be understood by playing with the code base. Fredrik Lundh, the author of Tkinter, asks us to imagine the root as an elastic sheet with a small opening at the center. The pack geometry manager makes a hole in the elastic sheet that is just large enough to hold the widget. The widget is placed along a given inner edge of the gap (the default is the top edge). It then repeats the process till all the widgets are accommodated.

Finally, when all the widgets have been packed in the elastic sheet, the geometry manager calculates the bounding box for all the widgets. It then makes the parent widget large enough to hold all the child widgets.

When packing child widgets, the pack manager distinguishes between the following three kinds of space:

- Unclaimed space
- Claimed but unused space
- Claimed and used space

The most commonly used options in pack include the following:

- `side`: LEFT, TOP, RIGHT, and BOTTOM (these decide the alignment of the widget)
- `fill`: X, Y, BOTH, and NONE (these decide whether the widget can grow in size)
- `expand`: Boolean values such as `tkinter.YES`/`tkinter.NO`, 1 / 0, and True/False
- `anchor`: NW, N, NE, E, SE, S, SW, W, and CENTER (corresponding to the cardinal directions)
- Internal padding (`ipadx` and `ipady`) for the padding inside widgets and external padding (`padx` and `pady`), which all default to a value of zero

Let's take a look at demo code that illustrates some of the pack features.

Two of the most commonly used pack options are `fill` and `expand`:

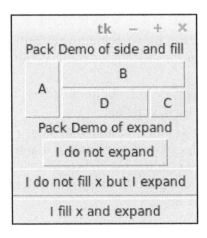

The following code (1.04.py) generates a GUI like the one shown in the preceding screenshot:

```
import tkinter as tk
root = tk.Tk()
frame = tk.Frame(root)
# demo of side and fill options
tk.Label(frame, text="Pack Demo of side and fill").pack()
tk.Button(frame, text="A").pack(side=tk.LEFT, fill=tk.Y)
tk.Button(frame, text="B").pack(side=tk.TOP, fill=tk.X)
tk.Button(frame, text="C").pack(side=tk.RIGHT, fill=tk.NONE)
tk.Button(frame, text="D").pack(side=tk.TOP, fill=tk.BOTH)
frame.pack()
# note the top frame does not expand or fill in X or Y directions
# demo of expand options - best understood by expanding the root
#vwidget and seeing the effect on all the three buttons below.
tk.Label (root, text="Pack Demo of expand").pack()
tk.Button(root, text="I do not expand").pack()
tk.Button(root, text="I do not fill x but I expand").pack(expand = 1)
tk.Button(root, text="I fill x and expand").pack(fill=tk.X, expand=1)
root.mainloop()
```

The following is a description of the preceding code:

- When you insert the A button in the root frame, it captures the leftmost area of the frame, expands, and fills the Y dimension. Because the fill option is specified as fill=tk.Y, it claims all the area that it wants and fills the Y dimension of its container frame.

- Because frame is itself packed with a plain pack() method with no mention of a pack option, it takes the minimum space required to accommodate all of its child widgets.

- If you increase the size of the root window by pulling it down or sideways, you will see that all the buttons within the frame do not fill or expand with the root window.

- The positioning of the B, C, and D buttons occurs on the basis of the side and fill options specified for each of them.

- The next three buttons (after B, C, and D) demonstrate the use of the expand option. A value of expand=1 means that the button moves its place on resizing the window. Buttons with no explicit expand options stay in their place and do not respond to changes in the size of their parent container (the root window, in this case).

- The best way to study this piece of code would be to resize the root window to see the effect that it has on various buttons.
- The anchor attribute (not used in the preceding code) provides a means to position a widget relative to a reference point. If the anchor attribute is not specified, the pack manager places the widget at the center of the available space or the packing box. The other options that are allowed include the four cardinal directions (N, S, E, and W) and a combination of any two directions. Therefore, valid values for the anchor attribute are CENTER (the default value), N, S, E, W, NW, NE, SW, and SE.

The values for most Tkinter geometry manager attributes can either be specified in capital letters without quotes (such as side=tk.TOP and anchor=tk.SE) or in small letters within quotes (such as side='top' and anchor='se').

We will use the pack geometry manager in some of our projects. Therefore, it will be worthwhile to get acquainted with pack and its options.

The pack manager is ideally suited for the following two kinds of situation:

- Placing widgets in a top-down manner
- Placing widgets side by side

1.05.py shows an example of both of these scenarios:

```
parent = tk.Frame(root)
# placing widgets top-down
tk.Button(parent, text='ALL IS WELL').pack(fill=tk.X)
tk.Button(parent, text='BACK TO BASICS').pack(fill=tk.X)
tk.Button(parent, text='CATCH ME IF U CAN').pack(fill=tk.X)
# placing widgets side by side
tk.Button(parent, text='LEFT').pack(side=tk.LEFT)
tk.Button(parent, text='CENTER').pack(side=tk.LEFT)
tk.Button(parent, text='RIGHT').pack(side=tk.LEFT)
parent.pack()
```

The preceding code produces a GUI, as shown in the following screenshot:

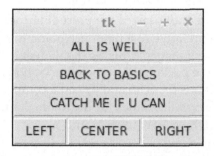

For a complete pack reference, type the following command in the Python shell:

```
>> import tkinter
>>> help(tkinter.Pack)
```

Besides getting interactive help with documentation, Python's REPL is also a great tool for iterating and quick prototyping of Tkinter programs.

Where should you use the pack() geometry manager?
Using the pack manager is somewhat complicated as compared to the `grid` method, which will be discussed next, but it is a great choice in situations such as the following:

- Having a widget fill the complete container frame
- Placing several widgets on top of each other or side by side (as shown in the preceding screenshot)

Although you can create complicated layouts by nesting widgets in multiple frames, you will find the grid geometry manager more suitable for most complex layouts.

The grid geometry manager

The grid geometry manager is easy to understand and perhaps the most useful geometry manager in Tkinter. The central idea of the grid geometry manager is to organize the container frame into a two-dimensional table that is divided into a number of rows and columns. Each cell in the table can then be targeted to hold a widget. In this context, a cell is an intersection of imaginary rows and columns.

Note that in the `grid` method, each cell can hold only one widget. However, widgets can be made to span multiple cells.

Within each cell, you can further align the position of the widget using the sticky option. The sticky option decides how the widget is expanded. If its container cell is larger than the size of the widget that it contains, the sticky option can be specified using one or more of the N, S, E, and W options or the NW, NE, SW, and SE options.

Not specifying stickiness defaults stickiness to the center of the widget in the cell.

Let's have a look at demo code that illustrates some features of the grid geometry manager. The code in `1.06.py` generates a GUI, as shown in the following screenshot:

The following code (`1.06.py`) generates the preceding GUI:

```
import tkinter as tk
root = tk.Tk()
tk.Label(root, text="Username").grid(row=0, sticky=tk.W)
tk.Label(root, text="Password").grid(row=1, sticky=tk.W)
tk.Entry(root).grid(row=0, column=1, sticky=tk.E)
tk.Entry(root).grid(row=1, column=1, sticky=tk.E)
tk.Button(root, text="Login").grid(row=2, column=1, sticky=tk.E)
root.mainloop()
```

The following is a description of the preceding code:

- Take a look at the grid position defined in terms of the row and column positions for an imaginary grid table spanning the entire frame. See how the use of `sticky=tk.W` on both the labels makes them stick on the left-hand side, thus resulting in a clean layout.
- The width of each column (or the height of each row) is automatically decided by the height or width of the widgets in the cell. Therefore, you need not worry about specifying the row or column width as equal. You can specify the width for widgets if you need that extra bit of control.
- You can use the `sticky=tk.NSEW` argument to make the widget expandable and fill the entire cell of the grid.

In a more complex scenario, your widgets may span across multiple cells in the grid. To make a grid to span multiple cells, the `grid` method offers handy options such as `rowspan` and `columnspan`.

Furthermore, you may often need to provide some padding between cells in the grid. The grid manager provides the `padx` and `pady` options to provide padding that needs to be placed around a widget.

Similarly, the `ipadx` and `ipady` options are used for internal padding. These options add padding within the widget itself. The default value of external and internal padding is 0.

Let's have a look at an example of the grid manager, where we use most of the common arguments to the grid method, such as `row`, `column`, `padx`, `pady`, `rowspan`, and `columnspan`.

`1.07.py` produces a GUI, as shown in the following screenshot, to demonstrate how to use the grid geometry manager options:

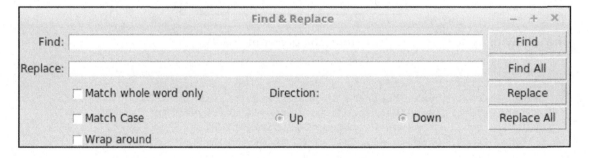

The following code (`1.07.py`) generates the preceding GUI:

```
import tkinter as tk
parent = tk.Tk()
parent.title('Find & Replace')
tk.Label(parent, text="Find:").grid(row=0, column=0, sticky='e')
tk.Entry(parent, width=60).grid(row=0, column=1, padx=2, pady=2,
                                sticky='we', columnspan=9)
tk.Label(parent, text="Replace:").grid(row=1, column=0, sticky='e')
tk.Entry(parent).grid(row=1, column=1, padx=2, pady=2, sticky='we',
                      columnspan=9)
tk.Button(parent, text="Find").grid( row=0, column=10, sticky='e' + 'w',
                                      padx=2, pady=2)
tk.Button(parent, text="Find All").grid(
                    row=1, column=10, sticky='e' + 'w', padx=2)
tk.Button(parent, text="Replace").grid(row=2, column=10, sticky='e' +
```

```
                              'w', padx=2)
tk.Button(parent, text="Replace All").grid(
                    row=3, column=10, sticky='e' + 'w', padx=2)
tk.Checkbutton(parent, text='Match whole word only').grid(
                    row=2, column=1, columnspan=4, sticky='w')
tk.Checkbutton(parent, text='Match Case').grid(
                    row=3, column=1, columnspan=4, sticky='w')
tk.Checkbutton(parent, text='Wrap around').grid(
                    row=4, column=1, columnspan=4, sticky='w')
tk.Label(parent, text="Direction:").grid(row=2, column=6, sticky='w')
tk.Radiobutton(parent, text='Up', value=1).grid(
                    row=3, column=6, columnspan=6, sticky='w')
tk.Radiobutton(parent, text='Down', value=2).grid(
                    row=3, column=7, columnspan=2, sticky='e')
parent.mainloop()
```

Note how just 14 lines of the core grid manager code generate a complex layout such as the one shown in the preceding screenshot. On the other hand, developing this with the pack manager would have been much more tedious.

Another grid option that you can sometimes use is the `widget.grid_forget()` method. This method can be used to hide a widget from the screen. When you use this option, the widget still exists at its former location, but it becomes invisible. The hidden widget may be made visible again, but the grid options that you originally assigned to the widget will be lost.

Similarly, there is a `widget.grid_remove()` method that removes the widget, except that in this case, when you make the widget visible again, all of its grid options will be restored.

For a complete grid reference, type the following command in the Python shell:

```
>>> import tkinter
>>> help(tkinter.Grid)
```

Where should you use the grid geometry manager?
The grid manager is a great tool for the development of complex layouts. Complex structures can be easily achieved by breaking the container widget into grids of rows and columns and then placing the widgets in grids where they are wanted. It is also commonly used to develop different kinds of dialog box.

Now we will delve into configuring a grid's column and row sizes.

Different widgets have different heights and widths. So, when you specify the position of a widget in terms of rows and columns, the cell automatically expands to accommodate the widget.

Normally, the height of all the grid rows is automatically adjusted so it's the height of its tallest cell. Similarly, the width of all the grid columns is adjusted so it's equal to the width of the widest widget cell.

If you then want a smaller widget to fill a larger cell or to stay on any one side of the cell, you can use the sticky attribute on the widget to control this aspect.

However, you can override this automatic sizing of columns and rows by using the following code:

```
w.columnconfigure(n, option=value, ...) AND
w.rowconfigure(n, option=value, ...)
```

Use these to configure the options for a given widget, w, in either the nth column or the nth row, specifying values for the options, minsize, pad, and weight. Note that the numbering of rows begins from 0 and not 1.

The options available are as follows:

Options	Descriptions
minsize	This is the minimum size of a column or row in pixels. If there is no widget in a given column or row, the cell does not appear in spite of this minsize specification.
pad	This is the external padding in pixels that will be added to the specified column or row over the size of the largest cell.
weight	This specifies the relative weight of a row or column and then distributes the extra space. This enables making the row or column stretchable. For example, the following code distributes two-fifths of the extra space to the first column and three-fifths to the second column: `w.columnconfigure(0, weight=2)` `w.columnconfigure(1, weight=3)`

The `columnconfigure()` and `rowconfigure()` methods are often used to implement the dynamic resizing of widgets, especially on resizing the root window.

 You cannot use the `grid` and `pack` methods together in the same container window. If you try doing that, your program will raise a `_tkinter.TclError` error.

The place geometry manager

The place geometry manager is the most rarely used geometry manager in Tkinter. Nevertheless, it has its uses in that it lets you precisely position widgets within their parent frame by using the (*x,y*) coordinate system.

The place manager can be accessed by using the `place()` method on any standard widget.

The important options for place geometry include the following:

- Absolute positioning (specified in terms of *x=N* or *y=N*)
- Relative positioning (the key options include `relx`, `rely`, `relwidth`, and `relheight`)

The other options that are commonly used with place include `width` and `anchor`(the default is NW).

Refer to `1.08.py` for a demonstration of common place options:

```
import tkinter as tk
root = tk.Tk()
# Absolute positioning
tk.Button(root, text="Absolute Placement").place(x=20, y=10)
# Relative positioning
tk.Button(root, text="Relative").place(relx=0.8, rely=0.2, relwidth=0.5,
                            width=10,  anchor=tk.NE)
root.mainloop()
```

You may not see much of a difference between the absolute and relative positions simply by looking at the code or the window frame. However, if you try resizing the window, you will observe that the **Absolute Placement** button does not change its coordinates, while the **Relative** button changes its coordinates and size to accommodate the new size of the root window:

For a complete `place` reference, type the following command in the Python shell:

```
>>> import tkinter
>>> help(tkinter.Place)
```

When should you use the place manager?
The place manager is useful in situations where you have to implement custom geometry managers, or where the widget placement is decided by the end user.

While the pack and grid managers cannot be used together in the same frame, the place manager can be used with any geometry manager within the same container frame.

The place manager is rarely used because, if you use it, you have to worry about the exact coordinates. If you make a minor change to a widget, it is very likely that you will have to change the *x,y* values for other widgets as well, which can be very cumbersome. We will use the place manager in Chapter 7, *Piano Tutor*.

This concludes our discussion on geometry management in Tkinter.

In this section, you had a look at how to implement the pack, grid, and place geometry managers. You also understood the strengths and weaknesses of each geometry manager.

You learned that pack is suitable for a simple side-wise or top-down widget placement. You also learned that the grid manager is best suited for the handling of complex layouts. You saw examples of the place geometry manager and explored the reasons behind why it is rarely used.

You should now be able to plan and execute different layouts for your programs using these Tkinter geometry managers.

Events and callbacks – adding life to programs

Now that you have learned how to add widgets to a screen and position them where you want, let's turn our attention to the third component of GUI programming.

This addresses the question of how to make widgets functional.

Making widgets functional involves making them responsive to events such as the pressing of buttons, the pressing of keys on a keyboard, and mouse clicks.

This requires associating callbacks with specific events. Callbacks are normally associated with specific widget events using command binding rules, which are discussed in the following section.

Command binding

The simplest way to add functionality to a button is called **command binding**, whereby a callback function is mentioned in the form of command = some_callback in the widget option. Note that the command option is available only for a few selected widgets.

Take a look at the following sample code:

```
def my_callback ():
    # do something when button is clicked
```

After defining the preceding callback, we can connect it to, say, a button with the command option referring to the callback, as follows:

```
tk.Button(root, text="Click me", command=my_callback)
```

A **callback** is a function memory reference (`my_callback` in the preceding example) that is called by another function (which is `Button` in the preceding example) and that takes the first function as a parameter. Put simply, a callback is a function that you provide to another function so that it can calling it.

Note that `my_callback` is passed without parentheses, `()`, from within the widget `command` option, because when the callback functions are set it is necessary to pass a reference to a function rather than actually call it.

If you add parentheses, `()`, as you would for any normal function, it would be called as soon as the program runs. In contrast, the callback is called only when an event occurs (the pressing of a button in this case).

Passing arguments to callbacks

If a callback does not take any argument, it can be handled with a simple function, such as the one shown in the preceding code. However, if a callback needs to take arguments, we can use the `lambda` function, as shown in the following code snippet:

```
def my_callback (argument)
    #do something with argument
```

Then, somewhere else in the code, we define a button with a command callback that takes some arguments, as follows:

```
tk.Button(root,text="Click", command=lambda: my_callback ('some argument'))
```

Python borrows a specific syntax from functional programming, called the `lambda` function. The `lambda` function lets you define a single-line, nameless function on the fly.

The format for using `lambda` is as follows:

```
lambda arg: #do something with arg in a single line
```

Here's an example:

```
square = lambda x: x**2
```

Now, we can call the `square` method, as follows:

```
>> print(square(5)) ## prints 25 to the console
```

Limitations of the command option

The command option that is available with the Button widget and a few other widgets is a function that can make the programming of a click-of-a-button event easy. Many other widgets do not provide an equivalent command binding option.

By default, the command button binds to the left-click and the spacebar. It does not bind to the *Return* key. Therefore, if you bind a button by using the command function, it will react to the space bar and not the *Return* key. This is counter-intuitive for many users. What's worse is that you cannot change the binding of the command function easily. The moral is that command binding, though a very handy tool, is not flexible enough when it comes to deciding your own bindings.

This brings us to the next method for handling events.

Event binding

Fortunately, Tkinter provides an alternative event binding mechanism called bind() to let you deal with different events. The standard syntax used to bind an event is as follows:

```
widget.bind(event, handler, add=None)
```

When an event corresponding to the event description occurs in the widget, it calls not only the associated handler, which passes an instance of the event object as the argument, but also the details of the event. If there already exists a binding for that event for this widget, the old callback is usually replaced with the new handler, but you can trigger both the callbacks by passing add='+' as the last argument.

Let's look at an example of the bind() method (code 1.09.py):

```
import tkinter as tk
root = tk.Tk()
tk.Label(root, text='Click at different\n locations in the frame
below').pack()

def callback(event):
    print(dir(event))
    print("you clicked at", event.x, event.y)

frame = tk.Frame(root, bg='khaki', width=130, height=80)
frame.bind("<Button-1>", callback)
frame.pack()
root.mainloop()
```

The following is a description of the preceding code:

- We bind the Frame widget to the `<Button-1>` event, which corresponds to the left-click. When this event occurs, it calls the `callback` function, passing an object instance as its argument.
- We define the `callback(event)` function. Note that it takes the `event` object generated by the event as an argument.
- We inspect the event object by using `dir(event)`, which returns a sorted list of attribute names for the event object passed to it. This prints the following list:

  ```
  [ '__doc__' , '__module__' , 'char' , 'delta' , 'height' ,
  'keycode' , 'keysym' , keysym_num' , 'num' , 'send_event' ,
  'serial' , 'state' ,'time' , 'type' , 'widget' , 'width' , 'x' ,
  'x_root' , 'y' , 'y_root' ]
  ```

- From the attributes list generated by the object, we use two attributes, `event.x` and `event.y`, to print the coordinates of the point of click.

When you run the preceding code (code `1.09.py`), it produces a window, as shown in the following screenshot:

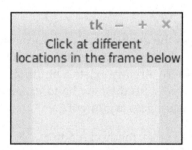

When you left-click anywhere in the yellow colored frame within the root window, it outputs messages to the console. A sample message passed to the console is as follows:

```
['__doc__', '__module__', 'char', 'delta', 'height', 'keycode', 'keysym',
'keysym_num', 'num', 'send_event', 'serial', 'state', 'time', 'type',
'widget', 'width', 'x', 'x_root', 'y', 'y_root']
 You clicked at 63 36.
```

Event patterns

In the previous example, you learned how to use the `<Button-1>` event to denote a left-click. This is a built-in pattern in Tkinter that maps it to a left-click event. Tkinter has an exhaustive mapping scheme that perfectly identifies events such as this one.

Here are some examples to give you an idea of event patterns:

The event pattern	The associated event
`<Button-1>`	Left-click of the mouse
`<KeyPress-B>`	A keyboard press of the *B* key
`<Alt-Control-KeyPress- KP_Delete>`	A keyboard press of *Alt + Ctrl + Del*

In general, the mapping pattern takes the following form:

```
<[event modifier-]...event type [-event detail]>
```

Typically, an event pattern will comprise the following:

- **An event type**: Some common event types include `Button`, `ButtonRelease`, `KeyRelease`, `Keypress`, `FocusIn`, `FocusOut`, `Leave` (when the mouse leaves the widget), and `MouseWheel`. For a complete list of event types, refer to the `event` types section at http://www.tcl.tk/man/tcl8.6/TkCmd/bind.htm#M7.
- **An event modifier** (optional): Some common event modifiers include `Alt`, `Any` (used like `<Any-KeyPress>`), `Control`, `Double` (used like `<Double-Button-1>` to denote a double-click of the left mouse button), `Lock`, and `Shift`. For a complete list of event modifiers, refer to the `event modifiers` section at http://www.tcl.tk/man/tcl8.6/TkCmd/bind.htm#M6.
- **The event detail** (optional): The mouse event detail is captured by the number 1 for a left-click and the number 2 for a right-click. Similarly, each key press on the keyboard is either represented by the key letter itself (say, *B* in `<KeyPress-B>`) or by using a key symbol abbreviated as `keysym`. For example, the up arrow key on the keyboard is represented by the `keysym` value of `KP_Up`. For a complete `keysym` mapping, refer to https://www.tcl.tk/man/tcl8.6/TkCmd/bind.htm.

Let's take a look at a practical example of event binding on widgets (refer to code 1.10.py for the complete working example):

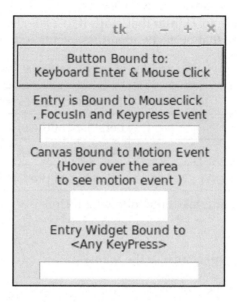

The following is a modified snippet of code; it will give you an idea of commonly used event bindings:

```
widget.bind("<Button-1>", callback) #bind widget to left mouse click
widget.bind("<Button-2>", callback) # bind to right mouse click
widget.bind("<Return>", callback)# bind to Return(Enter) Key
widget.bind("<FocusIn>", callback) #bind to Focus in Event
widget.bind("<KeyPress-A>", callback)# bind to keypress A
widget.bind("<KeyPress-Caps_Lock>", callback)# bind to CapsLock keysym
widget.bind("<KeyPress-F1>", callback)# bind widget to F1 keysym
widget.bind("<KeyPress-KP_5>", callback)# bind to keypad number 5
widget.bind("<Motion>", callback) # bind to motion over widget
widget.bind("<Any-KeyPress>", callback) # bind to any keypress
```

Rather than binding an event to a particular widget, you can also bind it to the top-level window. The syntax remains the same except that now you call it on the root instance of the root window such as root.bind().

Binding levels

In the previous section, you had a look at how to bind an event to an instance of a widget. This can be called an **instance-level binding**.

However, there may be times when you need to bind events to an entire application. At times, you may want to bind an event to a particular class of widget. Tkinter provides the following levels of binding options for this:

- **Application-level binding**: Application-level bindings let you use the same binding across all windows and widgets of an application as long as any one window of the application is in focus. The syntax for application-level bindings is as follows:

```
widget.bind_all(event, callback, add=None)
```

The typical usage pattern is as follows:

```
root.bind_all('<F1>', show_help)
```

Application-level binding here means that, irrespective of the widget that is currently under focus, pressing the *F1* key will always trigger the show_help callback as long as the application is in focus.

- **Class-level binding**: You can also bind events at a particular class level. This is normally used to set the same behavior for all instances of a particular widget class. The syntax for class-level binding is as follows:

```
w.bind_class(class_name, event, callback, add=None)
```

The typical usage pattern is as follows:

```
my_entry.bind_class('Entry', '<Control-V>', paste)
```

In the preceding example, all the entry widgets will be bound to the <Control-V> event, which will call a method named paste (event).

Event propagation
Most keyboard and mouse events occur at the operating system level. The event propagates hierarchically upward from its source until it finds a window that has the corresponding binding. The event propagation does not stop there. It propagates itself upwards, looking for other bindings from other widgets, until it reaches the root window. If it does reach the root window and no bindings are discovered by it, the event is disregarded.

Handling widget-specific variables

You need variables with a wide variety of widgets. You likely need a string variable to track what the user enters into the entry widget or text widget. You most probably need Boolean variables to track whether the user has checked off the Checkbox widget. You need integer variables to track the value entered in a Spinbox or Slider widget.

In order to respond to changes in widget-specific variables, Tkinter offers its own variable class. The variable that you can use to track widget-specific values must be subclassed from this Tkinter variable class. Tkinter offers some commonly used predefined variables. They are StringVar, IntVar, BooleanVar, and DoubleVar.

You can use these variables to capture and play with the changes in the values of variables from within your callback functions. You can also define your own variable type, if required.

Creating a Tkinter variable is simple. You simply have to call the constructor:

```
my_string = tk.StringVar()
ticked_yes = tk.BooleanVar()
group_choice = tk.IntVar()
volume = tk.DoubleVar()
```

Once the variable is created, you can use it as a widget option, as follows:

```
tk.Entry(root, textvariable=my_string)
tk.Checkbutton(root, text="Remember Me", variable=ticked_yes)
tk.Radiobutton(root, text="Option1", variable=group_choice,
value="option1")
tk.Scale(root, label="Volume Control", variable=volume, from =0, to=10)
```

Additionally, Tkinter provides access to the values of variables via the `set()` and `get()` methods, as follows:

```
my_var.set("FooBar") # setting value of variable
my_var.get() # Assessing the value of variable from say a callback
```

A demonstration of the Tkinter `variable` class is available in the `1.11.py` code file. The code generates a window, as shown in the following screenshot:

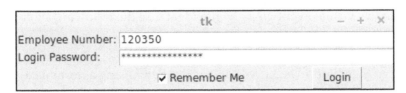

This concludes our brief discussion on events and callbacks. Here's a brief summary of the things that we discussed:

- Command binding, which is used to bind simple widgets to certain functions
- Event binding using the `widget.bind_all`(event, callback, add=None) method to bind keyboard and mouse events to your widgets and invoke callbacks when certain events occur
- The passing of extra arguments to a callback using the `lambda` function
- The binding of events to an entire application or to a particular class of widget by using `bind_all()` and `bind_class()`
- Using the Tkinter `variable` class to set and get the values of widget-specific variables

In short, you now know how to make your GUI program responsive to end-user requests!

Event unbinding and virtual events

In addition to the bind method that you previously saw, you might find the following two event-related options useful in certain cases:

- **Unbind:** Tkinter provides the unbind option to undo the effect of an earlier binding. The syntax is as follows:

    ```
    widget.unbind(event)
    ```

The following are some examples of its usage:

```
entry.unbind('<Alt-Shift-5>')
root.unbind_all('<F1>')
root.unbind_class('Entry', '<KeyPress-Del>')
```

- **Virtual events**: Tkinter also lets you create your own events. You can give these virtual events any name that you want. For example, let's suppose that you want to create a new event called <<commit>>, which is triggered by the *F9* key. To create this virtual event on a given widget, use the following syntax:

```
widget.event_add('<<commit>>', '<KeyRelease-F9>')
```

You can then bind <<commit>> to a callback by using a normal bind() method, as follows:

```
widget.bind('<<commit>>', callback)
```

Other event-related methods can be accessed by typing the following line in the Python Terminal:

```
>>> import tkinter
>>> help(tkinter.Event)
```

Now that you are ready to delve into real application development with Tkinter, let's spend some time exploring a few custom styling options that Tkinter offers. We will also have a look at some configuration options that are commonly used with the root window.

Doing it in style

So far, we have relied on Tkinter to provide specific platform-based styling for our widgets. However, you can specify your own styling of widgets, such as their color, font size, border width, and relief. A brief introduction to styling features that are available in Tkinter is supplied in the following section.

You may recall that we can specify widget options at the time of its instantiation, as follows:

```
my_button = tk.Button(parent, **configuration options)
```

Alternatively, you can specify the widget options by using configure() in the following way:

```
my_button.configure(**options)
```

Styling options are also specified as options to the widgets either at the time of creating the widgets, or later by using the `configure` option.

Specifying styles

Under the purview of styling, we will cover how to apply different colors, fonts, border widths, reliefs, cursors, and bitmap icons to widgets.

First, let's see how to specify the color options for a widget. You can specify the following two types of color for most widgets:

- The background color
- The foreground color

You can specify the color by using hexadecimal color codes for the proportion of red(*r*), green(*g*), and blue(*b*). The commonly used representations are `#rgb` (4 bits), `#rrggbb` (8 bits), and `#rrrgggbbb` (12 bits).

For example, `#fff` is white, `#000000` is black, `#f00` is red (R=0xf, G=0x0 , B=0x0), `#00ff00` is green (R=0x00, G=0xff, B=0x00), and `#000000fff` is blue (R=0x000 , G=0x000 , B=0xfff).

Alternatively, Tkinter provides mapping for standard color names. For a list of predefined named colors, visit `http://wiki.tcl.tk/37701` or `http://wiki.tcl.tk/16166`.

Next, let's have a look at how to specify fonts for our widgets. A font can be represented as a string by using the following string signature:

```
{font family} fontsize fontstyle
```

The elements of the preceding syntax can be explained as follows:

- `font family`: This is the complete font family long name. It should preferably be in lowercase, such as `font="{nimbus roman} 36 bold italic"`.
- `fontsize`: This is in the printer's point unit (`pt`) or pixel unit (`px`).
- `fontstyle`: This is a mix of normal/bold/italic and underline/overstrike.

The following are examples that illustrate the method of specifying fonts:

```
widget.configure (font='Times 8')
widget.configure(font='Helvetica 24 bold italic')
```

If you set a Tkinter dimension in a plain integer, the measurements take place in pixel units. Alternatively, Tkinter accepts four other measurement units, which are m(millimeters), c(centimeters), i(inches), and p(printer's points, which are about 1/72").

For instance, if you want to specify the wrap length of a button in terms of a printer's point, you can specify it as follows:

```
button.configure(wraplength="36p")
```

The default border width for most Tkinter widgets is 2 px. You can change the border width for widgets by specifying it explicitly, as shown in the following line:

```
button.configure(borderwidth=5)
```

The relief style of a widget refers to the difference between the highest and lowest elevations in a widget. Tkinter offers six possible relief styles—flat, raised, sunken, groove, solid, and ridge:

```
button.configure(relief='raised')
```

Tkinter lets you change the style of the mouse cursor when you hover over a particular widget. This is done by using the option cursor, as follows:

```
button.configure(cursor='cross')
```

For a complete list of available cursors, refer to https://www.tcl.tk/man/tcl8.6/TkCmd/cursors.htm.

Though you can specify the styling options at each widget level, sometimes it may be cumbersome to do so individually for each widget. Widget-specific styling has the following disadvantages:

- It mixes logic and presentation into one file, making the code bulky and difficult to manage
- Any change in styling has to be applied to each widget individually
- It violates the don't repeat yourself (DRY) principle of effective coding, as you keep specifying the same style for a large number of widgets

Fortunately, Tkinter now offers a way to separate presentation from logic and specify styles in what is called the **external option database**. This is just a text file where you can specify common styling options.

A typical option database text file looks like this:

```
*background: AntiqueWhite1
*Text*background: #454545
*Button*foreground: gray55
*Button*relief: raised
*Button*width: 3
```

In its simplest use, the asterisk (*) symbol here means that the particular style is applied to all the instances of the given widget. For a more complex usage of the asterisk in styling, refer to http://infohost.nmt.edu/tcc/help/pubs/tkinter/web/resource-lines.html.

These entries are placed in an external text (.txt) file. To apply this styling to a particular piece of code, you can simply call it by using the option_readfile() call early in your code, as shown here:

```
root.option_readfile('optionDB.txt')
```

Let's have a look at an example (see code 1.12.py) of using this external styling text file in a program:

```
import tkinter as tk
root = tk.Tk()
root.configure(background='#4D4D4D')#top level styling
# connecting to the external styling optionDB.txt
root.option_readfile('optionDB.txt')
#widget specific styling
mytext = tk.Text(root, background='#101010', foreground="#D6D6D6",
            borderwidth=18, relief='sunken',width=17, height=5)
mytext.insert(tk.END, "Style is knowing who you are, what you want to
                say, and not giving a damn.")
mytext.grid(row=0, column=0, columnspan=6, padx=5, pady=5)
# all the below widgets get their styling from optionDB.txt file
tk.Button(root, text='*').grid(row=1, column=1)
tk.Button(root, text='^').grid(row=1, column=2)
tk.Button(root, text='#').grid(row=1, column=3)
tk.Button(root, text='<').grid(row=2, column=1)
tk.Button(root, text='OK', cursor='target').grid(row=2, column=2)#changing
cursor style
tk.Button(root, text='>').grid(row=2, column=3)
tk.Button(root, text='+').grid(row=3, column=1)
tk.Button(root, text='v').grid(row=3, column=2)
tk.Button(root, text='-').grid(row=3, column=3)
for i in range(9):
    tk.Button(root, text=str(i+1)).grid(row=4+i//3, column=1+i%3)
root.mainloop()
```

The following is a description of the preceding code:

- The code connects to an external styling file called `optionDB.txt` that defines common styling for the widgets.
- The next segment of code creates a Text widget and specifies styling on the widget level.
- The next segment of code has several buttons, all of which derive their styling from the centralized `optionDB.txt` file. One of the buttons also defines a custom cursor.

Specifying attributes such as font sizes, the border width, the widget width, the widget height, and padding in absolute numbers, as we have done in the preceding example, can cause some display variations between different operating systems such as Ubuntu, Windows, and Mac respectively, as shown in the following screenshot. This is due to differences in the rendering engines of different operating systems:

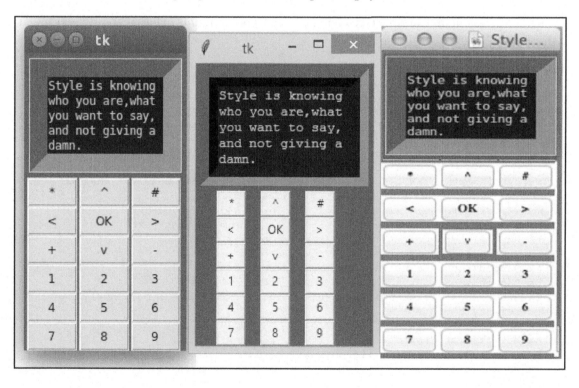

When deploying cross-platform, it is better to avoid specifying attribute sizes in absolute numbers. It is often the best choice to let the platform handle the attribute sizes.

Some common root window options

Now that we are done discussing styling options, let's wrap up with a discussion on some commonly used options for the root window:

Method	Description
`*root.geometry('142x280+150+200')`	You can specify the size and location of a root window by using a string of the `widthxheight + xoffset + yoffset` form.
`self.root.wm_iconbitmap('mynewicon.ico') OR` `self.root.iconbitmap('mynewicon.ico ')`	This changes the title bar icon to something that is different from the default Tk icon.
`root.overrideredirect(1)`	This removes the root border frame. It hides the frame that contains the minimize, maximize, and close buttons.

Let's explain these styling options in more detail:

- `root.geometry('142x280+150+200')`: Specifying the geometry of the root window limits the launch size of the root window. If the widgets do not fit in the specified size, they get clipped from the window. It is often better not to specify this and let Tkinter decide this for you.
- `self.root.wm_iconbitmap('my_icon.ico')` or `self.root.iconbitmap('my_icon.ico ')`: This option is only applicable to Windows. Unix-based operating systems do not display the title bar icon.

Getting interactive help

This section applies not only for Tkinter, but also for any Python object for which you may need help.

Let's say that you need a reference to the Tkinter pack geometry manager. You can get interactive help in your Python interactive shell by using the help command, as shown in the following command lines:

```
>>> import tkinter
>>> help(tkinter.Pack)
```

This provides detailed help documentation of all the methods defined under the `Pack` class in Tkinter.

You can similarly receive help for all the other individual widgets. For instance, you can check the comprehensive and authoritative help documentation for the Label widget in the interactive shell by typing the following command:

```
>>>help(tkinter.Label)
```

This provides a list of the following:

- All the methods defined in the `Label` class
- All the standard and widget-specific options for the `Label` widget
- All the methods inherited from other classes

Finally, when in doubt regarding a method, look into the source code of Tkinter, which is located at `<location-of-python-installation>\lib\`. For instance, the Tkinter source code is located in the `/usr/lib/python3.6.3/tkinter` directory on my Linux Mint operating system. You might also find it useful to look at the source code implementation of various other modules, such as the `color chooser`, `file dialogs`, and `ttk` modules, and the other modules located in the aforementioned directory.

Summary

This brings us to end of this chapter. This chapter aimed to provide a high-level overview of Tkinter. We worked our way through all the important concepts that drive a Tkinter program.

You now know what a root window is and how to set it up. You also know the 21 core Tkinter widgets and how to set them up. We also had a look at how to lay out our programs by using the `Pack`, `Grid`, and `Place` geometry managers, and how to make our programs functional by using `events` and `callbacks`. Finally, you saw how to apply custom styles to GUI programs.

To summarize, we can now start thinking about making interesting, functional, and stylish GUI programs with Tkinter! In the next chapter, we will build our first real application - a Text editor.

QA section

Before you proceed to the next chapter, make sure you can answer these questions to your satisfaction:

- What is a root window?
- What is the main loop?
- How do you create a root window?
- What are widgets? How do you create widgets in Tkinter?
- Can you list or identify all available widgets in Tkinter?
- What are geometry managers used for?
- Can you name all the available geometry managers in Tkinter?
- What are events in a GUI program?
- What are callbacks? How are callbacks different from regular functions?
- How do you apply callbacks to an event?
- How do you style widgets using styling options?
- What are the common configuration options for the root window?

Further reading

It would be a good idea to modify the examples from this chapter to lay out the widgets in different ways or to tweak the code to function in other ways to get your feet wet.

We recommend that you take a look at the documentation for all three geometry managers in your Python shell using the following commands:

```
>>> import tkinter
>>> help(tkinter.Pack)
>>> help(tkinter.Grid)
>>> help(tkinter.Place)
```

You can also find an excellent documentation of Tkinter at http://infohost.nmt.edu/tcc/help/pubs/tkinter/web/index.html.

2
Making a Text Editor

We got a fairly high-level overview of Tkinter in Chapter 1, *Meet Tkinter*. Now that we know some things about Tkinter's core widgets, geometry management, and the binding of commands and events to callbacks, let's use our skills in this project to create a text editor.

We will, in the process of creating a text editor, take a closer look at some widgets and learn how to tweak them to meet our specific needs.

The following are the key objectives for this project:

- Delving into some commonly used widgets, such as the Menu, Menubutton, Text, Entry, Checkbutton, and Button widgets
- Exploring the filedialog and messagebox modules of Tkinter
- Learning the vital concepts of indexing and tagging, as applied to Tkinter
- Identifying the different types of Toplevel windows

Project overview

The goal here is to build a text editor with some nifty features. Let's call it the **Footprint Editor**:

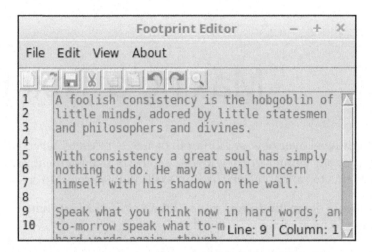

We intend to include the following features in the text editor:

- Creating new documents, opening and editing existing documents, and saving documents
- Implementing common editing options such as cut, copy, paste, undo, and redo
- Searching within a file for a given search term
- Implementing line numbering and the ability to show/hide line numbers
- Implementing theme selection to let a user choose custom color themes for the editor
- Implementing the about and help windows

Getting started – setting up the editor skeleton

Our first goal is to implement the broad visual elements of the text editor. As programmers, we have all used text editors to edit code. We are mostly aware of the common GUI elements of a text editor. So, without further ado, let's get started.

The first phase implements the Menu, Menubutton, Label, Button, Text, and Scrollbar widgets. Although we'll cover all of these in detail, you might find it helpful to look at the widget-specific options in the documentation of Tkinter maintained by its author, Frederick Lundh, at `http://effbot.org/tkinterbook/`. You can also use the interactive shell, as discussed in `Chapter 1`, *Meet Tkinter*.

You might also want to bookmark the official documentation page of Tcl/Tk at `http://www.tcl.tk/man/tcl8.6/TkCmd/contents.htm`. This site includes the original Tcl/Tk reference. While it does not relate to Python, it provides a detailed overview of each widget and is a useful reference. Remember that Tkinter is just a wrapper around Tk.

In this iteration, we will complete the implementation of broader visual elements of the editor.

We will use the `pack()` geometry manager to place all the widgets. We have chosen the pack manager because it is ideally suited for the placing of widgets, either in a side-by-side or top-down position.

Fortunately, in a text editor, we have all the widgets placed either side by side or in top-down positions. Thus, it is beneficial to use the pack manager. We can do the same thing with the grid manager as well.

A note on code styling

One of the key insights of the Python community is that code is read much more often than it is written. Following good naming conventions and consistency in code styling are key to maintaining readable and scalable programs. We will try to stick to the official Python styling guide, which is specified in the PEP8 documentation at `https://www.python.org/dev/peps/pep-0008`.

Some important styling conventions that we will stick to include the following:

- Use four spaces per indentation level
- Variable and function names will be lowercase, with words separated by underscores
- Class names will use the `CapWords` convention

Let's start by adding the Toplevel window using the following code:

```
from tkinter import Tk
root = Tk()
# all our code goes here
root.mainloop()
```

Note a slight difference in the way we import `tkinter` here. In the last chapter, we imported `tkinter` using this code:

```
import tkinter as tk
```

Since we used `tk` as an alias, we had to append the alias name to every call made to a class defined in Tkinter, as in `tk.Tk()`, `tk.Frame`, `tk.Button`, `tk.END`, and so on.

From this chapter onward, we will directly import the individual class that we will need for a given program. So, now that we need the `Tk()` class from Tkinter, we directly import it into our namespace as:

```
from tkinter import Tk
```

This, in turn, means that we can now directly reference it as the `Tk` class in our program without needing to append any alias name to it as in `root = Tk()`.

A third method is to import all (`*`) the classes from Tkinter into the namespace by using the following command:

```
from tkinter import *
```

The asterisk symbol means we want everything from `tkinter` to be imported into the namespace, regardless of whether we use it. This is, however, bad programming practice as it leads to namespace pollution. Furthermore, in larger programs, it can be hard to tell which module a particular class has been imported from, thus making debugging a difficult task.

Adding a menu and menu items

Menus offer a very compact way of presenting a large number of choices to the user without cluttering the interface. Tkinter offers the following two widgets to handle menus:

- **Menu widget**: This appears at the top of applications, which is always visible to end users
- **Menu items**: These show up when a user clicks on a menu

We will use the following code to add Toplevel menu buttons:

```
my_menu = Menu(parent, **options)
```

For example, to add a `File` menu, we will use the following code:

```
# Adding Menubar in the widget
menu_bar = Menu(root)
file_menu = Menu(menu_bar, tearoff=0)
# all file menu-items will be added here next
menu_bar.add_cascade(label='File', menu=file_menu)
root.config(menu=menu_bar)
```

The following screenshot is the result of the preceding code (`2.01.py`):

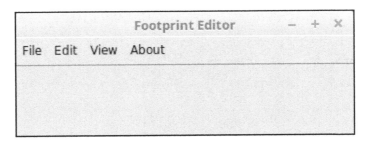

Similarly, we will add the **Edit**, **View**, and **About** menus (`2.01.py`).

We will also define a constant as follows:

```
PROGRAM_NAME = " Footprint Editor "
```

Then, we'll set the root window tile, as follows:

```
root.title(PROGRAM_NAME)
```

Most Linux platforms support **tear-off menus**. When `tearoff` is set to 1 (enabled), the menu appears with a dotted line above the menu options. Clicking on the dotted line enables the user to literally tear off or separate the menu from the top. However, as this is not a cross-platform feature, we have decided to disable tear-off, marking it as `tearoff = 0`.

Adding menu items

Next, we will add menu items in every individual menu. Not surprisingly, the code for the menu items needs to be added in the respective menu instance, as shown in the following screenshot:

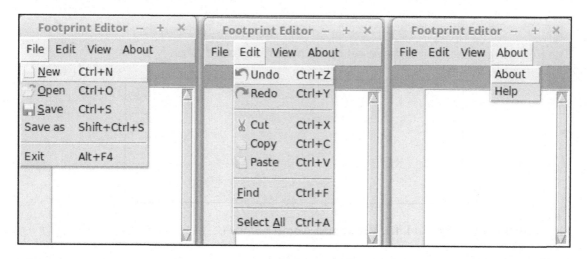

In our example, we will add menu items to the **File**, **Edit**, and **About** menus (2.02.py).

The **View** menu has certain menu item variations, which will be tackled in the following section and are therefore not dealt with here.

Menu items are added by using the add_command() method. The format used to add menu items is as follows:

```
my_menu.add_command(label="Menu Item Label", accelerator='KeyBoard
Shortcut', compound='left', image=my_image, underline=0, command=callback)
```

For example, you can create the **Undo** menu item by using the following syntax:

```
edit_menu.add_command(label="Undo", accelerator='Ctrl + Z',
compound='left', image=undo_icon, command=undo_callback)
```

Some new menu-specific options that are introduced in the preceding code are as follows:

- `accelerator`: This option is used to specify a string, typically a keyboard shortcut, that can be used to invoke a menu. The string specified as an `accelerator` appears next to the text of the menu item. Please note that this does not automatically create bindings for the keyboard shortcut. We will have to manually set them up. This will be discussed later.
- `compound`: Specifying a `compound` option for a menu item lets you add images beside a menu label. A specification such as `compound='left'`, `label= 'Cut'`, `image=cut_icon` means that the cut icon will appear to the left of the Cut menu label. The icons that we will use here are stored and referenced in a separate folder called `icons`.
- `underline`: The `underline` option lets you specify the index of a character in the menu text that needs to be underlined. The indexing starts at 0, which means that specifying `underline=1` underlines the second character of the text. Besides underlining, Tkinter also uses it to define the default bindings for the keyboard traversal of menus. This means that we can select the menu either with the mouse pointer or with the *Alt + <character_at_the_underlined_index>* shortcut.

To add the `New` menu item in the **File** menu, use the following code:

```
file_menu.add_command(label="New", accelerator='Ctrl+N', compound='left',
image=new_file_icon, underline=0, command=new_file)
```

Menu separators

Occasionally, in menu items, you will come across code such as `my_menu.add_separator()`. This widget displays a separator bar and is solely used to organize similar menu items in groups, separating groups by horizontal bars.

Next, we will add a Frame widget to hold the shortcut icons. We will also add a Text widget to the left to display line numbers, as shown in the following screenshot (2.02.py):

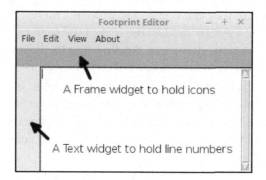

 When working with the pack geometry manager, it is important to add widgets in the order in which they will appear because pack() uses the concept of available space to fit the widgets. This is why the text content widget will appear lower in the code compared to the two label widgets.

Having reserved the space, we can later add shortcut icons or line numbers and keep the Frame widget as the parent widget. Adding frames is easy; we have done that in the past. The code is as follows (refer to 2.02.py):

```
shortcut_bar = Frame(root, height=25, background='light sea green')
shortcut_bar.pack(expand='no', fill='x')
line_number_bar = Text(root, width=4, padx=3, takefocus=0, border=0,
background='khaki', state='disabled', wrap='none')
line_number_bar.pack(side='left', fill='y')
```

We have applied a background color to these two widgets, for now, to differentiate them from the body of the Toplevel window.

Lastly, let's add the main Text widget and the Scrollbar widget, as follows (2.02.py):

```
content_text = Text(root, wrap='word')
content_text.pack(expand='yes', fill='both')
scroll_bar = Scrollbar(content_text)
content_text.configure(yscrollcommand=scroll_bar.set)
scroll_bar.config(command=content_text.yview)
scroll_bar.pack(side='right', fill='y')
```

The code is similar to how we instantiated all the other widgets so far. However, note that the scrollbar is configured to `yview` of the Text widget, and the Text widget is configured to connect to the Scrollbar widget. This way, the widgets are cross-connected to each other.

Now, when you scroll down the Text widget, the scrollbar reacts to it. Alternatively, when you move the scrollbar, the Text widget reacts in turn.

Implementing the View menu

Tkinter offers the following three varieties of menu item:

- **Checkbutton menu items**: These let you make a yes/no choice by checking/unchecking the menu item
- **Radiobutton menu items**: These let you choose an option from many different options
- **Cascade menu items**: These menu items only open up to show another list of choices

The following **View** menu shows these three menu item types in action:

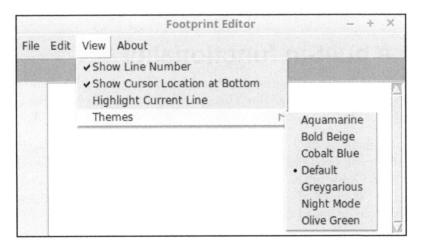

The first three menu items in the **View** menu let users make a definite yes or no choice by checking or unchecking thems. These are examples of the Checkbutton menu.

The **Themes** menu item in the preceding screenshot is an example of a **Cascade** menu. Hovering over this **Cascade** menu simply opens another list of menu items. However, we can also bind a menu item by using the postcommand=callback option. This can be used to manage something just before bringing up the cascading menu item's contents and is often used for dynamic list creation.

Within the **Cascade** menu, you are presented with a list of choices for your editor's theme. However, you can only select one theme. Selecting one theme deselects any previous selections. This is an example of the Radiobutton menu.

We will not present the entire code here (refer to the 2.03.py code in the code bundle). However, the example code used to add these three types of menu item is as follows:

```
view_menu.add_checkbutton(label="Show Line Number", variable=show_line_no)
view_menu.add_cascade(label="Themes", menu=themes_menu)
themes_menu.add_radiobutton(label="Default", variable=theme_name)
```

Now, we need to track whether a selection has been made by adding a variable, which can be BooleanVar(), IntVar(), or Stringvar(), as discussed in Chapter 1, *Meet Tkinter*.

This concludes our first iteration. In this iteration, we laid down the majority of the visual elements of the text editor. Now it's time to add some functionalities to the editor.

Adding a built-in functionality

Tkinter's Text widget comes with some handy built-in functionalities to handle common text-related functions. Let's leverage these functionalities to implement some common features in the text editor.

Let's start by implementing the cut, copy, and paste features. We now have the editor GUI ready. If you open the program and play with the Text widget, you will see that you can perform basic functions such as cut, copy, and paste in the text area by using *Ctrl + X*, *Ctrl + C*, and *Ctrl + V*, respectively. All of these functions exist without us having to add a single line of code for these functionalities.

The Text widget clearly comes with these built-in events. Now, we simply want to connect these events to their respective menu items.

The documentation of the Tcl/Tk universal widget methods tells us that we can trigger events without an external stimulus by using the following command:

```
widget.event_generate(sequence, **kw)
```

To trigger the Cut event, all we need is the following line in the code:

```
content_text.event_generate("<<Cut>>")
```

Let's call it by using a `cut` function and associate it with the Cut menu by using the callback command (`2.04.py`):

```
def cut():
    content_text.event_generate("<<Cut>>")
```

Then, define a callback command from the existing Cut menu, as follows:

```
edit_menu.add_command(label='Cut', accelerator='Ctrl+X', compound='left',
image=cut_icon, command=cut)
```

Similarly, trigger the `copy` and `paste` functions from their respective menu items.

Next, we will move on to the implementation of the `undo` and `redo` features. The Tcl/Tk text documentation tells us that the Text widget has an unlimited Undo and Redo mechanism provided we set the undo option to `true` or `1`. To leverage this option, let's first set the Text widget's undo option to `true` or `1`, as shown in the following code:

```
content_text = Text(root, wrap='word', undo=1)
```

Now, if you open the text editor and try out the `undo` feature by using *Ctrl + Z*, it should work well. Now, we only have to associate the events to functions and call back the functions from the Undo menu. This is similar to what we did for `cut`, `copy`, and `paste`. Refer to the code in `2.03.py`.

However, `redo` has a little quirk that needs to be addressed. By default, `redo` is not bound to the *Ctrl + Y* keys. Instead, *Ctrl + Y* is bound to the `paste` functionality. This is not how we expect the binding to behave, but it exists due to some historical reasons related to Tcl/Tk.

Fortunately, it is easy to override this functionality by adding an event binding, as follows:

```
content_text.bind('<Control-y>', redo) # handling Ctrl + small-case y
content_text.bind('<Control-Y>', redo) # handling Ctrl + upper-case y
```

Since an event binding like the one in the preceding code sends an event argument, the undo function must be able to handle this incoming parameter. Therefore, we'll add the event=None optional parameter to the redo function, as follows (2.04.py):

```
def redo(event=None):
  content_text.event_generate("<<Redo>>")
  return 'break'
```

Events propagate from the operating system level and are accessible to the window that subscribes to the event or wants to make use of it. The return 'break' expression in the preceding function tells the system that it has performed the event and that it should not be propagated further.

This prevents the same event from firing the paste event even though it is the default behavior in Tkinter. Now, *Ctrl + Y* fires the redo event instead of firing the paste event.

In fact, once we have performed an event, we do not want it to propagate further. Thus, we will add return break to all event-driven functions.

Indexing and tagging

Though we managed to leverage some built-in functionalities to gain a quick advantage, we need more control over the text area so that we can bend it to our will. This will require the ability to target each character or text location with precision.

We will need to know the exact position of each character, the cursor, or the selected area in order to do anything with the contents of the editor.

The Text widget offers us the ability to manipulate its content using **index**, **tags**, and **mark**, which let us target a position or place within the text area for manipulation.

Index

Indexing helps you target a particular place within a piece of text. For example, if you want to mark a particular word in bold, red, or in a different font size, you can do so if you know the index of the starting point and the index of the endpoint that needs to be targeted.

The index must be specified in one of the following formats:

The index format	Description
x.y	This refers to the character at row x and column y.
@x,y	This refers to the character that covers the x, y coordinate within the text's window.
end	This refers to the end of the text.
mark	This refers to the character after a named mark.
tag.first	This refers to the first character in the text that has been tagged with a given tag.
tag.last	This refers to the last character in the text that has been tagged with a given tag.
selection (SEL_FIRST, SEL_LAST)	This corresponds to the current selection. The SEL_FIRST and SEL_LAST constants refer to the start position and end position in the selection. Tkinter raises a TclError exception if there is no selection.
window_name	This refers to the position of the embedded window named window_name.
image_name	This refers to the position of the embedded image named image_name.
INSERT	This refers to the position of the insertion cursor.
CURRENT	This refers to the position of the character that is closest to the mouse pointer.

Note a small quirk here. The counting of rows in a Text widget starts at 1, while the counting of columns starts at 0. Therefore, the index for the starting position of the Text widget is 1.0 (that is, row number 1 and column number 0).

An index can be further manipulated by using modifiers and submodifiers. Some examples of modifiers and submodifiers are as follows:

- end - 1 chars or end - 1 c: This refers to the index of the character before the one at the end
- insert +5lines: This refers to the index five lines ahead of the insertion cursor
- insertwordstart - 1 c: This refers to the character just before the first one in a word containing the insertion cursor
- end linestart: This refers to the index of the line start of the end line

Indexes are often used as arguments to functions. Refer to the following list for some examples:

- `my_text.delete(1.0,END)` : This means that you can delete from line 1 , column 0 until the end
- `my_text.get(1.0, END)` : This gets the content from 1.0 (beginning) to the end
- `my_text.delete('insert-1c', INSERT)` : This deletes a character at the insertion cursor

Tags

Tags are used to annotate text with an identification string that can then be used to manipulate the tagged text. Tkinter has a built-in tag called **SEL**, which is automatically applied to the selected text. In addition to SEL, you can define your own tags. A text range can be associated with multiple tags, and the same tag can be used for many different text ranges.

Here are some examples of tagging:

```
my_text.tag_add('sel', '1.0', 'end') # add SEL tag from start(1.0) to end
my_text.tag_add('danger', "insert linestart", "insert lineend+1c")
my_text.tag_remove('danger', 1.0, "end")
my_text.tag_config('danger', background=red)
my_text.tag_config('outdated', overstrike=1)
```

You can specify the visual style for a given tag with `tag_config`, using options such as `background` (color), `bgstipple` (bitmap), `borderwidth` (distance), `fgstipple` (bitmap), `font` (font), `foreground` (color), `justify` (constant), `lmargin1` (distance), `lmargin2` (distance), `offset` (distance), `overstrike` (flag), `relief` (constant), `rmargin` (distance), `spacing1` (distance), `tabs` (string), `underline` (flag), and `wrap` (constant).

For a complete reference about text indexing and tagging, type the following command into the Python interactive shell:

```
>>> import Tkinter
>>> help(Tkinter.Text)
```

Equipped with a basic understanding of indexing and tagging, let's implement some more features in the code editor.

Implementing the Select All feature

We know that Tkinter has a built-in `sel` tag that applies a selection to a given text range. We want to apply this tag to the entire text in the widget.

We can simply define a function to handle this, as follows (`2.05.py`):

```
def select_all(event=None):
  content_text.tag_add('sel', '1.0', 'end')
  return "break"
```

After doing this, add a callback to the `Select All` menu item:

```
edit_menu.add_command(label='Select All', underline=7,
accelerator='Ctrl+A', command=select_all)
```

We also need to bind the function to the *Ctrl + A* keyboard shortcut. We do this by using the following key bindings (`2.05.py`):

```
content_text.bind('<Control-A>', select_all)
content_text.bind('<Control-a>', select_all)
```

The coding of the `Select All` feature is complete. To try it out, add some text to the text widget and then click on the menu item, `Select All`, or use *Ctrl + A* (`accelerator` shortcut key).

Implementing the Find Text feature

Next, let's code the `Find Text` feature (`2.05.py`). The following screenshot shows an example of the `Find Text` feature:

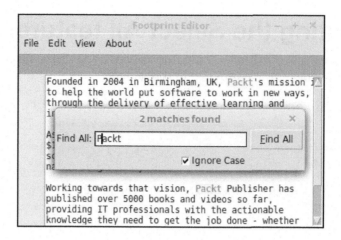

Here's a quick summary of the desired functionality. When a user clicks on the **Find** menu item, a new Toplevel window opens up. The user enters a search keyword and specifies whether the search needs to be case-sensitive. When the user clicks on the **Find All** button, all matches are highlighted.

To search through the document, we rely on the `text_widget.search()` method. The search method takes in the following arguments:

```
search(pattern, startindex, stopindex=None, forwards=None, backwards=None,
exact=None, regexp=None, nocase=None, count=None)
```

For the editor, define a function called `find_text` and attach it as a callback to the **Find** menu (`2.05.py`):

```
edit_menu.add_command(label='Find',underline= 0, accelerator='Ctrl+F',
command=find_text)
```

Also, bind it to the *Ctrl + F* shortcut, as follows:

```
content_text.bind('<Control-f>', find_text)
content_text.bind('<Control-F>', find_text)
```

Then, define the `find_text` function, as follows (`2.05.py`):

```
def find_text(event=None):
    search_toplevel = Toplevel(root)
    search_toplevel.title('Find Text')
    search_toplevel.transient(root)
    Label(search_toplevel, text="Find All:").grid(row=0,
                                    column=0,sticky='e')
    search_entry_widget = Entry(search_toplevel, width=25)
```

```
search_entry_widget.grid(row=0, column=1, padx=2, pady=2,
sticky='we')
search_entry_widget.focus_set()
ignore_case_value = IntVar()
.... more code here to crate checkbox and button
def close_search_window():
    content_text.tag_remove('match', '1.0', END)
    search_toplevel.destroy()
    search_toplevel.protocol('WM_DELETE_WINDOW',
    close_search_window)
    return "break"
```

The following is a description of the preceding code (2.05.py):

- When a user clicks on the **Find** menu item, it invokes a `find_text` callback.

- The first four lines of the `find_text()` function create a new Toplevel window, add a window title, specify its geometry (size, shape, and location), and set it as a *transient window*. Setting it as a transient window means that it is always drawn on top of its parent or root window. If you comment out this line and click on the root editor window, the **Find** window will go behind the root window.

- The next eight lines of code are pretty self-explanatory; they set the widgets of the **Find** window. They add the Label, Entry, Button, and Checkbutton widgets, and set up the `search_string` and `ignore_case_value` variables to track the value a user enters into the Entry widget and whether the user has checked off Checkbutton. The widgets are arranged by using the grid geometry manager to fit into the **Find** window.

- The **Find All** button has a command option that calls a `search_output` function, passing the search string as the first argument and whether the search needs to be case-sensitive as its second argument. The third, fourth, and fifth arguments pass the Toplevel window, the Text widget, and the Entry widget as parameters.

- We override the **Close** button of the **Find** window and redirect it to a callback named `close_search()`. The `close_search` function is defined within the `find_text` function. This function takes care of removing the match tag that was added during the search. If we do not override the **Close** button and remove these tags, the matched string will continue to be marked in red and yellow even after the search has ended.

Next, we define the `search_output` function, which does the actual searching and adds the match tag to the matching text. The code for this is as follows:

```
def search_output(needle, if_ignore_case, content_text,
  search_toplevel, search_box):
  content_text.tag_remove('match', '1.0', END)
  matches_found = 0
  if needle:
    start_pos = '1.0'
    while True:
        start_pos = content_text.search(needle, start_pos,
            nocase=if_ignore_case, stopindex=END)
        if not start_pos:
            break
        end_pos = '{}+{}c'.format(start_pos, len(needle))
        content_text.tag_add('match', start_pos, end_pos)
        matches_found += 1
        start_pos = end_pos
    content_text.tag_config('match', foreground='red', background='yellow')
  search_box.focus_set()
  search_toplevel.title('{} matches found'.format(matches_found))
```

The following is a description of the preceding code:

- This part of the code is the heart of the `search` function. It searches through the entire document by using the `while True` loop, breaking out of the loop only if no more text items remain to be searched.
- The code first removes the previous search-related match tags if there are any, as we do not want to append the results of the new search to the previous search results. The function uses the `search()` method, which is provided in Tkinter in the Text widget. The `search()` method takes the following arguments:

  ```
  search(pattern, index, stopindex=None, forwards=None,
  backwards=None, exact=None, regexp=None, nocase=None, count=None)
  ```

- The `search()` method returns the starting position of the first match. We store it in a variable named `start_pos`, calculate the position of the last character in the matched word, and store it in the `end_pos` variable.
- For every search match that it finds, it adds the match tag to the text ranging from the first position to the last position. After every match, we set the value of `start_pos` to be equal to `end_pos`. This ensures that the next search starts after `end_pos`.
- The loop also keeps track of the number of matches by using the `count` variable.

- Outside the loop, the tag match is configured to have a red font and yellow background. The last line of this function updates the title of the **Find** window with the number of matches that were found.

In case of event bindings, interaction occurs between input devices (keyboard/mouse) and your application. In addition to event binding, Tkinter also supports protocol handling.

The term protocol refers to the interaction between your application and the window manager. An example of a protocol is `WM_DELETE_WINDOW`, which handles the close window event for your window manager.

Tkinter lets you override these protocol handlers by mentioning your own handler for the root or Toplevel widget. To override the window exit protocol, we use the following command:

`root.protocol(WM_DELETE_WINDOW, callback)`

Once you add this command, Tkinter reroutes protocol handling to the specified callback/handler.

Types of Toplevel window

Previously in this chapter, we used the following line of code:

```
search_toplevel.transient(root)
```

Let's explore what it means here. Tkinter supports the following four types of Toplevel window:

- **The main Toplevel window**: This is the type we have been constructing so far.
- **The child Toplevel window**: This type is independent of the root. The Toplevel child behaves independently of its root, but it gets destroyed if its parent is destroyed.
- **The transient Toplevel window**: This always appears at the top of its parent, but it does not entirely grab the focus. Clicking again on the parent window allows you to interact with it. The transient window is hidden when the parent is minimized, and it is destroyed if the parent is destroyed. Compare this to what is called a **modal window**. A modal window grabs all the focus from the parent window and asks a user to first close the modal window before regaining access to the parent window.

- **The undecorated Toplevel window:** A Toplevel window is undecorated if it does not have a window manager decoration around it. It is created by setting the **overrideredirect** flag to 1. An undecorated window cannot be resized or moved.

Refer to the 2.06.py code for a demonstration of all four types of Toplevel window.

This concludes our second iteration. Congratulations! We have completed coding the Select All and Find Text functionality into our program.

More importantly, you have been introduced to indexing and tagging—two very powerful concepts associated with many Tkinter widgets. You will find yourself using these two concepts all the time in your projects.

We also explored the four types of Toplevel window and the use cases for each of them.

Working with forms and dialogs

The goal for this iteration is to implement the functionality of the **File** menu options: **Open**, **Save**, and **Save As**.

We can implement these dialogs by using the standard Tkinter widgets. However, since these are so commonly used, a specific Tkinter module called filedialog has been included in the standard Tkinter distribution.

Here's an example of a typical filedialog:

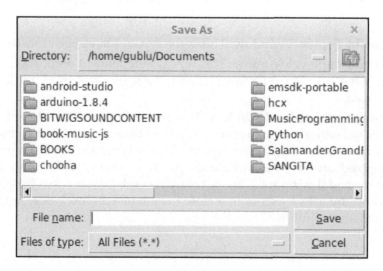

Tkinter defines the following common use cases for `filedialogs`:

Functions	Description
askopenfile	This returns the opened file object
askopenfilename	This returns the filename string, not the opened file object
askopenfilenames	This returns a list of filenames
askopenfiles	This returns a list of open file objects or an empty list if Cancel is selected
asksaveasfile	This asks for a filename to save as and returns the opened file object
asksaveasfilename	This asks for a filename to save as and returns the filename
askdirectory	This asks for a directory and returns the directory name

The usage is simple. Import the `filedialog` module and call the required function. Here's an example:

```
import tkinter.filedialog
```

We then call the required function using the following code:

```
file_object = tkinter.filedialog.askopenfile(mode='r')
```

Or, we use this code:

```
my_file_name = tkinter.filedialog.askopenfilename()
```

The `mode='r'` option specified in the preceding code is one of many configurable options that are available for dialogs.

You can specify the following additional options for `filedialog`:

File dialog	Configurable options
askopenfile (mode='r', **options)	parent, title, message, defaultextension, filetypes, initialdir, initialfile, and multiple
askopenfilename (**options)	parent, title, message, defaultextension, filetypes, initialdir, initialfile, and multiple
asksaveasfile (mode='w', **options)	parent, title, message, defaultextension, filetypes, initialdir, initialfile, and multiple

`asksaveasfilename` `(**options)`	`parent, title, message, defaultextension, filetypes,` `initialdir, initialfile,` and multiple
`askdirectory` `(**options)`	`parent, title,` and `initialdir` must exist

Equipped with a basic understanding of the `filedialog` module, let's now have a look at its practical usage. We'll begin by implementing the **File | Open** feature.

Let's start by importing the required modules, as follows:

```
import tkinter.filedialog
import os # for handling file operations
```

Next, let's create a global variable, which will store the name of the currently open file, as follows:

```
file_name = None
```

> The use of global variables is generally considered bad programming practice because it is very difficult to understand a program that uses lots of global variables.
>
> A global variable can be modified or accessed from many different places in the program. Therefore, it becomes difficult to remember or work out every possible use of the variable.
>
> A global variable is not subject to access control, which may pose security hazards in certain situations, say when this program needs to interact with third-party code.
>
> However, when you work on programs in a procedural style such as this one, global variables are sometimes unavoidable.
>
> An alternative approach to programming involves writing code in a class structure (also called **object-oriented programming**), where a variable can only be accessed by members of predefined classes. We will see a lot of examples of object-oriented programming in the chapters that follow.

The following code is present in `open_file` (`2.07.py`):

```
def open_file(event=None):
    input_file_name =
      tkinter.filedialog.askopenfilename(defaultextension=".txt",
        filetypes=[("All Files", "*.*"),("Text Documents", "*.txt")])
    if input_file_name:
      global file_name
```

```
file_name = input_file_name
root.title('{} - {}'.format(os.path.basename(file_name),PROGRAM_NAME))
content_text.delete(1.0, END)
with open(file_name) as _file:
  content_text.insert(1.0, _file.read())
on_content_changed()
```

Modify the **Open** menu to add a callback command to this newly defined method, as follows:

```
file_menu.add_command(label='Open', accelerator='Ctrl+O', compound='left',
image=open_file_icon, underline =0, command=open_file)
```

The following is a description of the preceding code:

- We declared a `file_name` variable in the `global` scope to keep track of the filename of the opened file. This is required to keep track of whether a file has been opened. We need this variable in the `global` scope as we want this variable to be available to other methods, such as `save()` and `save_as()`.
- Not specifying it as `global` would mean that it is only available within the function. So, the `save()` and `save_as()` functions would not be able to check whether a file is already open in the editor.
- We use `askopenfilename` to fetch the filename of the opened file. If a user cancels opening the file or no file is chosen, the `file_name` returned is None. In that case, we do nothing.
- However, if `filedialog` returns a valid filename, we isolate the filename using the `os` module and add it as the title of the root window.
- If the `Text` widget already contains some text, we delete it all.
- We then open the given file in read mode and insert its content into the Content widget.
- We use the context manager (the `with` command), which takes care of closing the file properly for us, even in the case of an exception.
- Finally, we add a command callback to the **File | Open** menu item.

This completes the coding of **File | Open**. If you now navigate to **File | Open**, select a text file, and click on **Open**, the content area will be populated with the content of the text file.

Next, we will have a look at how to save a file. There are two aspects to saving a file:

- **Save**
- **Save As**

If the Content text widget already contains a file, we do not prompt the user for a filename. We simply overwrite the contents of the existing file. If there is no filename associated with the current content of the text area, we prompt the user with a **Save As** dialog. Moreover, if the text area has an open file and the user clicks on **Save As**, we still prompt them with a **Save As** dialog to allow them to write the contents to a different filename.

The code for `save` and `save_as` is as follows (`2.07.py`):

```python
def save(event=None):
 global file_name
 if not file_name:
    save_as()
 else:
    write_to_file(file_name)
 return "break"

def save_as(event=None):
 input_file_name = tkinter.filedialog.asksaveasfilename
    (defaultextension=".txt", filetypes=[("All Files", "*.*"),
    ("Text Documents", "*.txt")])
 if input_file_name:
    global file_name
    file_name = input_file_name
    write_to_file(file_name)
    root.title('{} - {}'.format(os.path.basename(file_name),PROGRAM_NAME))
 return "break"

def write_to_file(file_name):
    try:
      content = content_text.get(1.0, 'end')
      with open(file_name, 'w') as the_file:
        the_file.write(content)
    except IOError:
      pass
      # pass for now but we show some warning - we do this in next section
```

Having defined the `save` and `save_as` functions, let's connect them to the respective menu callback:

```python
file_menu.add_command(label='Save', accelerator='Ctrl+S',  compound='left',
image=save_file_icon,underline=0, command= save)
file_menu.add_command(label='Save as',   accelerator='Shift+Ctrl+S',
command= save_as)
```

The following is a description of the preceding code:

- The `save` function first tries to check whether a file is open. If a file is open, it simply overwrites the contents of the file with the current contents of the text area. If no file is open, it simply passes the work to the `save_as` function.
- The `save_as` function opens a dialog by using `asksaveasfilename` and tries to get the filename provided by the user for the given file. If it succeeds, it opens the new file in write mode and writes the contents of the text under this new filename. After writing, it closes the current file object and changes the title of the window to reflect the new filename.
- If the user does not specify a filename or the user cancels the `save_as` operation, it simply ignores the process by using a pass command.
- We added a `write_to_file(file_name)` helper function to do the actual writing to the file.

While we are at it, let's complete the functionality of **File | New**. The code is simple (`2.07.py`):

```
def new_file(event=None):
    root.title("Untitled")
    global file_name
    file_name = None
    content_text.delete(1.0,END)
```

Now, add a callback command to this new function to the **File | New** menu item:

```
file_menu.add_command(label='New', accelerator='Ctrl+N', compound='left',
image=new_file_icon, underline=0, command=new_file)
```

The following is a description of the preceding code:

1. The `new_file` function begins by changing the title attribute of the root window to `Untitled`.
2. It then sets the value of the `global` filename variable to `None`. This is important because the `save` and `save_as` functionalities use this global variable name to track whether the file already exists or is new.
3. The function then deletes all the contents of the `Text` widget, creating a fresh document in its place.

Let's wrap up this iteration by adding keyboard shortcuts for the newly created features (2.07.py):

```
content_text.bind('<Control-N>', new_file)
content_text.bind('<Control-n>', new_file)
content_text.bind('<Control-O>', open_file)
content_text.bind('<Control-o>', open_file)
content_text.bind('<Control-S>', save)
content_text.bind('<Control-s>',save)
```

In this iteration, we implemented the coding functionality for the **New**, **Open**, **Save**, and **Save As** menu items. More importantly, we saw how to use the filedialog module to achieve certain commonly used file features in the program. We also had a look at how to use indexing to achieve a wide variety of tasks for programs.

Working with message boxes

Now, let's complete the code for the **About** and **Help** menus. The functionality is simple. When a user clicks on the **Help** or **About** menu, a message window pops up and waits for the user to respond by clicking on a button. Though we can easily code new Toplevel windows to show the **About** and **Help** messages, we will instead use a module called messagebox to achieve this functionality.

The messagebox module provides ready-made message boxes to display a wide variety of messages in applications. The functions available through this module include showinfo, showwarning, showerror, askquestion, askokcancel, askyesno, askyesnocancel, and askretrycancel, as shown in the following screenshot:

To use this module, we simply import it into the current namespace by using the following command:

```
import tkinter.messagebox
```

A demonstration of the commonly used functions of messagebox is provided in 2.08.py in the code bundle. The following are some common usage patterns:

```
import tkinter.messagebox as tmb
tmb.showinfo(title="Show Info", message="This is FYI")
tmb.showwarning(title="Show Warning", message="Don't be silly")
tmb.showerror(title="Show Error", message="It leaked")
tmb.askquestion(title="Ask Question", message="Can you read this?")
tmb.askokcancel(title="Ask OK Cancel", message="Say Ok or Cancel?")
tmb.askyesno(title="Ask Yes-No", message="Say yes or no?")
tmb.askyesnocancel(title="Yes-No-Cancel", message="Say yes no cancel")
tmb.askretrycancel(title="Ask Retry Cancel", message="Retry or what?")
```

Equipped with an understanding of the messagebox module, let's code the about and help functions for the code editor. The functionality is simple. When a user clicks on the **About** or **Help** menu item, a showinfomessagebox pops up.

To achieve this, include the following code in the editor (2.09.py):

```
def display_about_messagebox(event=None):
    tkinter.messagebox.showinfo("About", "{}{}".format(PROGRAM_NAME,
        "\nTkinter GUI Application\n Development Blueprints"))


def display_help_messagebox(event=None):
    tkinter.messagebox.showinfo("Help", "Help Book: \nTkinter GUI
        Application\n Development Blueprints", icon='question')
```

Then, attach these functions to the respective menu items, as follows:

```
about_menu.add_command(label='About', command=display_about_messagebox)
about_menu.add_command(label='Help', command=display_help_messagebox)
```

Next, we will add the quit confirmation feature. Ideally, we should have implemented file saving in the event the text content has been modified, but for the sake of simplicity I am not putting in that logic here and instead am displaying a prompt for the user to determine whether the program should be closed or kept open. Accordingly, when the user clicks on **File | Exit**, it prompts an Ok-Cancel dialog to confirm the quit action:

```
def exit_editor(event=None):
        if tkinter.messagebox.askokcancel("Quit?", "Really quit?"):
            root.destroy()
```

Then, we override the **Close** button and redirect it to the `exit_editor` function that we previously defined, as follows:

```
root.protocol('WM_DELETE_WINDOW', exit_editor)
```

Then, we add a callback command for all the individual menu items, as follows:

```
file_menu.add_command(label='Exit', accelerator='Alt+F4', command=
exit_editor)
about_menu.add_command(label='About', command = display_about_messagebox)
about_menu.add_command(label='Help', command = display_help_messagebox)
```

Finally, add the bindings for the keyboard shortcut to display help:

```
content_text.bind('<KeyPress-F1>', display_help_messagebox)
```

This completes the iteration.

The icons toolbar and View menu functions

In this iteration, we will add the following functionalities to the text editor:

- Showing shortcut icons on the toolbar
- Displaying line numbers
- Highlighting the current line
- Changing the color theme of the editor

Let's start with a simple task first. In this step, we will add shortcut icons to the toolbar, as shown in the following screenshot:

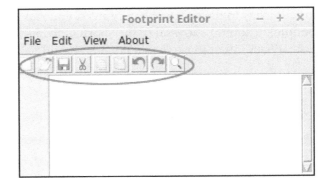

You may recall that we have already created a frame to hold these icons. Let's add these icons now.

While adding these icons, we have followed a convention. The icons have been named exactly the same as the corresponding function that handles them. Following this convention has enabled us to loop through a list, simultaneously apply the icon image to each button, and add the command callback from within the loop. All the icons have been placed in the icons folder.

The following code adds icons to the toolbar (2.10.py):

```
icons = ('new_file', 'open_file', 'save', 'cut', 'copy', 'paste', 'undo',
'redo', 'find_text')
for i, icon in enumerate(icons):
    tool_bar_icon = PhotoImage(file='icons/{}.gif'.format(icon))
    cmd = eval(icon)
    tool_bar = Button(shortcut_bar, image=tool_bar_icon, command=cmd)
    tool_bar.image = tool_bar_icon
    tool_bar.pack(side='left')
```

The following is a description of the preceding code:

- We have already created a shortcut bar in the first iteration. Now, we will simply add buttons with images in the frame.
- We create a list of icons, taking care to name them exactly the same as the name of the icons.
- We then loop through the list by creating a Button widget, adding an image to the button, and adding the respective callback command.
- Before adding the callback command, we have to convert the string to an equivalent expression by using the `eval` command. If we do not apply `eval`, it cannot be applied as an expression to the callback command.

Thus, we've added shortcut icons to the shortcut bar. Now, if you run the code (refer to `2.10.py` in the code bundle), it should show all of the shortcut icons. Moreover, as we have linked each button to its callback, all of these shortcut icons should work.

Displaying line numbers

Let's work toward showing line numbers to the left of the Text widget. This will require us to tweak the code in various places. So, before we start coding, let's look at what we are trying to achieve.

The **View** menu has a menu item that allows users to choose whether to **Show Line Number**. We only want to show line numbers if the option is selected, as shown in the following screenshot:

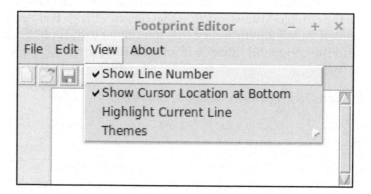

If the option is selected, we need to display line numbers in the left frame that we created earlier.

The line number should update every time a user enters a new line, deletes a line, cuts or pastes line text, performs an undo or a redo operation, opens an existing file, or clicks on the **New** menu item. In short, the line number should be updated after every activity results in a change of content. Therefore, we need to define a function called `on_content_changed()`. This function should be called after the definitions of every `press`, `cut`, `paste`, `undo`, `redo`, `new`, and `open` key, to check whether lines have been added or removed from the text area and accordingly update the line numbers.

We achieve this by using the following two strategies (refer to `2.10.py` in the code bundle):

```
def on_content_changed(event=None):
    update_line_numbers()
```

Bind a key press event to the `update_line_number()` function, as follows:

```
content_text.bind('<Any-KeyPress>', on_content_changed)
```

Next, add a call to the `on_content_changed()` function in each of the definitions of `cut`, `paste`, `undo`, `redo`, `new`, and `open`.

Then define a `get_line_numbers()` function that returns a string containing all the numbers until the last row, separated by line breaks.

So for instance, if the last non-empty row in the content widget is 5, this function returns us a string of the `1 /n 2 /n 3 /n 4/n 5 /n` form.

The following is the function definition:

```
def get_line_numbers():
    output = ''
    if show_line_number.get():
        row, col = content_text.index("end").split('.')
        for i in range(1, int(row)):
            output += str(i)+ '\n'
    return output
```

Now, let's define the `update_line_numbers()` function, which simply updates the text widget that displays the line using the string output from the previous function:

```
def update_line_numbers(event = None):
    line_numbers = get_line_numbers()
    line_number_bar.config(state='normal')
    line_number_bar.delete('1.0', 'end')
    line_number_bar.insert('1.0', line_numbers)
    line_number_bar.config(state='disabled')
```

The following is a description of the preceding code:

- You may recall that we assigned a `show_line_number` variable to the menu item earlier:
  ```
  show_line_number = IntVar()
  show_line_number.set(1)
  view_menu.add_checkbutton(label="Show Line
  Number", variable=show_line_number)
  ```
- If the `show_line_number` option is set to 1 (that is to say, it has been checked off in the menu item), we calculate the last line and last column in the text.
- We then create a text string consisting of numbers from 1 to the number of the last line, with each number separated by a line break (\n). This string is then added to the left label by using the `line_number_bar.config()` method.
- If `Show Line Number` is unchecked in the menu, the variable text remains blank, thereby displaying no line numbers.
- Finally, we update each of the previously defined `cut`, `paste`, `undo`, `redo`, `new`, and `open` functions to invoke the `on_content_changed()` function at its end.

We have finished adding the line number functionality to the text editor. However, I would like to add that this implementation, though simple, has some limitations in that it does not handle word wrapping and font size variability very well. A foolproof line numbering solution would require the use of the Canvas widget – something that we discuss Chapter 4 Game of Chess and onward. Meanwhile, if you are curious, take a look at a sample Canvas-based implementation at https://stackoverflow.com/a/16375233/2348704.

Lastly, in this iteration, we will implement a feature where a user can choose to highlight the current line (2.10.py).

The idea is simple. We need to locate the line of the cursor and add a tag to the line. We also need to configure the tag so that it appears with a differently colored background to highlight it.

You may recall that we have already provided a menu choice to users to decide whether to highlight the current line. We will now add a callback command from this menu item to a function that we will define as `toggle_highlight`:

```
to_highlight_line = BooleanVar()
view_menu.add_checkbutton(label='Highlight Current Line', onvalue=1,
offvalue=0,     variable=to_highlight_line, command=toggle_highlight)
```

Now, we define three functions to handle this for us:

```
def highlight_line(interval=100):
    content_text.tag_remove("active_line", 1.0, "end")
    content_text.tag_add("active_line",
                    "insert linestart", "insert lineend+1c")
    content_text.after(interval, toggle_highlight)

def undo_highlight():
    content_text.tag_remove("active_line", 1.0, "end")

def toggle_highlight(event=None):
    if to_highlight_line.get():
        highlight_line()
    else:
        undo_highlight()
```

The following is a description of the preceding code:

- Every time a user checks/unchecks **View** | **Highlight Current Line**, this invokes the `toggle_highlight` function. This function checks whether the menu item is checked. If it is checked, it invokes the `highlight_line` function. Otherwise, if the menu item is unchecked, it invokes the `undo_highlight` function.
- The `highlight_line` function simply adds a tag called `active_line` to the current line, and after every 100 milliseconds it calls the `toggle_highlight` function to check whether the current line should still be highlighted.
- The `undo_highlight` function is invoked when the user unchecks highlighting in the View menu. Once invoked, it simply removes the `active_line` tag from the entire text area.

Finally, we can configure the tag named `active_line` so that it is displayed with a different background color, as follows:

```
content_text.tag_configure('active_line', background='ivory2')
```

We used the .widget.after(ms, callback) handler in the code. Methods that let us perform some periodic actions are called **alarm handlers**. The following are some commonly used Tkinter alarm handlers:

- after(delay_ms, callback, args...): This registers a callback alarm, which can be called after a given number of milliseconds.
- after_cancel(id): This cancels the given callback alarm.
- after_idle(callback, args...): This calls back only when there are no more events to process in mainloop; that is, after the system becomes idle.

Adding the cursor information bar

The cursor information bar is simply a small label at the bottom-right corner of the Text widget that displays the current position of the cursor, as shown in the following screenshot:

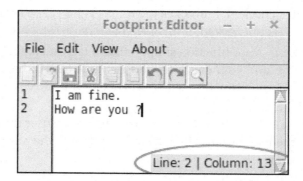

The user can choose to show/hide this info bar from the **View** menu (2.11.py).

Begin by creating a Label widget within the Text widget and pack it in the bottom-right corner, as follows:

```
cursor_info_bar = Label(content_text, text='Line: 1 | Column: 1')
cursor_info_bar.pack(expand=NO, fill=None, side=RIGHT, anchor='se')
```

In many ways, this is similar to displaying line numbers. Here, too, the positions must be calculated after every keystroke, after events such as cut, paste, undo, redo, new, and open, or activities that lead to a change in cursor positions. Because this too needs to be updated for all the changed content, for every keystroke, we will update on_content_changed to update this, as follows:

```
def on_content_changed(event=None):
 update_line_numbers()
 update_cursor_info_bar()

def show_cursor_info_bar():
 show_cursor_info_checked = show_cursor_info.get()
 if show_cursor_info_checked:
   cursor_info_bar.pack(expand='no', fill=None, side='right', anchor='se')
 else:
   cursor_info_bar.pack_forget()

def update_cursor_info_bar(event=None):
 row, col = content_text.index(INSERT).split('.')
 line_num, col_num = str(int(row)), str(int(col)+1) # col starts at 0
 infotext = "Line: {0} | Column: {1}".format(line_num, col_num)
 cursor_info_bar.config(text=infotext)
```

The code is simple. We get the row and column for the current cursor position by using the index(INSERT) method and update the labels with the latest row and column of the cursor.

Finally, the function is connected to the existing menu item by using a callback command:

```
view_menu.add_checkbutton(label='Show Cursor Location at Bottom',
                 variable=show_cursor_info, command=show_cursor_info_bar)
```

Adding themes

You may recall that, while defining the Themes menu, we defined a color scheme dictionary containing the name and hexadecimal color codes as a key-value pair, as follows:

```
color_schemes = {
'Default': '#000000.#FFFFFF',
'Greygarious':'#83406A.#D1D4D1',
'Aquamarine': '#5B8340.#D1E7E0',
'Bold Beige': '#4B4620.#FFF0E1',
'Cobalt Blue':'#ffffBB.#3333aa',
'Olive Green': '#D1E7E0.#5B8340',
```

```
'Night Mode': '#FFFFFF.#000000',
}
```

The theme choice menu has already been defined. Let's add a callback command to handle the selected menu (2.12.py):

```
themes_menu.add_radiobutton(label=k,
variable=theme_choice, command=change_theme).
```

Finally, let's define the change_theme function to handle the changing of themes, as follows:

```
def change_theme(event=None):
    selected_theme = theme_choice.get()
    fg_bg_colors = color_schemes.get(selected_theme)
    foreground_color, background_color = fg_bg_colors.split('.')
    content_text.config(background=background_color, fg=foreground_color)
```

The function is simple. It picks up the key-value pair from the defined color scheme dictionary. It splits the color into its two components and applies one color each to the Text widget foreground and background using widget.config().

Now, if you select a different color from the **Themes** menu, the background and foreground colors change accordingly.

This completes the iteration. We completed coding the shortcut icon toolbar and the functionality of the View menu in this iteration. In the process, we learned how to handle the Checkbutton and Radiobutton menu items. We also had a look at how to create compound buttons while reinforcing several Tkinter options that were covered in the previous sections.

Creating a context/pop-up menu

Let's complete the editor in this final iteration by adding a contextual menu to the editor (2.12.py), as shown in the following screenshot:

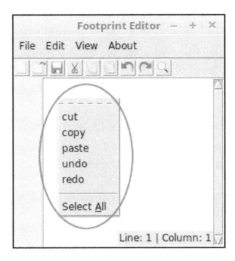

The menu that pops up on a right-click at the location of the cursor is called the **context menu** or the **pop-up menu**.

Let's code this feature in the text editor. First, define the context menu, as follows:

```
popup_menu = Menu(content_text)
for i in ('cut', 'copy', 'paste', 'undo', 'redo'):
    cmd = eval(i)
    popup_menu.add_command(label=i, compound='left', command=cmd)
    popup_menu.add_separator()
popup_menu.add_command(label='Select All',underline=7, command=select_all)
```

Then, bind the right-click of a mouse with a callback named show_popup_menu, as follows:

```
content_text.bind('<Button-3>', show_popup_menu)
```

Finally, define the show_popup_menu function in the following way:

```
def show_popup_menu(event):
    popup_menu.tk_popup(event.x_root, event.y_root)
```

You can now right-click anywhere on the Text widget in the editor to open the contextual menu.

This concludes the iteration as well as the chapter.

Summary

In this chapter, we covered the following points:

- We completed coding the editor in twelve iterations. We started by placing all the widgets on the Toplevel window.
- We then leveraged some built-in features of the Text widget to code some functionality.
- We learned the important concepts of indexing and tagging.
- We also saw how to use the `filedialog` and `messagebox` modules to quickly code some common features in programs.

Congratulations! You completed coding your text editor. In the next chapter, we will make a programmable drum machine.

QA section

Here are a few questions to reflect upon:

- What's the difference between the Checkbutton menu item and the Radio button menu item?
- What's the **Cascade** menu button used for?
- Identify different kinds of Toplevel window.
- List the different types of `filedialogs` and message boxes available in Tkinter.
- We used the pack geometry manager to build this text editor. Could we have built this using the grid geometry manager? How would the grid geometry manager fare against pack?
- How can we trigger events without an external stimulus in Tkinter?
- What are accelerator options in menu items?
- What is a transient window?

Further reading

The source code for the `filedialog` module can be found within the Tkinter source code in a separate file named `filedialog.py`. You are encouraged to take a look at its implementation.

If you are feeling adventurous and want to further explore the Text Editor program, I encourage you to have a look at the source code for Python's built-in editor named IDLE, which is written in Tkinter. The source code for IDLE can be found in your local Python library directory in a folder called `idlelib`. On Linux Mint, this is located at `/usr/lib/python3.4/idlelib`.

Read the official Python styling guide, which is specified in the PEP8 documentation at `https://www.python.org/dev/peps/pep-0008`.

If you like, try to implement syntax highlighting of Python code in the text editor. A naive implementation would first involve defining a list of keywords. Then we can bind the `<KeyRelease>` event to check whether the typed word is one of the keywords. We can then add a custom tag to the word using `tag_add`. Finally, we can change its color by using code such as `textarea.tag_config("the_keyword_tag", foreground="blue")`.

A slightly advanced idea to read up on and implement is called **lazy loading**. This is particularly helpful if you want to open a very large file in the text editor. In the present implementation, it may take very long time to open a very large file. In contrast, lazy loading will read only the section of the file that is currently visible in the text editor, thus making the program much more responsive.

3
Programmable Drum Machine

We looked at several common Tkinter widgets, such as Menu, Buttons, Label, and Text, in `Chapter 2`, *Making a Text Editor*. Let's now expand our experience with Tkinter to make some music. Let's build a cross-platform drum machine using Tkinter and some other Python modules.

Some of the key objectives for this chapter are:

- Learning to structure Tkinter programs in the **object-oriented style** of programming
- Delving deeper into a few more Tkinter widgets, such as Spinbox, Button, Entry, and Checkbutton
- Applying the grid geometry manager in a practical project
- Understanding the importance of choosing the right **data structure** for our programs
- Learning to bind **higher-order callback functions** to widgets
- Learning to use Tkinter in conjunction with some standard and third-party modules
- Understanding the need for **multithreading** and how to write multithreaded applications
- Learning about **object serialization** or **pickling**
- Learning about **ttk widgets**

Getting started

Our goal here is to build a programmable drum machine. Let's call it the `Explosion Drum Machine`.

The drum machine will let the user create an unlimited number of beat patterns using an unlimited number of drum samples. You can then store multiple riffs in a project and playback or edit the project later on. In its final form, the drum machine would look like the following screenshot:

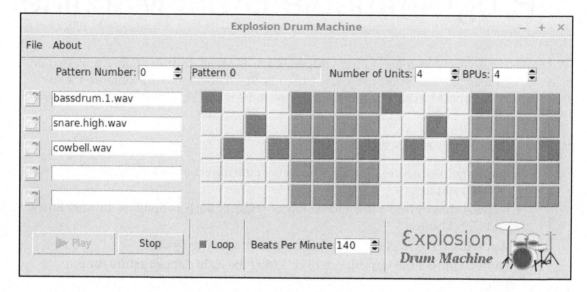

To create your own drum beat patterns, simply load some drum samples (which can be any audio file with a `.wav` or `.ogg` extension) using the buttons on the left. You can design your beat patterns by clicking on the buttons on the right.

You can decide the number of **beats per unit** (**BPU**). Most western beats have 4 BPU, a Waltz would have 3 BPU, and some Indian and Arabic rhythms that I composed on this machine had 3-16 BPU! You can also change the **beats per minute (BPM)**, which in turn decides the tempo of the rhythm.

A single pattern, as shown in the previous screenshot, constitutes a single beat pattern. You can design multiple beat patterns by changing the Pattern Number Spinbox widget in the top-left section.

Once you have made some beat patterns, you can even save the pattern and later replay or modify it. The saving and reloading of files are done from the **File** menu at the top.

A few drum samples are provided in the `Loops` subdirectory; however, you can load any other drum sample. You can download a large number of samples for free from the internet.

Technical requirements

We will use some more built-in libraries from the standard Python distribution for this chapter. This includes `tkinter`, `os`, `math`, `threading`, and `pickle` modules.

To verify that these modules exist, simply run the following statement in your Python3 IDLE interactive prompt:

```
>>> import tkinter, os, math, time, threading, pickle
```

This should not cause an error, as Python3 comes with these modules built into the distribution.

Other than this, you need to add an extra Python module called `pygame`. We will be using the version named 1.9.3 Package, which can be downloaded at `http://www.pygame.org/download.shtml`.

Linux users may additionally want to take a look at the following page for instructions on getting `pygame` to work with Python 3.x: `http://www.pygame.org/wiki/CompileUbuntu?parent=Compilation`.

`pygame` is a cross-platform package normally used for making games with Python. However, we will just be using a small module from the package named `pygame.mixer`, which is used for loading and playing sounds. The API documentation for this module can be found at `http://www.pygame.org/docs/ref/mixer.html`.

After you have installed the module, you can verify it by importing it:

```
>>> import pygame
>>> pygame.version.ver
```

If no errors are reported and the version output is 1.9.3, you are ready to program the drum machine. Let's start!

Setting up the GUI in OOP

The text editor we developed in the previous chapter was implemented in procedural code. Although it offered some benefits for quick coding, it had some typical limitations:

- We started encountering global variables
- The function definitions needed to be defined above the code that called them
- Most importantly, the code was not reusable

Therefore, we need some way to ensure that our code is reusable. This is why programmers prefer to use **object-oriented programming** (**OOP**) to organize their code into classes.

OOP is a programming paradigm that shifts the focus onto the objects we want to manipulate rather than the logic required to manipulate them. This is in contrast to procedural programming, which views a program as a logical procedure that takes input, processes it, and produces some output.

OOP provides several benefits, such as **data abstraction**, **encapsulation**, **inheritance**, and **polymorphism**. In addition, OOP provides a clear **modular structure** for programs. Code modification and maintenance are easy, as new objects can be created without modifying the existing ones.

Let's build our drum program using OOP to illustrate some of these features. An indicative OOP structure for our drum program could be as follows (code 3.01.py):

```python
from tkinter import Tk

PROGRAM_NAME = ' Explosion Drum Machine '

class DrumMachine:

    def __init__(self, root):
        self.root = root
        self.root.title(PROGRAM_NAME)

if __name__ == '__main__':
    root = Tk()
    DrumMachine(root)
    root.mainloop()
```

The description of the code is as follows:

- We create a class structure called `DrumMachine` and initialize the Toplevel window passed as an argument to it
- If the script is run as a standalone program, that is, `if __name__ == '__main__'`, a new `Tk()` root object is created and the root window is passed as an argument to the `DrumMachine` object
- We then initiate an object from the `DrumMachine` class to get a Toplevel window

Now that we have our Toplevel window ready, let's stop adding any more visual elements and think about something that is critical to how well our program will eventually turn out to be. Let's spend some time finalizing the data structure for our program.

Finalizing the data structure

As Linus Torvalds, the developer of Linux, once said:

> *"Bad programmers worry about the code. Good programmers worry about data structures and their relationships."*

What he means is that well-designed data structures make the code very easy to design, maintain, and scale up. In contrast, if you start with a poor data structure, you can't make up for that, even with the best of code.

Start with a good data structure and your code will naturally be more simple, elegant, and easy to maintain.

With that in mind, let's try to decide on a suitable data structure for our program. Go back and take a look at the previous screenshot (under the *Getting started* section). What kind of data structure, do you think, would be needed to capture all the necessary fields of information?

Well, first of all our drum machine needs to keep information about beat patterns. So let's start by creating a list named `all_patterns = []`.

Now, each of the patterns within the list needs to capture information about the drum files related to the pattern: the number of units in the pattern, the BPU for the pattern, the BPM, and the buttons clicked to form the pattern.

Accordingly, we need to come up with a data structure where `all_patterns` is a list where each item represents a single pattern. Each pattern is then denoted by a dictionary, as follows:

```
{
'list_of_drum_files': a list of location of audio drum files,
'number_of_units': an integer, 'bpu': an integer,
'beats_per_minute' : an integer,'button_clicked_list' : a 2
dimensional list of boolean values where True means button is
clicked and false means button is not clicked in the pattern
}
```

It is very important that you get familiar with the preceding data structure definition for our drum machine. Notice that, with just this data in hand, we can define the logic to display everything that you see in the finalized drum machine.

Also notice that this data structure does not contain information about any GUI elements, such as widget information or widget states. As far as possible, we should always strive to cleanly separate the data of the backend (program logic) from the data related to the frontend (user interfaces). Our data structure here merely represents the backend but is sufficient enough to allow us to lay out the logic to determine our frontend.

The preceding data structure was what I found to be a good representation of the data at hand. There could have been an equally valid but altogether different representation of the data. There is no one *correct answer* to the question of data representation. However, building the representation around built-in collections of a language allows us to work with highly optimized code and is generally a good idea. The choice of data structure directly affects the performance of an application—sometimes trivially but at other times very severely.

We modify our code accordingly (see code `3.02.py`) to initialize this data structure:

```
def init_all_patterns(self):
    self.all_patterns = [
        {
            'list_of_drum_files': [None] * MAX_NUMBER_OF_DRUM_SAMPLES,
            'number_of_units': INITIAL_NUMBER_OF_UNITS,
            'bpu': INITIAL_BPU,
            'is_button_clicked_list':
            self.init_is_button_clicked_list(
                MAX_NUMBER_OF_DRUM_SAMPLES,
                INITIAL_NUMBER_OF_UNITS * INITIAL_BPU
            )
        }
```

```
for k in range(MAX_NUMBER_OF_PATTERNS)]
```

We also initialize `is_button_clicked_list` with all values set to `False`, as follows:

```
def init_is_button_clicked_list(self, num_of_rows, num_of_columns):
    return [[False] * num_of_columns for x in range(num_of_rows)]
```

To support this structure, we define a few constants (see code `3.02.py`):

```
MAX_NUMBER_OF_PATTERNS = 10
MAX_NUMBER_OF_DRUM_SAMPLES = 5
INITIAL_NUMBER_OF_UNITS = 4
INITIAL_BPU = 4
INITIAL_BEATS_PER_MINUTE = 240
```

Now, if you run this program, you simply see a root window—nothing different from the previous code. But internally our code is reserving memory for all the data we will need to construct our logic. We have laid a strong foundation for our program to run. Believe it or not, we have done half the job.

Creating broader visual elements

Next, let's lay out the broader visual elements of our program. For the sake of modularity, we divide the program into four broad visual sections, as shown in the following diagram:

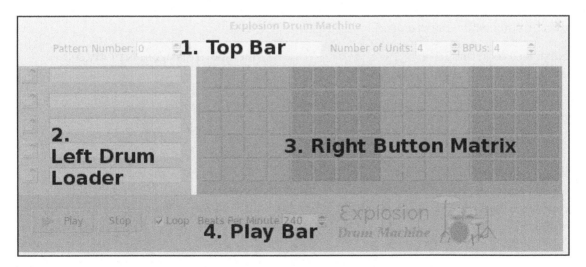

Let's define a method called `init_gui()`, which is called from within the `__init__` method as follows (see code `3.03.py`):

```
def init_gui(self):
    self.create_top_bar()
    self.create_left_drum_loader()
    self.create_right_button_matrix()
    self.create_play_bar()
```

We then proceed to define all four of these methods (`3.03.py`). The code is not discussed here, as we have done similar coding in previous chapters.

We begin with the **Top Bar** section. The Top Bar is simple. It has a few labels, three Spinboxes, and an Entry widget. We will not reproduce the entire code here (see code `3.03.py`) as we have already seen examples of creating Labels and Entry widgets several times in the previous chapters. For `Spinbox`, the options are specified as follows:

```
Spinbox(frame, from_=1, to=MAX_BPU,
width=5,command=self.on_bpu_changed).grid(row=0, column=7)
```

We set the class-level properties accordingly:

```
self.beats_per_minute = INITIAL_BEATS_PER_MINUTE
self.current_pattern_index = 0
```

Since we will allow multiple patterns to be designed, we need to keep track of the currently showing or active pattern. The `self.current_pattern_index` property keeps track of the currently active pattern.

Next, let's code the `create_left_drum_loader()` method. This again is pretty self-explanatory. We create a loop (see code `3.03.py`):

```
for i in range (MAX_NUMBER_OF_DRUM_SAMPLES):
    # create compound button here
    # create entry widgets here and keep reference to each entry widget in
    #a list for future update of values
```

Before we proceed to code the `create_right_button_matrix()` method, let's finish coding the `create_play_bar()` method, as it is the simpler of the two. All it contains is two Buttons, a Checkbutton, a Spinbox, and an image. We have coded similar widgets earlier in the book, and so I will leave it for you to explore on your own (see code `3.03.py`).

Next, let's code the `create_right_button_matrix()` method. This is the most complex of all.

The **right button matrix** comprises a two-dimensional array of rows and columns. The number of rows in the matrix equals the constant, `MAX_NUMBER_OF_DRUM_SAMPLES`, and the number of columns represents the number of beat units per cycle and is calculated by multiplying the number of units and the number of beats per unit.

The code that creates the button matrix looks like this (see code `3.03.py`):

```
self.buttons = [[None for x in range(self.find_number_of_columns())] for x
in range(MAX_NUMBER_OF_DRUM_SAMPLES)]
for row in range(MAX_NUMBER_OF_DRUM_SAMPLES):
    for col in range(self.find_number_of_columns()):
        self.buttons[row][col] = Button(right_frame,
                command=self.on_button_clicked(row, col))
        self.buttons[row][col].grid(row=row, column=col)
        self.display_button_color(row, col)
```

The associated code for the `find_number_of_columns()` method is as follows:

```
def find_number_of_columns(self):
    return int(self.number_of_units_widget.get()) *
        int(self.bpu_widget.get())
```

We have already created the button matrix, but we want the buttons to be colored in two alternating shades. Therefore, we define two constants:

```
COLOR_1 = 'grey55'
COLOR_2 = 'khaki'
```

This can be any hexadecimal color code or any color from Tkinter's predefined list of colors. We also require a third color to represent the button in a pressed state.

The constant `BUTTON_CLICKED_COLOR = 'green'` takes care of that.

We then define two methods:

```
def display_button_color(self, row, col):
    original_color = COLOR_1 if ((col//self.bpu)%2) else COLOR_2
    button_color = BUTTON_CLICKED_COLOR if
            self.get_button_value(row, col) else original_color
    self.buttons[row][col].config(background=button_color)

def display_all_button_colors(self):
    number_of_columns = self.find_number_of_columns()
    for r in range(MAX_NUMBER_OF_DRUM_SAMPLES):
```

```
for c in range(number_of_columns):
    self.display_button_color(r, c)
```

The idea is simple. A button is to be colored green if the value of the button is found to be `True` in our data structure, or else the button is to be shaded in patterns of `COLOR_1` and `COLOR_2` for each alternating unit of beats.

This alternating color is obtained by using this mathematical formula:

```
original_color = COLOR_1 if (col//bpu)%2 else COLOR_2
```

Remember that we had created a two-dimensional Boolean list called `is_button_clicked_list` as a dictionary item in our original data structure to hold this value.

We change the color of the button to `BUTTON_CLICKED_COLOR` if that value is found to be `True`. Accordingly, we define a `getter` method to get the value of the button:

```
def get_button_value(self, row, col):
    return
      self.all_patterns[self.current_pattern.get()]
        ['is_button_clicked_list'][row][col]
```

Now each button is attached to the command callback named `on_button_clicked`, which is coded as follows (see code `3.03.py`):

```
def on_button_clicked(self, row, col):
    def event_handler():
        self.process_button_clicked(row, col)
    return event_handler
```

Notice something fancy with this piece of code? This method defines a function within the function. It does not return a value as is typical of functions. Instead, it returns a function that can be executed at a later stage. These are called **higher-order functions** or, more precisely, **function closures**.

Why did we need to do this? We had to do this because each button is identified by its unique row and column-based indexes. The row values and column values are only available when the loop runs at the time of creating the buttons. The `row` and `col` variables are lost after that. We, therefore, need some way to keep these variables alive if we have to identify which button was clicked later on.

These callback functions come to our rescue as they encapsulate the row and column values in the function that they return at the time of creation.

Functions are first-class objects in Python. This means that you can pass a function to another function as a parameter and you can return a function from another function. In short, you can treat a function as any other object.

You can bind a method object to a particular context, as we did in the previous code, by nested scoping of a method within a method. Higher-order functions like these are a common way of associating functions with widgets in GUI programming.

You can find more information about function closures at `https://en.wikipedia.org/wiki/Closure_(computer_programming)`.

We then define a method called `process_button_clicked`:

```
def process_button_clicked(self, row, col):
    self.set_button_value(row, col, not self.get_button_value(row, col))
    self.display_button_color(row, col)

def set_button_value(self, row, col, bool_value):
    self.all_patterns[self.current_pattern.get()][
            'is_button_clicked_list'][row][col] = bool_value
```

The key section in the preceding code is the line that sets the button value opposite to its current value using the `not` operator. Once the value is toggled, the method calls the `display_button_color` method to recolor the buttons.

Finally, let's complete this iteration by defining some dummy methods for now and attach them as command callbacks to the respective widgets:

```
on_pattern_changed()
on_number_of_units_changed()
on_bpu_changed()
on_open_file_button_clicked()
on_button_clicked()
on_play_button_clicked()
on_stop_button_clicked()
on_loop_button_toggled()
on_beats_per_minute_changed()
```

That completes the iteration. Now if you run the program (see code `3.03.py`), it should display all the broad visual elements:

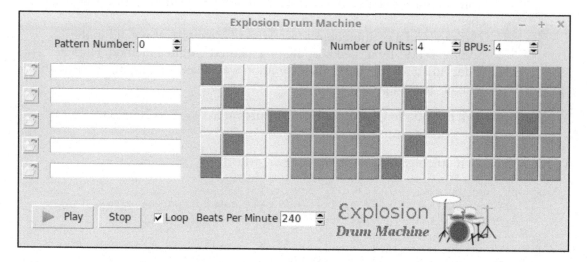

The buttons matrix should be colored in two alternating shades, and pressing the buttons should toggle its color between green and its previous color.

All other widgets remain non-functional at this stage as we have attached them to non-functional command callbacks. We will soon make them functional but, before we do that, let's do something to make all our future coding simple, clean, and elegant.

Defining getter and setter methods

In our previous section, we needed to know the value of a button in a given row and column of the button matrix for a given pattern. If the value was `True`, we colored the button green. If the value was `False`, we colored it in an alternative color.

We can get the value of the button by calling this line of code:

```
self.all_patterns[self.current_pattern.get()]['is_button_clicked_list'][row
][col]
```

Notice how this line has four sets of square brackets, `[]`. Since this nested super-scripting business can soon get ugly, we encapsulated this logic in a method named `get_button_value(row, col)`. Now, whenever we need to get a button's value, we can simply call this method with the right parameters.

Now our code will not be littered with those ugly nested superscripts. Whenever we want to get the value of a button, we can call the `get_button_value(row, col)` method, which has a nice indicative name for the work it does. Isn't this much more readable and comprehensible than its rather ugly counterpart?

One thing is for sure: all logic that we build from now onward will heavily rely on data we get from, or set to, our data structure. Given that we will need all this data all the time in our program, let's write its `getter` and `setter` methods in advance. This will certainly make our lives a lot easier.

The goal for this part of the iteration is simple—to define `getter` and `setter` methods for all the data that we have decided to store in our data structure.

The code is as follows (see `code 3.04.py`):

```
def get_current_pattern_dict(self):
    return self.all_patterns[self.current_pattern_index]

def get_bpu(self):
    return self.get_current_pattern_dict()['bpu']

def set_bpu(self):
    self.get_current_pattern_dict()['bpu'] = int(self.bpu_widget.get())

def get_number_of_units(self):
    return self.get_current_pattern_dict()['number_of_units']

def set_number_of_units(self):
    self.get_current_pattern_dict()['number_of_units']
            = int(self.number_of_units_widget.get())

def get_list_of_drum_files(self):
    return self.get_current_pattern_dict()['list_of_drum_files']

def get_drum_file_path(self, drum_index):
    return self.get_list_of_drum_files()[drum_index]

def set_drum_file_path(self, drum_index, file_path):
    self.get_list_of_drum_files()[drum_index] = file_path

def get_is_button_clicked_list(self):
    return self.get_current_pattern_dict()['is_button_clicked_list']

def set_is_button_clicked_list(self, num_of_rows, num_of_columns):
    self.get_current_pattern_dict()['is_button_clicked_list']
            = [[False] * num_of_columns for x in range(num_of_rows)]
```

That is all there is to coding the `getter` and `setter` methods. The code should be self-explanatory if you have understood the underlying data structure, as all that we do here is either get a value or set a value for various items in the data structure.

With these methods now handy, let's complete coding the functionality of widgets we had earlier left uncoded.

The number of units and beats per unit features

We earlier coded the matrix called `create_right_button_matrix`, which creates a two-dimensional matrix with the number of rows equal to `MAX_NUMBER_OF_DRUM_SAMPLES`. The number of columns would be decided by multiplying the number of units by the beats per unit values selected by the end user. Its formula can be given as follows:

Number of columns of buttons = Number of units x BPU

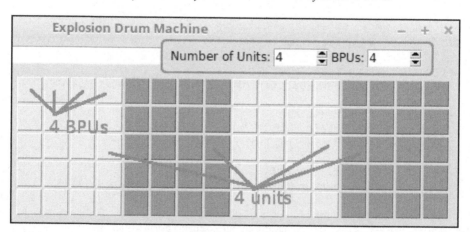

This means that every time the user changes the number of units or the beats per unit, the button matrix should be redrawn to change the number of columns. This change should also be reflected in our underlying data structure. Let's add this feature to our drum machine.

We had earlier defined two dummy methods—on_number_of_units_changed()
and on_bpu_changed(). We modify them now as follows (see code 3.04.py):

```
def on_number_of_units_changed(self):
  self.set_number_of_units()
  self.set_is_button_clicked_list(MAX_NUMBER_OF_DRUM_SAMPLES,
                  self.find_number_of_columns())
  self.create_right_button_matrix()

def on_bpu_changed(self):
  self.set_bpu()
  self.set_is_button_clicked_list(MAX_NUMBER_OF_DRUM_SAMPLES,
                  self.find_number_of_columns())
  self.create_right_button_matrix()
```

The preceding methods do two things:

- Modify the data structure to reflect the changes in BPU or number of units
- Call the create_right_button_matrix() method to recreate the button matrix

Now if you go and run the code (see code 3.04.py) and change either the values of number of units or BPU, the button matrix should redraw itself to reflect the change.

Loading drum samples

Our main objective is to play sound files in the order of a beat pattern decided by the user. To do this, we need to add sound files to the drum machine.

Our program does not have any preloaded drum files. Instead, we want to let the user select from a wide variety of drum files.

Thus, besides the normal drum, you can play a Japanese tsuzumi, an Indian tabla, Latin American bongo drums, or just about any other sound that you want to add to your rhythm. All you need is a small .wav or .ogg file containing that sound's sample.

The drum sample is to be loaded on the left bar, as shown in the following screenshot:

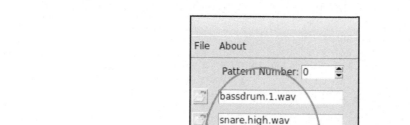

Let's code the ability to add drum samples to our program.

We have already created buttons with folder icons on the left-hand side of our drum pad. Now we need to make it functional. The desired functionality is simple. When a user clicks on any of the left buttons, they should open a file dialog letting the user choose a .wav or .ogg file. When the user selects the file and clicks on **Open**, the Entry widget next to that button should be populated with the name of the file.

Further, the location of the drum sample file should be added to our data structure at the appropriate place.

First, we will import the required modules.

We will use the filedialog module to ask the user to select drum files. We have already used the file dialog module in Chapter 2, *Making a Text Editor*. The functionality here is very similar. We will also need to extract the filename of the given sound sample using the os module. Let's begin by importing the two modules (see code 3.05.py):

```
import os
from tkinter import filedialog
```

The buttons we created for uploading drum files are attached to the
`on_open_file_button_clicked` method through a command callback. We created
a dummy method earlier by that name. We now modify that method to add the
required functionality (see `code 3.05.py`):

```
def on_open_file_button_clicked(self, drum_index):
    def event_handler():
        file_path = filedialog.askopenfilename
            (defaultextension=".wav", filetypes=[("Wave Files",
            "*.wav"), ("OGG Files", "*.ogg")])
        if not file_path:
            return
        self.set_drum_file_path(drum_index, file_path)
        self.display_all_drum_file_names()
    return event_handler
```

The preceding method again returns a function, as we need to track which of the drum files
was actually selected from all the rows of drum files.

The preceding code does three things:

- Asks the user for the file path using Tkinter's `filedialog`
- Modifies the underlying data structure to save the provided file path
- Calls another method to display the filename in the adjacent Entry widget

The next two methods are then responsible for displaying all drum names in the frontend
(see `code 3.05.py`):

```
def display_all_drum_file_names(self):
    for i, drum_name in enumerate(self.get_list_of_drum_files()):
        self.display_drum_name(i, drum_name)

def display_drum_name(self, text_widget_num, file_path):
    if file_path is None: return
    drum_name = os.path.basename(file_path)
    self.drum_load_entry_widget[text_widget_num].delete(0, END)
    self.drum_load_entry_widget[text_widget_num].insert(0, drum_name)
```

The preceding method uses `os.path.basename` from the `os` module to obtain the filename
from the file path.

This completes the section. Our code is now capable of loading drum samples and storing
records of all file paths in the data structure. Go ahead and try loading some drum samples
(see `code 3.05.py`) and the program should display the name of the drum file in the
adjacent Entry widget.

Playing the drum machine

Now that we have a mechanism to load drum samples and a mechanism to define beat patterns in place, let's add the ability to play these beat patterns. In many ways, this is the core of our program.

Let's first understand the functionality that we want to achieve here.

Once the user has loaded one or more drum samples and has defined a beat pattern using the toggle buttons, we need to scan each column of the pattern to see if it finds a green button (a True value in our data structure).

If the value is True for a given location in the matrix, our code should play the corresponding drum sample before moving ahead. If two or more drum samples are selected in the same column, all the samples should play almost simultaneously.

Moreover, there should be a fixed time gap between the playing of each successive column, which will define the tempo of the music.

To achieve this functionality, we need to import the pygame module to play the sounds, and the time module to define the temporal gap between them.

Initializing pygame

The pygame module is a set of highly portable modules that runs on most operating systems. We will use the mixer module from pygame to play the sound files.

Assuming that you have installed the package, let's begin by importing pygame (see code 3.06.py):

```
import pygame
```

According to the official API documentation of the mixer module at http://www.pygame. org/docs/ref/mixer.html, we need to initialize pygame before we can play back the audio files.

We initialize `pygame` in a new method called `init_pygame` (see code `3.06.py`):

```
def init_pygame(self):
    pygame.mixer.pre_init(44100, -16, 1, 512)
    pygame.init()
```

The `mixer.pre_init` method is a special requirement for our drum machine because the lack of it causes a lot of sound lagging. We will not get into the details of audio programming here, but suffice to say that the arguments to the `pre_init` method are as follows:

```
pre_init(frequency=22050, size=-16, channels=2, buffersize=512)
```

After `pygame` is initialized like this, the documentation suggests the following code to play the sound. Let's add this to our code as well (see code `3.06.py`):

```
def play_sound(self, sound_filename):
    if sound_filename is not None:
        pygame.mixer.Sound(sound_filename).play()
```

Playing complete patterns

Now our program has the ability to play any sound. But we don't just need to play a single sound. We need to play a pattern. Let's define a method called `play_pattern`, which reads our internal data structure and plays files accordingly (see code `3.06.py`):

```
import time
    def play_pattern(self):
        self.now_playing = True
        while self.now_playing:
            play_list = self.get_is_button_clicked_list()
            num_columns = len(play_list[0])
            for column_index in range(num_columns):
                column_to_play = self.get_column_from_matrix(
                    play_list, column_index)
                for i, item in enumerate(column_to_play):
                    if item:
                        sound_filename = self.get_drum_file_path(i)
                        self.play_sound(sound_filename)
                time.sleep(self.time_to_play_each_column())
                if not self.now_playing: break
            if not self.loop: break
        self.now_playing = False
```

We also add an associated method that returns the ith column from a matrix:

```
def get_column_from_matrix(self, matrix, i):
    return [row[i] for row in matrix]
```

The description of the preceding code is as follows:

- We create a class attribute called `self.keep_playing` to decide whether the pattern is to be played just once or continuously in a loop.

- We create another class attribute called `self.now_playing` to track whether a beat is currently playing. This will help us to make some decisions on how to handle a sudden close of program or change of pattern by the user.

- We then fetch the two-dimensional Boolean list from our data structure and scan each column of the list to look for `True` values. We get the column data from the matrix by defining a separate method called `get_column_from_matrix(self, matrix, i)`.

- For every column, if a `True` value is encountered, we fetch the corresponding drum file path and call the `self.play_sound()` method to play the file.

- The code sleeps for a fixed duration of time before reading the second column. This sleep duration defines the tempo of the drum beat. If the code does not sleep for some time between each column, all the patterns would play almost immediately and would not even sound like a rhythm. We need to import the `time` module to use the `time.sleep()` method.

- The amount of time the code sleeps between scanning each column is decided by another method called `self.time_to_play_each_column()`, which we define next.

Determining the tempo of a rhythm

The mathematics of defining the tempo of a rhythm is simple. We get the value associated with the `beats_per_minute` attribute and divide it by 60 to get the beats per second. Then, the time to play each beat (or group of beats simultaneously for a given column) is the reciprocal of `beats_per_second`.

The code is as follows (see code 3.06.py):

```
def time_to_play_each_column(self):
  beats_per_second = self.beats_per_minute/60
  time_to_play_each_column = 1/beats_per_second
  return time_to_play_each_column
```

While we are handling the tempo for the pattern, let's also complete coding of the command callback attached to our beats per minute Spinbox widget (see code 3.06.py):

```
def on_beats_per_minute_changed(self):
    self.beats_per_minute = int(self.beats_per_minute_widget.get())
```

Now let's code the functionality related to the loop Checkbox. We have already factored in the looping issue in our play_pattern method using the self.loop variable. We simply need to set the value of the self.loop attribute by reading the value of the Spinbox widget (see code 3.06.py):

```
def on_loop_button_toggled(self):
  self.loop = self.loopbuttonvar.get()
```

With that out of the way, let's code the command callback attached to our **Play** button and the **Stop** button (see code 3.06.py):

```
def on_play_button_clicked(self):
  self.start_play()

def start_play(self):
  self.init_pygame()
  self.play_pattern()

def on_stop_button_clicked(self):
  self.stop_play()

def stop_play(self):
  self.now_playing = False
```

Our drum machine is now operational (see code 3.06.py). You can load drum samples and define beat patterns, and when you click on the **Play** button, the drum machine plays that beat pattern!

However, there is a small problem. The play_sound method blocks the main loop of our Tkinter program. It does not relinquish control back to the main loop until it is done playing the sound sample.

Since our `self.loop` variable is set to `True`, this means that `pygame` never returns back control to Tkinter's main loop and our play button and program is stuck! This can be seen in the following screenshot:

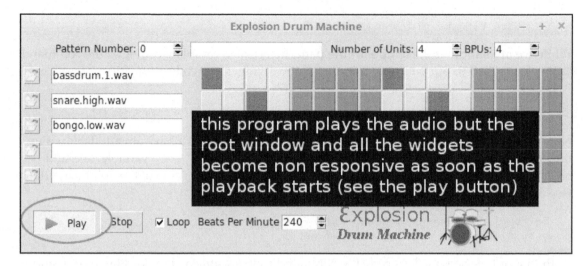

This means that if you now want to click on the **Stop** button or change some other widget, or even close the window, you will have to wait for the play loop to complete, which never happens in our case.

This is clearly a glitch. We need some method to confer back the control to the Tkinter main loop while the play is still in progress.

That brings us to the next iteration, where we discuss and implement **multithreading** in our application.

Tkinter and threading

One of the simplest ways that we can make our root window responsive is to use the `root.update()` method within our `play_pattern` loop. This updates the `root.mainloop()` method after each sound sample is played.

However, this is an inelegant method because the control is passed to the main loop with some staggering experienced in the GUI. Thus, you may experience a slight delay in the responses of other widgets in the Toplevel window.

Further, if some other event causes the method to be called, it could result in a nested event loop.

A better solution would be to run the play_pattern method from a separate **thread**.

Let's use the threading module of Python to play the pattern in a separate thread. This way, pygame will not interfere with Tkinter's main loop.

A thread is a coding construct that can advance two or more separate sets of logical workflow together within an instance of a running program (process), **context-switching** between the workflows. Each thread in a running program gets its own stack and its own program counter, but all threads in a process share the same memory.

In contrast to threads, processes are independent execution instances of programs, each maintaining its own state information and address space. Processes can only interact with other processes using interprocess communication mechanisms.

Threading is a topic for a book in itself. However, we will not get into the details and instead will use the threading module from the Python standard library. The threading module provides a higher-level threading interface to hide away the inner complexities of implementing a multithreaded program. To use the module, let's first import the threading module into our namespace (see code 3.07.py):

```
import threading
```

Now, let's create a method, play_in_thread(), as follows (3.07.py):

```
def play_in_thread(self):
    self.thread = threading.Thread(target = self.play_pattern)
    self.thread.start()
```

Finally, change the start_play method to call the play_in_thread rather than calling the play_pattern directly:

```
def start_play(self):
    self.init_pygame()
    self.play_in_thread() # deleted direct call to self.play_pattern()
```

Now if you load some drum samples, define the beat patterns, and hit the **Play** button, the sound will play in a separate thread without causing other widgets to become unresponsive (see code 3.07.py).

However, this poses a new problem. What happens if the user clicks the **Play** button multiple times? That would spawn multiple threads of beat patterns all playing simultaneously.

We can overcome this problem by disabling the **Play** button when the audio is playing. This can be achieved by defining `toggle_play_button_state()` (see code 3.07.py):

```
def toggle_play_button_state(self):
  if self.now_playing:
    self.play_button.config(state="disabled")
  else:
    self.play_button.config(state="normal")
```

We then attach this state toggling method onto the Play, Stop, and Loop widget command callbacks, as follows (3.07.py):

```
def on_play_button_clicked(self):
  self.start_play()
  self.toggle_play_button_state()

def on_stop_button_clicked(self):
  self.stop_play()
  self.toggle_play_button_state()

def on_loop_button_toggled(self):
  self.loop = self.to_loop.get()
  self.keep_playing = self.loop
  if self.now_playing:
    self.now_playing = self.loop
    self.toggle_play_button_state()
```

We also modify our `play_pattern()` method to include a call to `toggle_play_button_state()` at the end (see code 3.07.py). This will ensure that when the pattern has ended playing, the **Play** button returns to its normal state.

The **Play** button now remains in a disabled state as long as some audio is playing. It returns to a normal state when audio isn't playing.

Tkinter and thread safety

Tkinter is not thread safe. The Tkinter interpreter is valid only in the thread that runs the main loop. Any calls to widgets must ideally be done from the thread that created the main loop. Invoking widget-specific commands from other threads is possible but is not reliable.

When you call a widget from another thread, the events get queued for the interpreter thread, which executes the command and passes the result back to the calling thread. If the main loop is running but not processing events, it sometimes results in unpredictable exceptions.

In fact, if you find yourself calling a widget from a thread other than the main loop, chances are that you have not separated the visual elements from the underlying data structure. You are possibly doing it wrong.

Before we complete this iteration, let's take care of a small detail. What happens if a beat is currently playing and the user hits the Close button on the window? The main loop will die and our audio-playing thread will be left in an orphaned state. This can lead to ugly error messages thrown at the user.

Let's, therefore, override the Close button and stop the audio play before we quit the window. To override the Close button, we add a small line to our class __init__ method, as follows (see code 3.07.py):

```
self.root.protocol('WM_DELETE_WINDOW', self.exit_app)
```

Then, we define a method called exit_app(), as follows (see code 3.07.py):

```
def exit_app(self):
  self.now_playing = False
  if messagebox.askokcancel("Quit", "Really quit?"):
    self.root.destroy()
```

This completes the project iteration.

To summarize, we refined our start_play() method to play the audio files on a separate thread. We also made sure to disable the **Play** button as long as the audio plays. Finally, we overrode the Close button to handle exiting when some audio is currently playing.

We used Python's built-in threading module to play the loops in a separate thread. We also looked at some of the threading-related limitations of Tkinter. However, threading is a vast topic in itself and we have just scratched the surface here.

You can find more details about the threading module at https://docs.python.org/3/library/threading.html.

Support for multiple beat patterns

Our drum program is now functional. You can load drum samples and define a beat pattern and our drum machine will play it.

Let's now extend our drum machine to create more than one pattern in the same program. This will provide us with the ability to play different patterns simply by changing the pattern number. This gives the user the ability to make different beats for the intro, verse, chorus, bridge, and other parts of a song. The pattern-changing user interface is highlighted in red in the following screenshot:

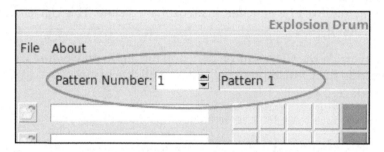

At the very outset, we have an Entry widget adjacent to the Pattern Number Spinbox widget. We want to display the current pattern number in that Entry widget. We accordingly create a method, `display_pattern_name()`, which does this task (see code 3.08.py):

```
def display_pattern_name(self):
    self.current_pattern_name_widget.config(state='normal')
    self.current_pattern_name_widget.delete(0, 'end')
    self.current_pattern_name_widget.insert(0,
            'Pattern {}'.format(self.current_pattern_index))
    self.current_pattern_name_widget.config(state='readonly')
```

We want the pattern name to display in the text widget when the program initially launches. Therefore, we modify our `create_top_bar()` method to include a call to this newly defined method (see code 3.08.py).

A change of pattern requires several changes. First of all, let's modify the `on_pattern_changed()` command callback to call a new method, `change_pattern()`, as follows (see code 3.08.py):

```
def on_pattern_changed(self):
    self.change_pattern()
```

Next, let's define the `change_pattern()` method:

```
def change_pattern(self):
    self.current_pattern_index = int(self.pattern_index_widget.get())
    self.display_pattern_name()
    self.create_left_drum_loader()
    self.display_all_drum_file_names()
    self.create_right_button_matrix()
    self.display_all_button_colors()
```

The preceding code should almost read like plain English and the steps involved in a change of pattern should be self-explanatory.

This completes coding our drum machine to support multiple beat patterns. Go ahead and run code `3.08.py`. Load some drum files, define the first beat pattern, and play it. Change the beat pattern using the Spinbox widget at the top left,
load new drums, and define a new pattern. Then, play that pattern. While it is playing, try switching to your first beat pattern. The change should happen seamlessly.

Saving beat patterns

In the preceding iteration, we added the capability to define multiple beat patterns.

However, the beat patterns can be played only on a single script run. When the program is closed and restarted, all previous pattern data is lost.

We need a way to persist or store the beat patterns beyond a single program run. We need the ability to store values in some form of file storage and reload, play, and even edit the patterns. We need some form of **object persistence**.

Python provides several modules for object persistence. The module that we will use for persistence is called the `pickle` module. Pickle is a standard library of Python.

An object represented as a string of bytes is called a **pickle** in Python. **Pickling**, also known as object **serialization**, let's us convert our object into a string of bytes. The process of reconstructing the object from the string of bytes is called **unpickling** or **deserialization**.

More information about the `pickle` module is available at http://docs.python.org/3/library/pickle.html.

Let's illustrate it with a simple example:

```
import pickle
party_menu= ['Bread', 'Salad', 'Bordelaise', 'Wine', 'Truffles']
pickle.dump(party_menu, open("my_menu", "wb"))
```

First, we serialize or pickle our list, `party_menu`, using `pickle.dump`, and save it in an external file, `my_menu`.

We later retrieve the object using `pickle.load`:

```
import pickle
menu= pickle.load( open( "my_menu", "rb" ) )
print(menu) # prints ['Bread', 'Salad', 'Bordelaise', 'Wine', 'Truffles']
```

Coming back to our drum machine—if we need to store and reuse the beat patterns, we only need to pickle our data structure list, named `self.all_patterns`. Having saved the object, we can later easily unpickle the file to reconstruct our beat patterns.

We first need to add three top-menu items to our program, as shown in the following screenshot:

The three top-menu items are:

- **File | Load Project**
- **File | Save Project**
- **File | Exit**

While we are creating our menu items, let's also add an **About** menu item.

Here, we are particularly interested in saving the project (pickling), and loading the project back (unpickling). The code for menu items is defined in a separate method called `create_top_menu`, as shown in the following code (see code `3.09.py`):

```
def create_top_menu(self):
  self.menu_bar = Menu(self.root)
  self.file_menu = Menu(self.menu_bar, tearoff=0)
  self.file_menu.add_command(
      label="Load Project", command=self.load_project)
  self.file_menu.add_command(
      label="Save Project", command=self.save_project)
  self.file_menu.add_separator()
  self.file_menu.add_command(label="Exit", command=self.exit_app)
  self.menu_bar.add_cascade(label="File", menu=self.file_menu)
  self.about_menu = Menu(self.menu_bar, tearoff=0)
  self.about_menu.add_command(label="About",command=self.show_about)
  self.menu_bar.add_cascade(label="About", menu=self.about_menu)
  self.root.config(menu=self.menu_bar)
```

The code is self-explanatory. We have created similar menu items in our last two projects. Finally, to display this menu, we call this method from our `init_gui()` method.

To pickle our object, we first import the pickle module into the current namespace, as follows (`3.09.py`):

```
import pickle
```

The **Save Project** menu has a command callback attached to `self.save_project`, which is where we define the pickling process:

```
def save_project(self):
  saveas_file_name = filedialog.asksaveasfilename
              (filetypes = [('Explosion Beat File','*.ebt')],
            title="Save project as...")
  if saveas_file_name is None: return
  pickle.dump( self.all_patterns, open(saveas_file_name, "wb"))
  self.root.title(os.path.basename(saveas_file_name) +PROGRAM_NAME)
```

The description of the code is as follows:

- The `save_project` method is called when the user clicks on the **Save Project** menu; hence, we need to give the user an option to save the project in a file.
- We have chosen to define a new file extension (`.ebt`) to keep track of our beat patterns. This is a completely arbitrary choice of extension name.

- When the user specifies the filename, it is saved with a .ebt extension. The file contains the serialized list self.all_patterns, which is dumped into the file using pickle.dump.
- Lastly, the title of the Toplevel window is changed to reflect the filename.

We are done pickling the object. Let's now code the unpickling process. The unpickling process is handled by a method, load_project, which is called from the **Load Project** menu, as follows:

```
def load_project(self):
    file_path = filedialog.askopenfilename(
    filetypes=[('Explosion Beat File', '*.ebt')], title='Load Project')
    if not file_path:
        return
    pickled_file_object = open(file_path, "rb")
    try:
        self.all_patterns = pickle.load(pickled_file_object)
    except EOFError:
        messagebox.showerror("Error", "Explosion Beat file seems corrupted
or invalid !")
    pickled_file_object.close()
    try:
      self.change_pattern()
      self.root.title(os.path.basename(file_path) + PROGRAM_NAME)
    except:
      messagebox.showerror("Error",
       "An unexpected error occurred trying to process the beat file")
```

The description of the code is as follows:

- When a user clicks on the **Load Project** menu, it triggers a command callback connected to this load_project method.
- The first line of the method prompts the user with an **Open File** window. When the user specifies a previously pickled file with a .ebt extension, the filename is stored in a variable called pickled_file_object.
- If the filename returned is None because the user cancels the **Open File** dialog, nothing is done. The file is then opened in read mode, and the contents of the file are read into self.all_patterns using pickle.load.
- self.all_patterns now contains the list of beat patterns defined in the previous pickle.
- The file is closed and the first pattern of self.all_patterns is reconstructed by calling our previously defined change_pattern() method.

This should load the first pattern on our drum machine. Try playing any of the patterns, and you should be able to replay the pattern exactly as it was defined at the time of pickling.

Note, however, that the pickled .ebt files are not portable from one computer to another. This is because we have just pickled the file path for our drum files. We have not pickled the actual audio files. So if you try to run the .ebt file on another machine or if the file path to the audio files has changed since the pickling, our code will not be able to load the audio files and will report an error.

The process of pickling uncompressed audio files like those in .wav files, .ogg files, or PCM data is the same as the preceding process. After all, these uncompressed audio files are nothing but lists of numbers.

However, trying to pickle audio files here would require us to deviate a lot from our current topic. Therefore, we have not implemented it here.

Pickling, though great for serialization, is vulnerable to malicious or erroneous data. You may want to pickle only if the data is from a trusted source, or if proper validation mechanisms are in place. You may also find the json module useful for serializing objects in JSON. Also, the ElementTree and xml.minidom libraries are relevant for parsing XML data.

To end this section, let's complete coding the response to clicking on the **About** menu item:

```
def show_about(self):
    messagebox.showinfo(PROGRAM_NAME,
                    "Tkinter GUI Application\n Development  Blueprints")
```

This is self-explanatory. We have done similar coding in our previous project.

To summarize this iteration, we used Python's built-in pickle module to pickle and unpickle the beat patterns defined by the user.

This now lets us save our beat patterns. We can later load, replay, and edit these saved patterns in our drum machine (see code 3.09.py).

Working with ttk-themed widgets

We are almost done programming our drum machine. However, we would like to end this chapter by introducing you to ttk-themed widgets.

Tkinter does not bind to the native platform widgets on many platforms, such as Microsoft Windows and X11.

The Tk toolkit (and Tkinter) originally appeared on **X-Window systems;** hence, it adopted the motif style that was the *de facto* standard for GUI development on X-Window systems.

When Tk was ported to other platforms, such as Windows and Mac OS, this motif style started appearing out of place with the look of these platforms.

Due to this, some even argue that Tkinter widgets are rather ugly and do not integrate well with such desktop environments.

Another criticism of Tkinter is based on the fact that Tkinter mixes logic and styling by allowing both to be changed as widget options.

Tkinter was also criticized for lacking any kind of theming support. Although we saw an example of centralized styling via the option database, the method required styling to be done at the widget level. It does not allow for selective styling of two Button widgets differently, for example. This made it difficult for developers to implement visual consistency for similar groups of widgets while differentiating them from other groups of widgets.

As a result of this, many GUI developers moved to Tkinter alternatives, such as **wxPython**, **PySide**, and **PyQT**.

With Tkinter 8.5, the makers of Tkinter have tried to address all these concerns by introducing the **ttk module**, which may be considered as an advance to the original Tkinter module.

Let's take a look at some of the features offered by the ttk-themed widgets module.

One of the first things that ttk does is provide a set of built-in themes that allows Tk widgets to look like the native desktop environment in which the application is running.

Additionally, it introduces 6 new widgets—**Combobox, Notebook, Progressbar, Separator, Sizegrip**, and **Treeview** to the list of widgets, in addition to supporting 11 core Tkinter widgets, which are Button, Checkbutton, Entry, Frame, Label, LabelFrame, Menubutton, PanedWindow, Radiobutton, Scale, and Scrollbar.

To use the ttk module, we first import it into the current namespace:

```
from tkinter import ttk
```

You can display the ttk widgets as follows (see code 3.10.py):

```
ttk.Button(root, text='ttk Button').grid(row=1, column=1)
ttk.Checkbutton(root, text='tkCheckButton').grid(row=2, column=1)
```

Code 3.10.py provides a comparison of displays between the normal Tkinter widgets and the counterpart ttk widgets, as shown in the following screenshot:

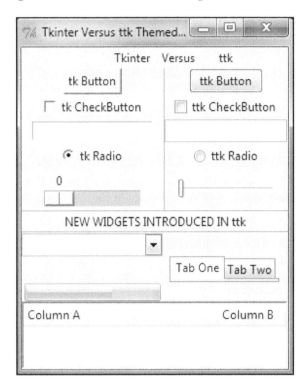

Notice that the preceding screenshot is taken on a Microsoft Windows platform as the differences are more marked on systems that do not explicitly use the X-Window system. Notice how Tkinter widgets (on the left) look out of place on Microsoft Windows as compared to ttk widgets (on the right), which is the native Microsoft Windows look and feel (see code 3.10.py).

You can even override the basic Tkinter widgets by importing ttk after Tkinter as follows:

```
from tkinter import *
from tkinter.ttk import *
```

This causes all widgets common to Tk and ttk to be replaced by ttk widgets.

This has the direct benefit of using the new widgets, which gives a better look and feel across platforms.

However, the disadvantage of this kind of import is that you cannot distinguish the module from which the widget classes are imported. This is important because the Tkinter and ttk widget classes are not completely interchangeable. In this case, an unambiguous solution is to import them, as shown in the following code:

```
import tkinter as tk
from tkinter import ttk
```

Although most of the configuration options for Tkinter and ttk widgets are common, ttk-themed widgets do not support styling options such as fg, bg, relief, and border. This is purposefully removed from ttk in an attempt to keep logic and styling in different controls.

Instead, all styling-related options are handled by the respective style names. In a standard ttk module, each widget has an associated style name. You can retrieve the default style name of a widget using the `widget.winfo_class()` method.

For instance, consider a ttk Button:

```
>>> my_button = ttk.Button()
>>> my_button.winfo_class()
```

This prints `Tbutton`, which is the default style name for `ttk.Button`. For a list of default ttk style names for different widgets, refer to `http://infohost.nmt.edu/tcc/help/pubs/tkinter/web/ttk-style-layer.html`.

In addition to the default style, you can assign a custom style class to a widget or group of widgets. To set up a new style, you use the following:

```
style = ttk.Style()
```

To configure the style options for a default style, you use the command:

```
style.configure('style.Defaultstyle', **styling options)
```

To create a new style from the built-in styles, define a style name of the form `newName.oldName`. For instance, to create an Entry widget to hold a date, you can call it `Date.Tentry`.

To use the new style on a widget, you use the command:

```
ttk.Widget(root, style='style.Defaultstyle')
```

Next, we will discuss **ttk theming**.

The `Style` is used to control the appearance for individual widgets. Themes, on the other hand, control the appearance of the entire GUI. More simply put, a theme is a collection of styles. Grouping styles into themes lets the user switch designs for the entire GUI all at once. Like styles, all themes are uniquely identified by their name.

The list of available themes can be obtained as follows:

```
>> from tkinter.ttk import *
>>> style = Style()
>>> style.theme_names()
('winnative', 'clam', 'alt', 'default', 'classic', 'xpnative')
To obtain the name of the currently active theme:
>>> style.theme_use()
'default'
```

You can change to another theme from the `style.theme_names()` list; use the following:

```
style.theme_use('your_new_theme_name')
```

To explore various styling and theming-related options of ttk, refer to the dummy example (see `code 3.11.py`):

```
from tkinter import Tk
from tkinter import ttk
root = Tk()
style = ttk.Style()
# defining the global style - applied when no other style is defined
style.configure('.', font='Arial 14', foreground='brown',
  background='yellow')
# this label inherits the global style as style option not specified for
it
ttk.Label(root, text='I have no style of my own').pack()
# defining a new style named danger and configuring its style only for the
# button widget
style.configure('danger.TButton', font='Times 12', foreground='red',
padding=1)
ttk.Button(root, text='Styled Dangerously',
```

```
style='danger.TButton').pack()
 # Different styling for different widget states
 style.map("new_state_new_style.TButton", foreground=[('pressed', 'red'),
('active', 'blue')])
 ttk.Button(text="Different Style for different
states",style="new_state_new_style.TButton").pack()
 # Overriding current theme styles for the Entry widget
 current_theme = style.theme_use()
 style.theme_settings( current_theme,
     {"TEntry":
         {"configure":
           {"padding": 10},
           "map": {"foreground": [("focus", "red")] }
         }
     })
 print(style.theme_names())
 print(style.theme_use())
 # this is effected by change of themes even though no style specified
 ttk.Entry().pack()
 root.mainloop()
```

The description of the code is as follows:

- The first three lines of code import Tkinter and ttk, and set up a new root window.
- The next line, `style = ttk.Style()`, defines a new style.
- The next line configures a program-wide style configuration using `style.configure`. The dot character (`.`), which is the first argument of `configure`, means that this style would apply to the `Toplevel` window and to all its child elements. This is the reason why all of our widgets get to have a yellow background.
- The next line creates an extension (`danger`) to the default style (`TButton`). This is how you create custom styles, which are variations on a base default style.
- The next line creates a `ttk.Label` widget. Since we have not specified any style for this widget, it inherits the global style specified for the Toplevel window.
- The next line creates a `ttk.button` widget and specifies it to be styled using our custom style definition of `danger.TButton`. This is why the foreground color of this button turns red. Notice how it still inherits the background color, yellow, from the global Toplevel style that we defined earlier.

- The next two lines of code demonstrate how ttk allows for styling different widget states. In this example, we styled different states for a `ttk.Button` widget to display in different colors. Go ahead and click on this second button to see how different styles apply to different states of a button. Here, we use `map(style, query_options, **kw)` to specify dynamic values of style for changes in the state of the widget.
- The next line fetches the current applicable theme. It then overrides some of the options for the theme's Entry widget using `style.theme_settings('themename', ***options)`.
- The next line defines an Entry widget but does not specify any style to it. It, therefore, inherits its properties from the theme we configured earlier. If you now type anything in this Entry widget, you will notice that it gets a padding of 10 px and the foreground text color is red inside the Entry widget.

Now that we know how to make our widgets look more like native platform widgets, let's change the **Play** and **Stop** buttons for our drum machine to `ttk.button`. Let's also change the `Loop` Checkbutton from `Tkinter` Checkbutton to `ttk` Checkbutton and add a few separators in the Play Bar section.

The following screenshots show the Play Bar before and after making the changes:

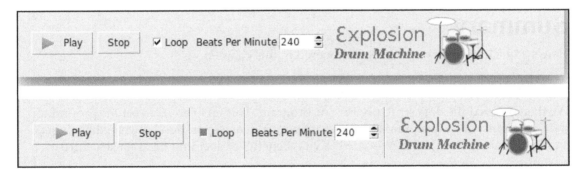

We first import `ttk` into our namespace and append `ttk` to the **Play** and **Stop** buttons as follows (code `3.12.py`):

```
from tkinter import ttk
```

We then simply modify the buttons and Checkbutton in the `create_play_bar`, replacing `button` with `ttk.Button`, and `loopbutton` with `ttk.Checkbutton`:

```
button = ttk.Button()
loopbutton = ttk.Checkbutton(**options)
```

Note that these changes make the Buttons and the Checkbutton look more like the native widgets of your working platform.

Finally, let's add `ttk.separators` to our Play Bar (see code `3.12.py`). The format for adding separators is as follows:

```
ttk.Separator(playbar_frame, orient='vertical').grid(row=start_row, column
= 5, sticky="ns", padx=5)
```

Note that we cannot change the buttons in the right-button matrix from button to `ttk.Button`. This is because ttk buttons do not support specifying options like background color.

This concludes the last iteration of this project. In this iteration, we first saw how and why to use **ttk-themed** widgets to improve the look and feel of our programs.

We then used ttk Buttons and ttk Checkbuttons in our drum program to improve its look. We also saw the reasons why certain Tkinter Buttons in our program could not be replaced by ttk Buttons.

That brings us to the end of this chapter.

Summary

Here's a quick summary of things we covered in this chapter.

We started by learning how to structure the Tkinter program as classes and objects.

We then decided the data structure for our program. This enabled us to set the ground for writing the rest of the program logic, maintaining a clean separation between data, logic, and its visual representation. We saw the vital benefits of deciding the data structure in advance.

We also worked with more Tkinter widgets such as Spinbox, Button, Entry, and Checkbutton. We also saw the grid geometry manager in action in the chapter.

We then saw how to bind widgets to higher-order functions using command callbacks. This is a very common technique used in GUI programming.

We then understood multithreaded programming in the context of Tkinter. We moved the audio playback onto a separate thread. This enabled us to keep the audio playing without hampering Tkinter's main loop in any way.

We then understood how to persist an object's state with the pickle module and then how to unpickle it later to retrieve the state of the object.

Finally, we saw how to use ttk-themed widgets to ensure that our GUI feels native on the platform where it is run.

Congratulations! You have now completed coding your drum machine.

QA section

Before you proceed to the next chapter, make sure you can answer these questions to your satisfaction:

- How do you organize a Tkinter program in an object-oriented fashion? What are the advantages of using an object-oriented structure as apposed to writing pure procedural code? What are the disadvantages?
- At what stage of programming should you consider drafting a data structure for your GUI program? What are the benefits of having a data structure or model in place?
- What are higher-order functions?
- Why is threading required? What are its advantages and disadvantages?
- What is the difference between a process and a thread?
- What is object persistence?
- How do you pickle and unpickle objects in Python?
- Besides pickling, what are the other common modes of persisting objects?
- What are ttk widgets? Why are they used?

Further reading

Read about object-oriented programming terminologies like class, objects, constructor, inheritance, encapsulation, class methods, static methods, getters, setters, and their specific implementation in Python. A good place to start would be the official documentation of classes at `https://docs.python.org/3/tutorial/classes.html`.

Read the official documentation of Python object serialization at https://docs.python.org/3/library/pickle.html.

Read more about threading, context switching, and thread-based parallelism in general, along with its specific implementation in Python. The official documentation for threading is located at https://docs.python.org/3/library/threading.html.

4
Game of Chess

Let's build a game of chess in Tkinter. If you already know the basic rules of chess, you are ready to write this program. However, if you do not know the rules, you should read them before you start programming this application.

Some of the key objectives of this chapter are as follows:

- Learning how to structure a program in a **Model-View-Controller** (**MVC**) architecture
- Learning how to tame complexity by implementing programs in a modular structure
- Taking a look at the versatility and power of the Tkinter Canvas widget
- Learning the basic usage of canvas coordinates, object IDs, and tags
- Learning the recommended error-handling practices
- Learning how to extend Python's built-in data types
- Using object inheritance to code classes with similar attributes and behavior
- Using Python's built-in `configparser` module to store program preferences
- Getting acquainted with several Python modules that you will often use in a variety of application development projects

An overview of the chapter

We will now implement a *human* versus *human* chess game. Our chess game will enforce all the standard rules that are applicable to a game of chess. Some advanced rules such as castling and en passant are left as an exercise for you.

In its final form, our chess program will look like this:

Module requirements for this chapter

We will not use any external third-party modules in this chapter. However, we will use several built-in Python modules.

To check whether all the required libraries are indeed provided by your Python distribution, type the following command in your Python command line:

```
>> import tkinter, copy, sys, configparser
```

This should be executed without an error message. If no errors are thrown back, you are ready to build the chess application. Let's get started!

Structuring our program

In this section, we decide on an overall structure for our program.

The development of large applications generally starts with recording the **software requirement specifications** (**SRS**). This is generally followed by a graphical representation of constructs, such as the class, composition, inheritance, and the hiding of information using several modeling tools. These tools can be flow charts, **Unified Modeling Language** (**UML**) tools, data flow diagrams, Venn diagrams (for database modeling), and so on.

These tools are very useful when the problem domain is not very clear. However, if you have ever played the game of chess, you should be very well acquainted with the problem domain. Furthermore, our chess program can be classified as a medium-sized program spanning a few hundred lines of code. Therefore, let's bypass these visual tools and get to the actual program design.

All of our previous projects have been structured as a single file. However, as programs grow in complexity, we need to break programs into modules and class structures.

One of the key objectives of this chapter is to learn to write programs in the **MVC** architecture. Some of the central aspects of the MVC architecture are as follows:

- A model handles backend data and logic
- A view handles the frontend presentation
- The model and view never interact directly
- Whenever the view needs to access backend data, it requests the controller to intervene with the model and fetch the required data

Given these aspects, let's create three files for our chess program: model.py, view.py, and controller.py (see 4.01.py).

Now, let's create an empty Model class, an empty View class, and a Controller class in their respective files, as follows:

```
class Model(): #in model.py
  def __init__(self):
    pass

class View(): #in view.py
  def __init__(self):
    pass

class Controller(): # in controller.py
  def __init__(self):
    self.init_model()

  def init_model(self):
    self.model = model.Model()
```

Note that since the Controller class needs to fetch data from the Model class, we instantiated a new Model class from within the Controller class. This now provides us with a way to fetch data from the Model class as and when needed.

Let's also add a separate file called exceptions.py. This will be our central place for the handling of all errors and exceptions. Within this file, add the following single line of code:

```
class ChessError(Exception): pass
```

We created a custom ChessError class that was inherited from the standard Exception class. This simple line of code now allows the ChessError class and all of its children to raise errors, which can then be handled by using the try...except block. All the new error classes that will be defined in our code from now on will derive from this ChessError base class.

With this boilerplate code out of the way, let's create another blank file called configurations.py (4.01). We will use this file to store all the constants and configurable values in one place.

Let's define some constants right away, as follows (see code 4.01—configurations.py):

```
NUMBER_OF_ROWS = 8
NUMBER_OF_COLUMNS = 8
DIMENSION_OF_EACH_SQUARE = 64 # denoting 64 pixels
BOARD_COLOR_1 = "#DDB88C"
BOARD_COLOR_2 = "#A66D4F"
```

To make these constant values available to all files, let's import them in to the model.py, view.py, and controller.py folders (see 4.01):

```
from configurations import *
```

As per the tenets of the MVC architecture, the View class is never supposed to interact directly with the Model class. It should always interact with the Controller class, and the Controller class is then responsible for fetching data from the Model class. Accordingly, let's import the controller in the View class and the model in the Controller class, as follows:

```
import controller # in view.py
import model # in controller.py
```

Let's start by editing the view.py file to display a chessboard (see 4.01—view.py). Our goal for this iteration is to display the empty chessboard as shown in the following screenshot:

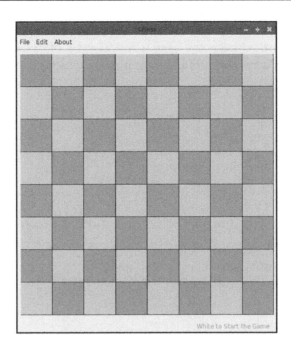

Take a look at the code implementation in `view.py` (see 4.01).

The __init__ method of the `View` class calls a method called `create_chess_base`, which is defined as follows:

```
def create_chess_base(self):
  self.create_top_menu()
  self.create_canvas()
  self.draw_board()
  self.create_bottom_frame()
```

We will not reproduce the code responsible for the creation of the root window, the menu at the top, or the frame at the bottom. We have implemented similar widgets in previous chapters (see 4.01—`view.py` for a complete reference).

However, we will discuss the code that creates the chessboard:

```
def create_canvas(self):
  canvas_width = NUMBER_OF_COLUMNS * DIMENSION_OF_EACH_SQUARE
  canvas_height = NUMBER_OF_ROWS * DIMENSION_OF_EACH_SQUARE
  self.canvas = Canvas(self.parent, width=canvas_width,
height=canvas_height)
  self.canvas.pack(padx=8, pady=8)
```

Nothing fancy here. Creating a Canvas widget is similar to creating other widgets in Tkinter. The Canvas widget takes the `width` and `height` of two configurable options. Next, paint the Canvas widget in alternating shades to form the chessboard (`view.py`):

```
def draw_board(self):
  current_color = BOARD_COLOR_2
  for row in range(NUMBER_OF_ROWS):
    current_color = self.get_alternate_color(current_color)
    for col in range(NUMBER_OF_COLUMNS):
        x1, y1 = self.get_x_y_coordinate(row, col)
        x2, y2 = x1 + DIMENSION_OF_EACH_SQUARE, y1 +DIMENSION_OF_EACH_SQUARE
        self.canvas.create_rectangle(x1, y1, x2, y2, fill=current_color)
        current_color = self.get_alternate_color(current_color)

def get_x_y_coordinate(self, row, col):
        x = (col * DIMENSION_OF_EACH_SQUARE)
        y = ((7 - row) * DIMENSION_OF_EACH_SQUARE)
        return (x, y)

def get_alternate_color(self, current_color):
        if current_color == self.board_color_2:
          next_color = self.board_color_1
        else:
          next_color = self.board_color_2
        return next_color
```

The following is the description of the code:

- We used the Canvas widget's `create_rectangle()` method to draw alternating shades of squares to resemble a chessboard.
- The rectangles are drawn from point x1, y1, and they extend to x2, y2. These values correspond to two diagonally opposite corners of the rectangle (coordinates of the upper-left and lower-right edges).
- The x and y values are calculated by using a newly defined method called `get_x_y_coordinate()`, which performs simple mathematics depending on the dimensions of each square that was defined in pixel units earlier.
  The y value is calculated by first subtracting a row from (7-row) because the Canvas widget measures the coordinates starting from the top left. The top-left corner of the canvas has the coordinates (0, 0).
- The `get_alternate_color` method is a helper method that, not surprisingly, returns the alternate color.

The Tkinter Canvas widget lets you draw a line, an oval, a rectangle, an arc, and polygon shapes at a given coordinate. You can also specify various configuration options, such as fill, outline, width, and so on for each of these shapes.

The Canvas widget uses a coordinate system to specify the position of objects on the widget. Coordinates are measured in pixels. The top-left corner of the canvas has the coordinates (0, 0).

The objects drawn on the Canvas widget are usually handled by assigning them an ID or a tag. We will see an example of this later in the chapter.

If an object on the Canvas widget is tagged to multiple tags, the options defined for tags at the top of the stack have precedence. However, you can change the precedence of tags by using `tag_raise(name)` or `tag_lower(name)`.

For a complete list of Canvas widget-related options, refer to the interactive help for the Canvas widget using `help(Tkinter.Canvas)` in the command line, as follows:

```
>>> import tkinter
>>> help(tkinter.Canvas)
```

Next, let's bind the mouse click to the Canvas widget from the __init__ method of the View class (see `4.01—view.py`), as follows:

```
self.canvas.bind("<Button-1>", self.on_square_clicked)
```

The bound method calls another method called `get_clicked_row_column()`, and for now it prints the result on the console as follows:

```
def on_square_clicked(self, event):
    clicked_row, clicked_column =  self.get_clicked_row_column(event)
    print("Hey you clicked on", clicked_row, clicked_column)
```

The `get_clicked_row_column()` method is defined as follows:

```
def get_clicked_row_column(self, event):
    col_size = row_size = DIMENSION_OF_EACH_SQUARE
    clicked_column = event.x // col_size
    clicked_row = 7 - (event.y // row_size)
    return (clicked_row, clicked_column)
```

Now, if you run the code (see `4.01—view.py`) and click on different squares, it should output a message like this to the console:

```
Hey you clicked on 0 7
Hey you clicked on 3 3
```

This completes our first iteration. In this iteration, we determined the broader file structure for the chess program. We created the `model`, `view`, and `controller` classes. We also decided to keep all the constants and configuration values in a separate file called `configurations.py`.

We have now had a first taste of the Canvas widget. We created a blank canvas and then added square areas using the `canvas.create_rectangle` method to create a chessboard.

Now, if you run `4.01—view.py`, you will see an empty chessboard. You will also find out that the *File* menu and the *Edit* menu dropdowns are not functional. The *About* menu should show a standard `messagebox` widget.

Before you proceed to the next section, you are encouraged to go and explore the code in the `4.01` folder in its entirety.

Modeling the data structure

Coming back to the old adage, data structures, not algorithms, are central to writing good programs. Therefore, it is important that we spend some time defining the data structure.

The key data that the model needs to record is the position of the chess pieces on the chessboard. Accordingly, we first need a way to define these locations and a unique way to identify the chess pieces. Let's first agree to the naming conventions that we will stick to in the program.

Convention on naming chess pieces

Every chess piece is identified by a single letter (pawn = p, knight = n (yes knight with an n!), bishop = b, rook = r, queen = q, and king = k).

The *white* chess pieces are represented by *uppercase* letters (PNBRQK), and the *black* chess pieces are represented by *lowercase* letters (pnbrqk).

Convention for naming locations on the chessboard

In order to assign unique identifiers to every square on the chessboard, we will mark the squares along the *x* axis by using the letters A to H. We will mark the *y* axis by using the numbers 1 to 8.

Accordingly, the squares on the chessboard will be identified as follows:

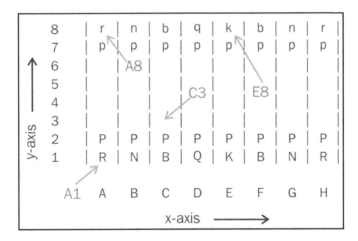

Thus, **A1** denotes the leftmost square at the bottom of the chessboard. Currently, it is occupied by a white rook. The **C3** position is currently empty, **E8** has a black king, and **A8** has a black rook.

Let's add this to the configurations.py file (see 4.02):

```
X_AXIS_LABELS = ('A', 'B', 'C', 'D', 'E', 'F', 'G', 'H')
Y_AXIS_LABELS = (1, 2, 3, 4, 5, 6, 7, 8)
```

Now, if you want to represent the chessboard at any point in time, all you need is a mapping of the location to the chess piece at that location. Looks like a perfect candidate for storing as a Python dictionary.

Thus, the initial position of all the chess pieces on the chessboard can be represented as follows:

```
START_PIECES_POSITION = {
"A8": "r", "B8": "n", "C8": "b", "b", "G8": "n", "H8": "r",
"A7": "p", "B7": "p", "C7": "p", "p", "G7": "p", "H7": "p",
"A2": "P", "B2": "P", "C2": "P", "P", "G2": "P", "H2": "P",
"A1": "R", "B1": "N", "C1": "B", "D8": "q", "E8": "k", "F8":
"D7": "p", "E7": "p", "F7": "D2": "P", "E2": "P", "F2":
"D1": "Q", "E1": "K", "F1":"B", "G1": "N", "H1": "R"
}
```

We need this data to get started. So, let's add this as a constant to the `configurations.py` file (see `4.02`).

Now, let's move on to code the `Model` class for our program. We have already decided that we will use a Python dictionary to store the position of chess pieces on the chessboard. We can go ahead and add a dictionary attribute to the class.

However, we will take a slightly different approach.

Let's make the `Model` class a child class of the built-in dictionary class, as follows:

```
class Model(dict):
```

Thus, the `self` variable that refers to the current class object instance will also have all the properties and methods that are available to the dictionary. All the methods that are available to the standard dictionary class can now be called on the `Model` object (`self`).

So now we can define a method that returns the short name of the chess piece at that position when it's given a position on the chessboard, as follows (see `4.02—model.py`):

```
def get_piece_at(self, position):
    return self.get(position)
```

If there is no chess piece at the position, this returns `None` rather than giving a `KeyError` exception.

Next, let's add some more important attributes to the `Model` class, as follows (see `4.02—model.py`):

```
captured_pieces = { 'white': [], 'black': [] }
player_turn = None
halfmove_clock = 0
fullmove_number = 1
history = []
```

The `half-move_clock` keeps a track of the number of turns played since the last pawn's advance or the last capture. This is used to determine whether a draw can be claimed under the `fifty-move` rule.

The `full-move` number is a count that is incremented by 1 after every move of a black piece. This is used to track the overall length of a game.

Finally, let's add another method that, given the row-column tuple for a square, returns its alphanumeric position (for example, an input of (1, 2) returns B3):

```
def get_alphanumeric_position(self, rowcol):
  if self.is_on_board(rowcol):
    row, col = rowcol
    return "{}{}".format(X_AXIS_LABELS[col], Y_AXIS_LABELS[row])
```

Next, let's define an associated helper method to ensure that we only process mouse clicks that occur on the Canvas widget and not anywhere else in the root window, as follows:

```
def is_on_board(self, rowcol):
    row, col = rowcol
    return 0 <= row <= 7 and 0 <= col <= 7
```

There is not much that can be added to the `Model` class for now until we lay down the code logic to handle the chess pieces.

We can define the rules for all the chess pieces within the `Model` class, but that would make the `Model` class too bulky.

Therefore, let's define the chess piece-related logic in a new file named `piece.py`. Since this is inherently a part of the `Model` class but it is defined in a new file, let's add a reference to the `Model` class within this file.
(see `4.02—piece.py`)

Let's do this next.

Creating a Piece class

Think about it. We need to define rules for all the different chess pieces. Some attributes and methods, such as color, will be common to all the chess pieces, while other attributes/methods, such as rules for movement, will vary for each chess piece.

First, we'll define a new `Piece` class. This class will have the attributes and methods that are common to all the chess pieces. Then, we will define classes for every individual piece as a subclass of this parent `Piece` class. We can then override all the attributes and methods in these individual classes. The code will look like this (see `4.02—piece.py`):

```
from configurations import *

class Piece():
  def __init__(self, color):
    self.name = self.__class__.__name__.lower()
    if color == 'black':
      self.name = self.name.lower()
    elif color == 'white':
      self.name = self.name.upper()
      self.color = color

def keep_reference(self, model):
    self.model = model

class King(Piece):
  pass

class Queen(Piece):
  pass

class Rook(Piece):
  pass

class Bishop(Piece):
  pass

class Knight(Piece):
  pass

class Pawn(Piece):
  pass
```

Note that the `Piece` class needs `color` as an argument for object creation. We create two attributes, named `self.name` and `self.color`, in the class.

Also note the `keep_reference(self, model)` method definition. Since the `Piece` class is nothing but an extension of the `Model` class, we need to get a reference to the `Model` class in this method to communicate with it.

Similarly, the `Model` class needs a reference to the new `Piece` class. Accordingly, we add this as an import to the `Model` class, as follows (see 4.02—`model.py`):

```
import piece
```

Finally, we need a method that takes a string pertaining to the name of a given piece object and creates a new piece object. For example, we need a method that, given the arguments (Pawn, black) or simply (`"p"`), dynamically creates a new `Pawn` object with the color attribute defined as black.

Accordingly, let's define a helper method in the `piece.py` file but outside the `Piece` class, as follows (see 4.02—`piece.py`):

```
def create_piece (piece, color='white'):
    if isinstance(piece, str):
        if piece.upper() in SHORT_NAME.keys():
            color = "white" if piece.isupper() else "black"
            piece = SHORT_NAME[piece.upper()]
        piece = piece.capitalize()
        if piece in SHORT_NAME.values():
            return eval("{classname} (color)".format(classname=piece))
    raise exceptions.ChessError("invalid piece name: '{}'".format(piece))
```

To support the preceding method, add the following constant to the `configurations.py` file (see 4.02):

```
SHORT_NAME = {
 'R':'Rook', 'N':'Knight', 'B':'Bishop', 'Q':'Queen', 'K':'King',
'P':'Pawn'
 }
```

The preceding code simply takes a single character as an input. It then gets the full name for the corresponding piece class (for example, if a p is given, it gets the full name, which is `Pawn`). It then checks the case of the character and defines the color variable as *white* if the input character is uppercase. Otherwise, the color is set to *black*. It then dynamically creates a corresponding piece object.

This concludes the iteration. We have created the `Piece` class and all of its subclasses, and we have the ability to create `Piece` objects dynamically from a given input character. This class is simply an extension of the `Model` class, and each of the two classes can access each other's methods by keeping a reference to each other.

Displaying chess pieces on the chessboard

Now, let's turn our attention to displaying all the chess pieces on the chessboard.

First, we'll define a method named `draw_single_piece`, which draws a chess piece at the given position when it's given a position, and the character representing the chess piece as follows (see `4.03—view.py`):

```
def draw_single_piece(self, position, piece):
    x, y = self.controller.get_numeric_notation(position)
    if piece:
        filename = "../pieces_image/{}_{}.png".format(piece.name.lower(),
piece.color)
        if filename not in self.images:
            self.images[filename] = PhotoImage(file=filename)
        x0, y0 = self.calculate_piece_coordinate(x, y)
        self.canvas.create_image(x0, y0, image=self.images[filename],
                        tags=("occupied"), anchor="c")
```

The following is a description of the preceding code:

- The images of the chess pieces are stored in a folder named `pieces_image` and are named with the chess piece's name in `lowercase` + `_` + `color.png` format. So for instance, the black queen is saved by the name `queen_black.png`.
- The images are added to the chessboard by using the `canvas.create_image()` method, which takes the *x, y* coordinates and a `PhotoImage()` object that relies on the location of the image file as its argument.
- We used Tkinter's `PhotoImage` class to reference the `.png` files.
- In addition to creating and displaying a chess piece on the chessboard, we also *tagged* them with a custom tag called `occupied`. Tagging is an important feature of the Canvas widget which lets us uniquely identify items placed on the Canvas widget.

We used the following helper method in the preceding code (see `4.03—view.py`):

```
def calculate_piece_coordinate(self, row, col):
    x0 = (col * DIMENSION_OF_EACH_SQUARE) + int(DIMENSION_OF_EACH_SQUARE / 2)
    y0 = ((7 - row) * DIMENSION_OF_EACH_SQUARE) +
        int(DIMENSION_OF_EACH_SQUARE / 2)
    return (x0, y0)
```

We also define another helper method that returns the numeric notation for the position of a piece (see `4.03—controller.py`):

```
def get_numeric_notation(self, position):
  return piece.get_numeric_notation(position)
```

This is just a wrapper around the following code from 4.03—piece.py:

```
def get_numeric_notation(rowcol):
  row, col = rowcol
  return int(col)-1, X_AXIS_LABELS.index(row)
```

Now, it's time simply to call the preceding draw_single_piece method on all the chess pieces (4.03—view.py):

```
def draw_all_pieces(self):
 self.canvas.delete("occupied")
 for position, piece in  self.controller.get_all_pieces_on_chess_board():
   self.draw_single_piece(position, piece)
```

A key aspect that you need to note here is that when we needed some data from the Model class, say, a dictionary containing all the chess pieces on the chessboard, we did not directly call the Model class for the data. Instead, we requested the controller get us the data from the model. The get_all_pieces_on_chess_board() controller method is simply a wrapper around the actual method from the Model class (see 4.03—controller.py):

```
def get_all_pieces_on_chess_board(self):
  return self.model.items()
```

Great! We now have the methods required to draw all the chess pieces on the chessboard. But merely defining them does not help. These methods need to be called from somewhere. Therefore, let's define a new method named start_new_game() and call it from the __init__ method of the View class, as follows (see 4.03—view.py):

```
 def start_new_game(self):
   self.controller.reset_game_data()
   self.controller.reset_to_initial_locations()
   self.draw_all_pieces()
```

In addition to calling the draw_all pieces() method, this method also resets the Model via calls to two wrapper controller methods (see 4.03—controller.py):

```
def reset_game_data(self):
  self.model.reset_game_data()

def reset_to_initial_locations(self):
  self.model.reset_to_initial_locations()
```

The actual methods are defined in the `Model` class, as follows:

```
def reset_game_data(self):
    captured_pieces = {'white': [], 'black': []}
    player_turn = None
    halfmove_clock = 0
    fullmove_number = 1
    history = []

def reset_to_initial_locations(self):
    self.clear()
    for position, value in START_PIECES_POSITION.items():
        self[position] = piece.create_piece(value)
        self[position].keep_reference(self)
        self.player_turn = 'white'
```

The `reset_game_data()` method is simple. It just resets all the attributes of the `Model` class to their initial states.

The `reset_to_initial_locations()` method initializes all the chess piece locations to reflect the starting position of the game. This too should be self-explanatory if you are aware of the data structure that we discussed earlier.

Now, when you go ahead and run the code (see `4.03—view.py`), the chessboard should display all the chess pieces at the starting position of the game, as shown in the following screenshot:

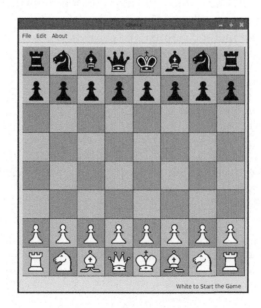

This completes the current iteration. The next iteration will define the rules for the movement of the chess pieces on the chessboard. We need this part done before we can think of moving the chess pieces around.

Defining rules for the chess pieces

Different chess pieces have different rules of movement. Let's try to tabulate the rules:

Name of the chess piece	Orthogonal movement	Diagonal movement	The maximum number of places the chess piece is allowed to move
King	Yes	Yes	1
Queen	Yes	Yes	8
Rook	Yes	No	8
Bishop	No	Yes	8
Knight	N/A	N/A	N/A
Pawn	Yes, but it captures diagonally	No	1 or 2

As evident from the table, the rules for all the chess pieces except for *Knight* and *Pawn* are pretty straightforward.

Knights are different from the others. They must move two squares in one direction, and then one more move at a 90-degree angle, following the shape of an L. Knights are also the only chess pieces that can jump over other chess pieces.

Pawns move forward, but they capture diagonally. Pawns can only move forward one square at a time, except for their very first move, where they can move forward by two squares. Pawns can only capture one square diagonally in front of them.

Rules for the king, queen, rooks, and bishops

Let's first take a look at simple cases of orthogonally and diagonally moving chess pieces, which are the king, queen, rooks, and bishops. We need somehow to figure out a way to change the position of these chess pieces by using a mathematical rule.

The following diagram shows what it takes to move a chess piece from its current position (say *x, y*) both orthogonally and diagonally:

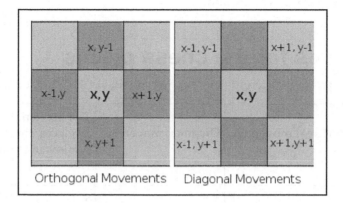

If you look at the preceding diagram, *x* represents the column number and *y* represents the row number. It is clear that we can represent the orthogonal movements by adding to the current position the items from the tuples (−1, 0), (0, 1), (1, 0), (0, −1).

Similarly, diagonal movements can be represented by adding to the tuples (−1, 1), (1, 1), (1, −1), (−1, −1).

Let's add these two tuples to `configurations.py` (see 4.04), as follows:

```
ORTHOGONAL_POSITIONS = ((-1,0),(0,1),(1,0),(0, -1))
DIAGONAL_POSITIONS = ((-1,-1),(-1,1),(1,-1),(1,1))
```

If a chess piece can move both orthogonally and diagonally, such as the *queen,* the representative tuple is simply an addition of the preceding two tuples.

If a chess piece can be moved by more than one square, it's simply a matter of multiplying the representative tuple by an integer to get all the other allowed positions on the chessboard.

With this information in mind, let's code a `moves_available` method that, given the current position of the chess piece, the directions tuple relevant to the chess piece, and the maximum distance that the chess piece can move, returns a list of all the `allowed_moves`, as follows (see 4.04—`piece.py`):

```
def moves_available(self, current_position, directions,distance):
    model = self.model
    allowed_moves = []
    piece = self
```

```
start_row, start_column = get_numeric_notation(current_position)
for x, y in directions:
  collision = False
  for step in range(1, distance + 1):
    if collision: break
    destination = start_row + step * x, start_column + step * y
    if self.possible_position(destination) not in
      model.all_occupied_positions():
        allowed_moves.append(destination)
    elif self.possible_position(destination) in
                      model.all_positions_occupied_by_color
                        (piece.color):
      collision = True
    else:
      allowed_moves.append(destination)
      collision = True
allowed_moves = filter(model.is_on_board, allowed_moves)
return map(model.get_alphanumeric_position, allowed_moves)
```

The following is a description of the preceding code:

- Depending on the arguments, the method collects all the allowed moves for a given chess piece in a list named `allowed_moves`.
- The code iterates through all the locations to detect a possible collision. If a collision is detected, it breaks out of the loop. Otherwise, it appends the coordinate to the `allowed_moves` list.
- The second to last line filters out the moves that fall outside the chessboard, and the last line returns the equivalent position in alphanumeric notations for all the allowed moves.

We can also define a few helper methods to support the preceding method, as follows:

```
def possible_position(self, destination): #4.04 piece.py
  return self.model.get_alphanumeric_position(destination)

def all_positions_occupied_by_color(self, color): #4.04 model.py
  result = []
  for position in self.keys():
    piece = self.get_piece_at(position)
    if piece.color == color:
      result.append(position)
  return result

def all_occupied_positions(self): #4.04 model.py
  return self.all_positions_occupied_by_color('white') +\
         self.all_positions_occupied_by_color('black')
```

Next, let's modify the `Piece` child classes of king, queen, rooks, and bishops as follows (see `4.04—piece.py`):

```
class King(Piece):
    directions = ORTHOGONAL_POSITIONS + DIAGONAL_POSITIONS
    max_distance = 1

    def moves_available(self,current_position):
        return super().moves_available(current_position, self.directions,
self.max_distance)

class Queen(Piece):
    directions = ORTHOGONAL_POSITIONS + DIAGONAL_POSITIONS
    max_distance = 8

    def moves_available(self,current_position):
      return super(Queen, self).moves_available
                (current_position, self.directions, self.max_distance)

class Rook(Piece):
    directions = ORTHOGONAL_POSITIONS
    max_distance = 8
    def moves_available(self,current_position):
        return super(Rook, self).moves_available(current_position,
                            self.directions, self.max_distance)

class Bishop(Piece):
    directions = DIAGONAL_POSITIONS
    max_distance = 8

    def moves_available(self,current_position):
        return super(Bishop, self).moves_available
                (current_position, self.directions, self.max_distance)
```

Rules for the Knight

The knight is a different beast because it does not move orthogonally or diagonally. It can also jump over chess pieces.

Like the rules that we followed earlier to arrive at ORTHOGONAL_POSITIONS and DIAGONAL_POSITIONS, we can similarly arrive at the rules that are required to determine the KNIGHT_POSITIONS tuple. This is defined in `4.04—configurations.py`, as follows:

```
KNIGHT_POSITIONS =
 ((-2,-1),(-2,1),(-1,-2),(-1,2),(1,-2),(1,2),(2,-1),(2,1))
```

Next, let's override the `moves_available` method from the `Knight` class (see code `4.04—piece.py`):

```
class Knight(Piece):

  def moves_available(self, current_position):
    model = self.model
    allowed_moves = []
    start_position = get_numeric_notation(current_position.upper())
    piece = model.get(pos.upper())
    for x, y in KNIGHT_POSITIONS:
      destination = start_position[0] + x, start_position[1] + y
      if(model.get_alphanumeric_position(destination) not
            in model.all_positions_occupied_by_color(piece.color)):
        allowed_moves.append(destination)
    allowed_moves = filter(model.is_on_board, allowed_moves)
    return map(model.get_alphanumeric_position, allowed_moves)
```

The following is a description of the preceding code:

- The method is quite similar to the previous superclass method. However, unlike the superclass method, the changes are represented as capture moves using the `KNIGHT_POSITIONS` tuple.
- Unlike the superclass, we do not need to track collisions, because knights can jump over other chess pieces.

Rules for a pawn

A pawn has a unique movement too in that it moves forward, but it captures diagonally. Let's similarly override the `moves_available` class from within the `Pawn` class, as follows (see `4.04—piece.py`):

```
class Pawn(Piece):

  def moves_available(self, current_position):
    model = self.model
    piece = self
    if self.color == 'white':
      initial_position, direction, enemy = 1, 1, 'black'
    else:
      initial_position, direction, enemy = 6, -1, 'white'
    allowed_moves = []
    # Moving
    prohibited = model.all_occupied_positions()
```

```
start_position = get_numeric_notation(current_position.upper())
forward = start_position[0] + direction, start_position[1]
if model.get_alphanumeric_position(forward) not in prohibited:
  allowed_moves.append(forward)
  if start_position[0] == initial_position:
    # If pawn is in starting position allow double  moves
    double_forward = (forward[0] + direction, forward[1])
    if model.get_alphanumeric_position(double_forward) not in
      prohibited:
        allowed_moves.append(double_forward)
# Attacking
for a in range(-1, 2, 2):
  attack = start_position[0] + direction,
  start_position[1] + a
  if model.get_alphanumeric_position(attack) in
          model.all_positions_occupied_by_color(enemy):
      allowed_moves.append(attack)
allowed_moves = filter(model.is_on_board, allowed_moves)
return map(model.get_alphanumeric_position, allowed_moves)
```

The following is a description of the preceding code:

- We first assigned the `initial_row_position`, direction, and enemy variables depending on whether the pawn is black or white.
- Similar to the previous `moves_allowed` methods, this method collects all the allowed moves in a blank list named `allowed_moves`.
- Then, we collected a list of all the prohibited moves by concatenating two lists of squares occupied by all the black and white chess pieces.
- We defined a variable named `forward` which holds the position of the square immediately ahead of the current position of the pawn.
- A pawn cannot move forward if there is a chess piece in front of it. If the forward position is not prohibited, the position is appended to the `allowed_moves` list. A pawn can move two places forward from its starting position. We check whether the current position is the starting position, and if it is the starting position, we append the double move to the `allowed_moves` list.
- A pawn can capture only the diagonally adjacent chess pieces in front of it. Therefore, we assigned a variable attack to track the diagonally adjacent positions on the chessboard. If the diagonally adjacent square is occupied by an enemy, that position qualifies to be appended to the `allowed_moves` list.
- Then, we filtered the list to remove all the positions that may fall outside the chessboard. The last line returns all the allowed moves as a list of corresponding alphanumeric notations, as we did in all the previous definitions.

This completes the current iteration. We coded the logic needed to enforce the rules related to the movement of chess pieces on the chessboard.

Movement validation of chess pieces

Before we allow chess pieces to move, we must have a record of all the possible movement options on the chessboard. At every move, we also need to check whether it is a legitimate turn for a given player and the proposed move should not cause check on the current player's king.

Now, check may occur on the king not only from a chess piece that was moved, but from any other chess piece on the chessboard as a consequence of such a movement. Thus, after every move, we need to calculate the possible moves for all the chess pieces of the opponent.

Accordingly, we will need two methods to do the following:

- Keep a track of all the available moves for a player
- Check whether there is check on the king

Let's add two new methods in the `Model` class (see `4.05—model.py`).

Tracking all available moves

The code needed to keep track of all the available moves for a player is as follows:

```
def get_all_available_moves(self, color):
  result = []
  for position in self.keys():
    piece = self.get_piece_at(position)
    if piece and piece.color == color:
      moves = piece.moves_available(position)
      if moves:
        result.extend(moves)
  return result
```

The description of the code is as follows:

- We have already coded the `moves_available` method in the previous iteration
- The preceding method simply iterates through every item in the dictionary and appends the `moves_available` result for every chess piece of a given color in a list named `result`

Finding out the current position of the king

Before we code the method that checks whether a king is in check, we first need to know the exact position of the king. Let's define a method to find out the current position of the king, as follows (see `4.05—model.py`):

```
def get_alphanumeric_position_of_king(self, color):
    for position in self.keys():
        this_piece = self.get_piece_at(position)
        if isinstance(this_piece, piece.King) and this_piece.color == color:
            return position
```

The preceding code simply iterates through all the items in the dictionary. If a given position is an instance of the `King` class, it simply returns its position.

Checking whether the king is in check

Let's define a method to check whether the king is in check from the opponent, as follows:

```
def is_king_under_check(self, color):
    position_of_king = self.get_alphanumeric_position_of_king(color)
    opponent = 'black' if color =='white' else 'white'
    return position_of_king in self.get_all_available_moves(opponent)
```

The following is a description of the preceding code:

- First, we obtained the current position of the king and the color of the opponent.
- We then found out all the possible moves for all the chess pieces of the opponent. If the position of the king coincides with any position from all the possible moves, the king is in check and we return `True`. Otherwise, we return `False`.

This accomplishes the objectives for the iteration. We are now in a position to check all the available moves for a player at a given point in the game. We can also check whether a king is in check from the opponent.

Making the game functional

Now that we have all the chess pieces and chessboard-related validation rules in place, let's add life to our chess program. In this iteration, we will make our chess game fully functional.

The objective of this iteration is to move the chess pieces with a click of the left mouse button. When a player clicks on a chess piece, the code should first check whether it is a legitimate turn for that chess piece.

On the first click, the chess piece that needs to be moved is selected, and all the allowed moves for that chess piece are highlighted on the chessboard. The second click should be performed on the destination square. If the second click is done on a valid destination square, the chess piece should move from the source square to the destination square.

We also need to code the events of capturing chess pieces and the king being in check. The other attributes that need to be tracked include a list of the captured chess pieces, the half-move clock count, the full-move number count, and the history of all the previous moves.

You may recall that we created a dummy method which is bound to the left-click event. The method, for now, simply prints the row and column value on the console.

Let's modify this method, as follows (see 4.06—view.py):

```python
def on_square_clicked(self, event):
    clicked_row, clicked_column = self.get_clicked_row_column(event)
    position_of_click = self.controller.get_alphanumeric_position
                                ((clicked_row, clicked_column))
    if self.selected_piece_position: # on second click
        self.shift(self.selected_piece_position, position_of_click)
        self.selected_piece_position = None
    self.update_highlight_list(position_of_click)
    self.draw_board()
    self.draw_all_pieces()
```

The following is a description of the preceding code:

- The first part of the code calculates the coordinates for the chess piece on which you clicked. Based on the calculated coordinates, it stores the corresponding letter notation in a variable named `position_of_click`.
- It then tries to assign the piece variable to the corresponding piece instance. If there is no piece instance on the clicked square, it simply ignores the click.
- The second part of the method checks whether this is the second click that was intended to move a chess piece to a destination square. If this is the second click, it calls the `shift` method, passing the source and destination coordinates as its two arguments.
- If the `shift` method succeeds, it sets all the previously set attributes to their original empty values and calls the `draw_board` and `draw_pieces` methods to redraw the chessboard and chess pieces.

While coding the desired functionality for the `on_square_clicked` method, we called several new methods from within it. We need to define these new methods.

Keep an eye on the `on_square_clicked` method. This is the central method around which all the other methods will evolve over the course of our attempts to make the chess game functional.

Getting the source and destination position

We have called the `shift` method from the `on_square_clicked` method. The code for the `shift` method is responsible for the collection of the necessary arguments that are required for the `shift` operation.

The code for the `shift` method is as follows:

```
def shift(self, start_pos, end_pos):
    selected_piece = self.controller.get_piece_at(start_pos)
    piece_at_destination =  self.controller.get_piece_at(end_pos)
    if not piece_at_destination or piece_at_destination.color
                    != selected_piece.color:
        try:
            self.controller.pre_move_validation(start_pos, end_pos)
        except exceptions.ChessError as error:
            self.info_label["text"] = error.__class__.__name__
    else:
        self.update_label(selected_piece, start_pos, end_pos)
```

The code first checks whether a chess piece exists at the destination. If a chess piece does not exist at the destination square, it calls on a method, `shift`, from the *controller,* which is a wrapper around the actual `shift` method from the `Model` class.

Collecting a list of the moves that need to be highlighted

We also called the `update_highlight_list(position)` method from the `on_square_clicked` method. The purpose of this method is to collect all the possible moves for a given chess piece in a list named `all_squares_to_be_highlighted`.

The actual focusing of the available moves takes place in the `draw_board` method of the GUI class. The code for this is as follows (see `4.06—view.py`):

```
def update_highlight_list(self, position):
  self.all_squares_to_be_highlighted = None
  try:
    piece = self.controller.get_piece_at(position)
  except:
    piece = None
  if piece and (piece.color == self.controller.player_turn()):
    self.selected_piece_position = position
  self.all_squares_to_be_highlighted =
list(map(self.controller.get_numeric_notation,
self.controller.get_piece_at(position).moves_available(position)))
```

Highlighting allowed moves

In the `on_square_clicked` method, we called the `draw_board` method to take care of the redrawing or changing of the chess pieces' coordinates. The current `draw_board` method is not equipped to handle this because we only designed it in the first iteration to provide us with a blank chessboard.

First, let's add a `HIGHLIGHT_COLOR` constant to the `configurations.py` file, as follows:

```
HIGHLIGHT_COLOR = "#2EF70D"
```

Then, modify the `draw_board` method to handle this, as follows (see `4.06—view.py`):

```
def draw_board(self):
  current_color = BOARD_COLOR_2
```

```
for row in range(NUMBER_OF_ROWS):
    current_color = self.get_alternate_color(current_color)
    for col in range(NUMBER_OF_COLUMNS):
        x1, y1 = self.get_x_y_coordinate(row, col)
        x2, y2 = x1 + DIMENSION_OF_EACH_SQUARE, y1 +
          DIMENSION_OF_EACH_SQUARE
        if(self.all_squares_to_be_highlighted and (row, col) in
                      self.all_squares_to_be_highlighted):
            self.canvas.create_rectangle(x1, y1, x2, y2,
              fill=HIGHLIGHT_COLOR)
        else:
            self.canvas.create_rectangle(x1, y1, x2, y2, fill=current_color)
        current_color = self.get_alternate_color(current_color)
```

Pre-move validation

The chess piece must only be moved if it does not violate the rules of the game. For example, a chess piece can move to a valid location only if that location is not already occupied by a chess piece of the same color. Similarly, a piece can move only if it is the player's turn to move. Another rule states that a piece can only move if the resulting move does not result in check for the king of the same color.

This `pre_move_validation` method is responsible for checking all the rules. If all validations pass, it calls the `move` method to update the move, as follows (see `4.06—model.py`):

```
def pre_move_validation(self, initial_pos, final_pos):
    initial_pos, final_pos = initial_pos.upper(), final_pos.upper()
    piece = self.get_piece_at(initial_pos)
    try:
        piece_at_destination = self.get_piece_at(final_pos)
    except:
        piece_at_destination = None
    if self.player_turn != piece.color:
        raise exceptions.NotYourTurn("Not " + piece.color + "'s turn!")
    enemy = ('white' if piece.color == 'black' else 'black')
    moves_available = piece.moves_available(initial_pos)
    if final_pos not in moves_available:
        raise exceptions.InvalidMove
    if self.get_all_available_moves(enemy):
        if self.will_move_cause_check(initial_pos, final_pos):
            raise exceptions.Check
    if not moves_available and self.is_king_under_check(piece.color):
        raise exceptions.CheckMate
    elif not moves_available:
```

```
            raise exceptions.Draw
        else:
            self.move(initial_pos, final_pos)
            self.update_game_statistics(
                piece, piece_at_destination, initial_pos, final_pos)
            self.change_player_turn(piece.color)
```

If the rules are not being followed, this code raises several exceptions, which are defined in the exceptions class as follows (see `4.06—exceptions.py`):

```
class Check(ChessError): pass
class InvalidMove(ChessError): pass
class CheckMate(ChessError): pass
class Draw(ChessError): pass
class NotYourTurn(ChessError): pass
```

We could have further coded the error classes, but we chose not to because we simply updated the name of the error class to the bottom label, which is sufficient for our current purpose. The error message is displayed from the shift method of the `View` class, as follows (see `4.06—view.py`):

```
self.info_label["text"] = error.__class__.__name__
```

Check whether a move will cause check on the King

Though a major part of the validation check done in the preceding lines is simple, one of the validation steps needs to check whether a movement will cause the king to be in check. This is a tricky situation. We can only find this out after we have made the actual move. However, we cannot allow that movement to happen on the chessboard.

To do this, the `pre_move_validation` method calls a method named `will_move_cause_check`, which creates a copy of the `Model` class. Then, it performs a move on the new temporary copy to check whether it does cause a king to be in check. The code for this is as follows (`4.06—model.py`):

```
def will_move_cause_check(self, start_position, end_position):
    tmp = deepcopy(self)
    tmp.move(start_position, end_position)
    return tmp.is_king_under_check(self[start_position].color)
```

Note that when you create a copy by simple assignment, Python creates a shallow copy. In a shallow copy, the two variables now share the same data. So, a modification in one place affects the other as well. In contrast to this, deep copies create a copy of everything—the structure as well as the elements. We need to create a deep copy of the chessboard because we want to check whether the king makes a valid move before it actually moves, and we want to do this without modifying the original object's state in any way.

Recording a move in the data structure

The `shift` method defined in `view.py` is responsible for the actual moving of a chess piece on the chessboard. However, this brings about a change in the underlying data structure. The `move` method of the `Model` class is then responsible for updating the data structure. This `move` method is called from the previously defined `pre_move_validation()` method if and only if no errors are raised, as follows (`4.06—model.py`):

```
def move(self, start_pos, final_pos):
  self[final_pos] = self.pop(start_pos, None)
```

Note that as soon as this update is complete, the control returns to the `on_square_clicked()` method in `view.py`. The method then calls the `draw_all_pieces()` method, which updates the view.

Keep game statistics

The `pre_move_validation()` method also calls another method called `update_game_statistics()` on successfully recording a move (see `4.06—model.py`):

```
def update_game_statistics(self, piece, dest, start_pos, end_pos):
    if piece.color == 'black':
        self.fullmove_number += 1
    self.halfmove_clock += 1
    abbr = piece.name
    if abbr == 'pawn':
        abbr = ''
        self.halfmove_clock = 0
    if dest is None:
        move_text = abbr + end_pos.lower()
    else:
```

```
                move_text = abbr + 'x' + end_pos.lower()
                self.halfmove_clock = 0
        self.history.append(move_text)
```

Congratulations, our chess game is now functional!

Let's complete the iteration by binding the **File** | **New Game** menu item to start a new game. Earlier, we defined the `start_new_game()` method. Now, it's simply a matter of calling it from the `on_new_game_menu_clicked()` method, as follows (`4.06—view.py`):

```
def on_new_game_menu_clicked(self):
    self.start_new_game()
```

Managing user preferences

A very common theme in several GUI programs involves letting the user set the program's preferences.

For example, what if we want users to be able to customize the chessboard colors? What if we want users to select colors and, once selected, it is saved as a user preference and it is loaded the next time the program is run? Let's implement this as a feature.

Python offers a standard module called `configparser` that lets us save user preferences. Let's see the `configparser` module in action.

To begin with, import the `ConfigParser` class from the `configparser` module in the `configurations.py` file, as follows (see `4.07 preferenceswindow.py`):

```
from configparser import ConfigParser
```

The `configparser` module uses the `.ini` files to store and read the configuration values. The file consists of one or more named sections. These sections contain individual options with names and values.

To illustrate this, let's create a file called `chess_options.ini` in the project's root folder (see `4.07`). The file looks like this:

```
[chess_colors]
board_color_1 = #DDB88C
board_color_2 = #A66D4F
highlight_color = #2EF70D
```

The first line of the file enclosed in square brackets ([chess_colors] in our example) is called a **section**. A .ini file can have multiple sections. This file has a single section. Each section can have multiple *key-value* options, as specified in the example.

We can read these values in our program by using the getter methods, as follows (see 4.07—configurations.py):

```
config = ConfigParser()
config.read('chess_options.ini')
BOARD_COLOR_1 = config.get('chess_colors', 'board_color_1',
    fallback="#DDB88C")
BOARD_COLOR_2 = config.get('chess_colors', 'board_color_2', fallback =
    "#A66D4F")
HIGHLIGHT_COLOR =config.get('chess_colors', 'highlight_color', fallback
    = "#2EF70D")
```

The preceding code replaces the three color constants that we defined earlier in the code.

Now, if you change the options in the .ini file, the color of the chessboard changes accordingly. However, we cannot expect end users to be conversant with editing the .ini files. Therefore, we will let them choose the colors using the **color chooser** module of Tkinter. A color that a user chooses gets reflected in the .ini file and consequently on the chessboard.

When a user clicks on the **Edit | Preference** menu item, we want to open a *transient window* with three different buttons to choose two chessboard colors and one highlight color. Clicking on a single button opens a color select window, as shown in the following screenshot:

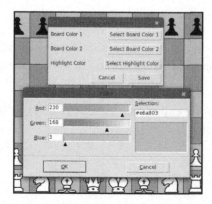

We created this transient window in a new file called `preferenceswindow.py` (see `4.07.py`). We will not discuss the code that creates this window, as this should be an easy task for you now.

Note that this window is converted into a transient window with respect to the top-level window by using the following code:

```
self.pref_window.transient(self.parent)
```

As a reminder, a transient window is one that always stays at the top of its parent window. It gets minimized when its parent window is minimized. For a quick refresher on transient windows, refer to `Chapter 2`, *Making a Text Editor,*—`2.06.py`.

As we have created the window in `preferencewindow.py`, we'll import it into the `View` class as follows (see `2.07—view.py`):

```
import preferenceswindow
```

Then, command bind the preference menu by using the following two methods:

```
def on_preference_menu_clicked(self):
    self.show_prefereces_window()

def show_prefereces_window(self):
    preferenceswindow.PreferencesWindow(self)
```

When a user clicks on the **Cancel** button, we simply want the settings window to close. To do this, use the following code (see `4.07—preferencewindow.py`):

```
def on_cancel_button_clicked(self):
    self.pref_window.destroy()
```

When a user changes the colors and clicks on the **Save** button, the method calls the `set_new_values()` method, which first writes the new values to the `.ini` file and then returns the values to the `View` class to update the chessboard immediately:

```
def set_new_values(self):
    color_1 = self.board_color_1.get()
    color_2 = self.board_color_2.get()
    highlight_color = self.highlight_color.get()
    config = ConfigParser()
    config.read('chess_options.ini')
    config.set('chess_colors', 'board_color_1',color_1)
    config.set('chess_colors', 'board_color_2',color_2)
    config.set('chess_colors', 'highlight_color', highlight_color)
    configurations.BOARD_COLOR_1 = self.board_color_1.get()
    configurations.BOARD_COLOR_2 = self.board_color_2.get()
```

```
configurations.HIGHLIGHT_COLOR = self.highlight_color.get()
with open('chess_options.ini', 'w') as config_file:
    config.write(config_file)
```

When the preceding code writes the new values to the `.ini` file, call the `reload_colors()` method from the `View` class to update the chessboard's color immediately. If you do not do this, the color change will take place the next time the chess program is run (see `4.07—view.py`):

```
def reload_colors(self, color_1, color_2, highlight_color):
    self.board_color_1 = color_1
    self.board_color_2 = color_2
    self.highlight_color = highlight_color
    self.draw_board()
    self.draw_all_pieces()
```

Having changed these attributes, we call `draw_board()` and `draw_all_pieces()` to repaint the chessboard in the newly defined colors. (see `4.07—view.py`).

This concludes the iteration. The users of the program can change the colors to match their preferences, and the program will remember the chosen values.

Summary

We have come to the end of this chapter. So, what is it that we achieved here? Let's have a look at all the key things that we learned from the chapter.

We learned how to structure programs using the MVC architecture.

We took a peek at the versatility and power of the Tkinter Canvas widget. This included a tour through the basic usage of the canvas coordinates, object IDs, and tags.

We discussed how to handle complexity by implementing programs in a modular structure. We achieved this modularity by breaking down the code into several smaller files. We handled the entire configuration from a single file and all the errors in another file.

We explored how to extend Python's built-in error class to define a custom error and exceptions. We also had a look at how we can extend Python's built-in data types, as in the case of the `Model` class, which directly extended the `dict` class.
We studied how to use object inheritance to code classes with similar attributes and behavior when building the `Piece` class and all its subclasses.

Finally, you learned how to use Python's built-in `configparser` module to store user preferences.

We will create an audio player in the next chapter. In addition to this, we'll work with several new widgets. We will also take a look at how to create our own widgets!

QA section

Before you proceed to the next chapter, make sure you can answer these questions to your satisfaction:

- What are the central tenets of the model-view-controller framework?
- What is modularity in programming? Why is modularity good?
- What are the advantages and disadvantages of using class inheritance in programs?
- While inheritance provided us with a tool to reuse our code, multiple inheritance is frowned upon by many experts. What could be the reason for this?
- What are `tags` used for in the Tkinter Canvas widget?
- Why do we use a `configparser` module? What are some of the alternatives to using a `configparser` module?

Further reading

MVC is a popular software **architectural pattern**, but there are many more architectural patterns that suit different use cases. Read about different architectural patterns at `https://en.wikipedia.org/wiki/Architectural_pattern`.

If chess enthuses you, or if you would like to get started in artificial intelligence, you might attempt to implement a chess engine that plays as an opponent. This would require some reading on optimal search algorithms. Here's a tutorial that walks us through the process: `https://medium.freecodecamp.org/simple-chess-ai-step-by-step-1d55a9266977`. The tutorial engine has been implemented in JavaScript, but we can use it as a reference to build our own engine in Python.

5

Building an Audio Player

Let's build an audio player! Our application should have the features offered by typical audio players, such as play, pause, fast forward, rewind, next, mute, volume scale, time seek, and more. It should let listeners easily access media files or a media library on their local drive. The audio player should do all this and more. Let's begin!

The following are the key objectives of this chapter:

- Exploring Tkinter widgets, namely Slider, Listbox, Radiobutton, and Canvas
- Creating new widgets in Tkinter by extending the existing widgets
- Understanding virtual events and their usage
- Learning the most common coding pattern used in Tkinter-based animations
- Learning some common Tkinter extensions such as Pmw, WCK, and TIX

An overview of the chapter

Let's call our audio player *Achtung Baby*.

The audio player will be capable of playing audio files in **AU**, **MP2**, **MP3**, **OGG/Vorbis**, **WAV**, and **WMA** formats. It will have all the controls that you would expect of a small media player.

We will use cross-platform modules to write the code. This will ensure that the player can play audio files on Windows, macOS X, and Linux platforms.

On completion, the audio player will look as follows:

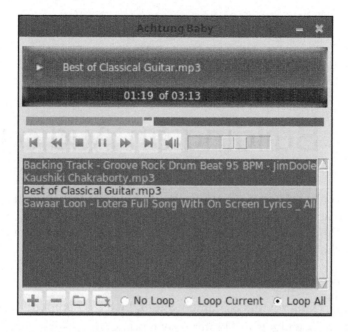

Perhaps the most important takeaway from this chapter is to learn how to create your own widgets in Tkinter.

The seek bar in the preceding screenshot is an example of a custom-made widget that was not natively available in Tkinter, but was handcrafted for this particular use case.

After you learn how to create custom widgets, what you can then create will only be limited by what you can imagine.

External library requirements

In addition to the several built-in modules of Python, we will use the following two external modules in this project:

1. The `pyglet` library for audio manipulation
2. **Pmw** (short for **Python megawidget**) for the widgets that are not available in core Tkinter

The pyglet module

Pyglet is a cross-platform windowing and multimedia library for Python. It can be downloaded at `https://bitbucket.org/pyglet/pyglet/wiki/Download`.

Pyglet can be installed using the pip installer, which is the default package manager for Python by using the following command:

```
pip3 install pyglet
```

Windows users can also download and install binary packages for `pyglet` from `http://www.lfd.uci.edu/~gohlke/pythonlibs/#pyglet`.

Pyglet needs another module called `AVbin` to support playback of file formats such as MP2 and MP3. `AVbin` can be obtained for Windows, Linux, and macOS from the download section at `http://avbin.github.io`.

Pmw Tkinter extension

We will use the Pmw Tkinter extension to code some widget features that are not available in core Tkinter. Pmw can be installed by using the pip command-line tool, as follows:

```
pip3 install pmw
```

Pmw can also be installed from the source package for all the platforms. The package can be downloaded from `http://sourceforge.net/projects/pmw/`.

After installing `pyglet`, `AVbin`, and Pmw, execute the following command from the Python shell:

```
>> import pyglet, Pmw
>>> pyglet.version
 '1.3.0'
>>> Pmw.version()
 '2.0.1'
```

If the commands execute without an error message and the version of `pyglet` and Pmw are the same as what's shown in the preceding code, you are ready to code your audio player.

Program structure and broadview skeleton

Our first goal is to build the broad modular structure for the program. As usual, we will keep the data structure, audio-related logic, and the presentation logic in three separate files. Therefore, we will create three separate files named `model.py`, `player.py`, and `view.py` (see `code 5.01`).

Let's create an empty `Model` class and an empty `Player` class in their respective files. The following is the code for `5.01—model.py`:

```
class Model:
  def __init__(self):
    pass
```

Here's the code for `5.01—player.py`:

```
import pyglet
class Player():
  def __init__(self):
    pass
```

Next, let's create the `View` class. We will leave the `Model` and `Player` classes empty for now. However, we will complete this iteration by coding the majority of the view elements for the player.

Let's begin by importing the required modules in the `View` class, as follows:

```
import tkinter as tk
import tkinter.filedialog
import tkinter.messagebox
import tkinter.ttk
```

Also, import the blank `Model` and `Player` classes in the `View` namespace (see code `5.01—view.py`):

```
import model
import player
```

However, since we do not want to mix the logic with its representation, we do not import `View` in the `Model` class. In short, the `Model` class knows nothing about how its data will be presented to the frontend user.

Note that we are not using the `Controller` class in this program. We saw how to use controllers in `Chapter 4`, *Game of Chess*. While controllers are a great way to avoid direct coupling between the `Model` and `View` classes, they can be an overkill for small programs like this one.

Now, let's create the top-level window. Also, we'll create instances of the `Model` and `Player` classes and pass them as arguments to the `View` class, as follows (see code `5.01—view.py`):

```
if __name__ == '__main__':
    root = Tk()
    root.resizable(width=False, height=False)
    player = player.Player()
    model = model.Model()
    app = View(root, model, player)
    root.mainloop()
```

Now that the boilerplate code is written, let's start coding the actual `View` class, as follows (see code `5.01—view.py`):

```
class View:
    def __init__(self,root, model, player):
        self.root = root
        self.model = model
        self.player = player
        self.create_gui()

    def create_gui(self):
        self.root.title(AUDIO_PLAYER_NAME)
        self.create_top_display()
        self.create_button_frame()
        self.create_list_box()
        self.create_bottom_frame()
        self.create_context_menu()
```

The __init__ method should look familiar to you by now. The final line of the __init__ calls a method called `create_gui`, which is responsible for the creation of the entire GUI. The `create_gui` method in turn simply calls five different methods, where each method is responsible for the creation of different sections of the GUI.

We also made the root window nonresizable by adding `root.resizable(width=False, height=False)` to the code.

We will not reproduce the entire code that creates the GUI, since we have coded similar widgets in the past. But all of these five methods, when combined, create the GUI shown in the following screenshot:

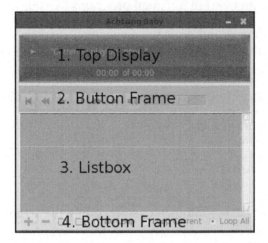

For the sake of separation, we have also marked the four sections differently in the preceding screenshot. The fifth method creates the right-click context menu and is not visible here.

The code used to create all of these GUI elements should be familiar to you by now. However, note a few things about the code (see code 5.01—view.py):

- All the images used in the preceding code have been stored in a separate folder named icons.
- We have used the grid geometry manager to place all the elements on the top-level window.
- The Top Display section creates a Canvas widget and places an overlay image using the canvas.create_image() method. The currently playing text and the timer displayed in the top display have been created by using the canvas.create_text() method. The coordinates used to place these elements have been decided on a trial-and-error basis. As a reminder, the canvas coordinates are measured from the top-left corner.
- The **Button Frame** section simply creates buttons and uses images instead of text, using the following code:

  - ```
    button=tk.Button(parent, image=previous_track_icon)
    ```
    ```

- The **Button Frame** section also uses a ttk Scale widget, which can be used as a volume slider. This has been created by using the following code:

  - ```
    self.volume_scale = tkinter.ttk.Scale(frame, from_=0.0, to=1.0,
    command=self.on_volume_scale_changed)
    ```

- The `from` and `to` values for the Scale widget have been chosen as `0.0` and `1.0` because these are the numbers that the `pyglet` library uses to denote the minimum and maximum volume, which will be seen in the following section.
- The Listbox section creates a playlist by using the Tkinter Listbox widget, which uses the following code:

  - ```
    self.list_box = tk.Listbox(frame, activestyle='none',
    cursor='hand2', bg='#1C3D7D', fg='#A0B9E9', selectmode=tk.EXTENDED,
    height=10)
    ```

- The `select mode=EXTENDED` option in the preceding code means that this list box will allow multiple list items to be selected at once. If this line is omitted, the default behavior of the Listbox widget is to allow only a single selection at a time.
- The `activestyle='none'` option means that we do not want to underline the selected item.
- The Listbox section is attached to the Scrollbar widget, which is similar to what we have done in the earlier chapters.
- The **Bottom Frame** section adds a few image buttons as we did earlier. It also creates three Radiobutton widgets using a `for` loop.
- Finally, note that we have completely skipped the creation of the seek bar, as it is a custom widget that is not natively defined in Tkinter. This is something that we will create in a dedicated section of its own.

The Listbox widget offers the following four selection modes via the selectmode option:

- `SINGLE`: This allows only a single row to be selected at a time
- `BROWSE` (the default mode): This is similar to `SINGLE`, but it allows you to move a selection by dragging the mouse
- `MULTIPLE`: This allows for multiple selections by clicking on items one at a time
- `EXTENDED`: This allows for the selection of a multiple range of items using the *Shift* and *Ctrl* keys

In addition to creating all of these widgets, we have also added a command callback to most of these widgets. These command callbacks currently point to the following empty, nonfunctional methods (see code 5.01—view.py):

```
on_previous_track_button_clicked()
on_rewind_button_clicked()
on_play_stop_button_clicked()
on_pause_unpause_button_clicked()
on_mute_unmute_button_clicked()
on_fast_forward_button_clicked()
on_next_track_button_clicked()
on_volume_scale_changed(, value)
on_add_file_button_clicked()
on_remove_selected_button_clicked()
on_add_directory_button_clicked()
on_empty_play_list_button_clicked()
on_remove_selected_context_menu_clicked()
on_play_list_double_clicked(event=None)
```

None of these methods are functional now. We will end the iteration here, as there are a few other things that we need to do before we can think of making the widgets functional.

Deciding the data structure

Sticking to the model first philosophy, let's spend some time on deciding the appropriate data structure or model for the program.

The data structure of the audio player is fairly simple. All that we expect of the model is to keep a track of playlists. The main data then is a list called play_list, and the Model class is then simply responsible for the addition and removal of items to and from the playlist.

Accordingly we came up with the following Model class for the program (see code 5.02—model.py):

```
class Model:
    def __init__(self):
        self.__play_list = []

    @property
    def play_list(self):
        return self.__play_list

    def get_file_to_play(self, file_index):
        return self.__play_list[file_index]
```

```
def clear_play_list(self):
    self.__play_list.clear()

def add_to_play_list(self, file_name):
    self.__play_list.append(file_name)

def remove_item_from_play_list_at_index(self, index):
    del self.__play_list[index]
```

Nothing fancy in the preceding code. The object simply consists of a Python list with various utility methods that can be used to add and remove items from the list.

The `play_list` method has been declared as a property so that we need not write the `getter` method for the playlist. This is definitely more Pythonic because a statement such as `play_list = self.play_list` is more readable than `play_list = self.get_play_list()`.

Creating the Player class

Now, let's write the code for the `Player` class. This class will be responsible for the handling of audio playback and its related functions, such as pause, stop, seek, fast forward, rewind, change of volume, mute, and so on.

We will use the `pyglet` library to handle these functions.

Pyglet is a cross-platform library that uses the `AVbin` module to support a large variety of audio files.

You might want to look at the API documentation of the pyglet player, which is available at `https://bitbucket.org/pyglet/pyglet/wiki/Home`.

You can also access the documentation for the pyglet media player class by typing the following two lines in the Python interactive shell:

```
>>> import pyglet
>>> help(pyglet.media)
```

The online documentation at `https://pyglet.readthedocs.org/` tells us that we can play an audio file by using the following code:

```
player= pyglet.media.Player()
source = pyglet.media.load(<<audio file to be played>>)
player.queue(source)
```

```
    player.play()
```

Accordingly, the code for the Player class is as follows (see code 5.02—player.py):

```
import pyglet

FORWARD_REWIND_JUMP_TIME = 20

class Player:
  def __init__(self):
    self.player = pyglet.media.Player()
    self.player.volume = 0.6

 def play_media(self, audio_file):
   self.reset_player()
   self.player = pyglet.media.Player()
   self.source = pyglet.media.load(audio_file)
   self.player.queue(self.source)
   self.player.play()

 def reset_player(self):
   self.player.pause()
   self.player.delete()

def is_playing(self):
  try:
    elapsed_time = int(self.player.time)
    is_playing = elapsed_time < int(self.track_length)
  except:
    is_playing = False
  return is_playing

def seek(self, time):
  try:
   self.player.seek(time)
  except AttributeError:
   pass

@property
def track_length(self):
  try:
    return self.source.duration
  except AttributeError:
    return 0

@property
def volume(self):
  return self.player.volume
```

```python
    @property
    def elapsed_play_duration(self):
      return self.player.time

  @volume.setter
  def volume(self, volume):
    self.player.volume = volume

  def unpause(self):
    self.player.play()

  def pause(self):
    self.player.pause()

  def stop(self):
    self.reset_player()

  def mute(self):
    self.player.volume = 0.0

  def unmute(self, newvolume_level):
    self.player.volume = newvolume_level

  def fast_forward(self):
    time = self.player.time + FORWARD_REWIND_JUMP_TIME
    try:
      if self.source.duration > time:
        self.seek(time)
      else:
        self.seek(self.source.duration)
    except AttributeError:
      pass

  def rewind(self):
    time = self.player.time - FORWARD_REWIND_JUMP_TIME
    try:
      self.seek(time)
    except:
      self.seek(0)
```

The preceding code is built on the `pyglet` API, which is quite intuitive. We will not get into the details of audio programming here and trust the `pyglet` library as a black box that delivers what it says, namely, to be able to play and control audio.

The following are the important things that you should note about the preceding code:

- We defined the `play_media` method, which is responsible for the playing of audio. All the other methods support other functions related to playback, such as pause, stop, rewind, forward, mute, and so on.
- Note that the code defines a new pyglet `Player` class every time it wants to play an audio file. Though we could have used the same player instance to play multiple audio files, it turns out that the `pyglet` library does not have a `stop` method. The only way we can stop an audio file from playing is by killing the `Player` object and creating a fresh `Player` object for the next audio file playback.
- When it came to choosing an external implementation as we did for the audio API here, we first searched through the Python standard library at `https://docs.python.org/3.6/library/`.
- Because the standard library does not have a suitable package for us, we turned our attention to the Python package index to check whether there exists another high-level audio interface implementation. The Python package index can be found at `http://pypi.python.org/`.
- Fortunately, we came across several audio packages. After comparing the packages against our needs and seeing how active their communities were, we settled for `pyglet`. The same program could have been implemented with several other packages, though this would be done with varying levels of complexity.

> In general, the lower you go down the protocol stack, the more complex your programs will get.
> However, at the lower layers of the protocol, you will get a finer control over the implementation at the cost of increasing learning curves.
> Also, note that most of the audio libraries change over a period of time. While this current audio library may become nonfunctional over time, you can easily modify the `Player` class to use some other audio library and still be able to use this program as long as you keep the interface defined in the `Player` class.

This concludes the iteration. We now have a functional `Player` class that can manipulate audio files. We have a data structure that consists of a `play_list` with various methods to add and remove files from a playlist. We will next look at how to add and remove files from a playlist from the frontend of the program.

Adding and removing items from a playlist

Let's write some code for a feature that allows us to add and remove items from a playlist. To be more specific, we will write the code for a function for the four buttons marked in the following screenshot:

The four buttons, from left to right, perform the following functions:

- The first button from the left adds individual audio files to a playlist
- The second button deletes all the selected items from the playlist
- The third button scans a directory for audio files and adds all the found audio files to the playlist
- The last button empties the playlist

Since adding these features requires us to interact with the Listbox widget of Tkinter, let's spend some time getting to know the Listbox widget:

We can create a Listbox widget like we'd create any other widget, as follows:

```
play_list = tk.ListBox(parent, **configurable options)
```

When you initially create a Listbox widget, it is empty. To insert one or more lines of text into the Listbox, use the `insert()` method, which takes two arguments, namely an index of the position where the text needs to be inserted and the actual string that needs to be inserted, as follows:

```
play_list.insert(0, "First Item")
play_list.insert(1, "Second Item")
play_list.insert(END, "Last Item")
```

The `curselection()` method returns the index of all the items selected in the list, and the `get()` method returns the list item for a given index, as follows:

```
play_list.curselection() # returns a tuple of all selected items
play_list.curselection()[0] # returns first selected item
play_list.get(1) # returns second item from the list
play_list.get(0, END) # returns all items from the list
```

In addition to this, the Listbox widget has several other configurable options.

For a complete Listbox widget reference, type the following into the Python interactive shell:

```
>>> import tkinter
>>> help(tkinter.Listbox)
```

Now that we know how to add and remove items from the Listbox widget, let's code these functions into the player.

Let's begin by modifying the command callback attached to the four buttons, as follows (see code 5.03—view.py):

```
def on_add_file_button_clicked(self):
 self.add_audio_file()

def on_remove_selected_button_clicked(self):
 self.remove_selected_file()

def on_add_directory_button_clicked(self):
 self.add_all_audio_files_from_directory()

def on_clear_play_list_button_clicked(self):
 self.clear_play_list()

def on_remove_selected_context_menu_clicked(self):
 self.remove_selected_file()
```

All that these four methods do is call four other methods that do the actual task of adding or removing items to the playlist. All the methods will update the `play_list` items at the following two places:

- In the visible Listbox widget
- In the backend data structure playlist maintained by the `Model` class

Let's define the four new methods.

Adding a single audio file

Adding a file involves asking for the location using Tkinter `filedialog` and updating the frontend and backend, as follows (see code 5.03—view.py):

```
def add_audio_file(self):
```

```
audio_file = tkinter.filedialog.askopenfilename(filetypes=[(
      'All supported', '.mp3 .wav'), ('.mp3 files', '.mp3'),('.wav files',
'.wav')])
if audio_file:
  self.model.add_to_play_list(audio_file)
  file_path, file_name = os.path.split(audio_file)
  self.list_box.insert(tk.END, file_name)
```

Removing the selected files from a playlist

Since the Listbox allows for multiple selections, we iterate through all the selected items, removing them from the frontend Listbox widget as well as from the model `play_list`, as follows (see code `5.03—view.py`):

```
def remove_selected_files(self):
 try:
  selected_indexes = self.list_box.curselection()
  for index in reversed(selected_indexes):
    self.list_box.delete(index)
    self.model.remove_item_from_play_list_at_index(index)
 except IndexError:
   pass
```

Note that we reverse the tuple before removing items from the playlist because we want to start removing items from the end, as a removal causes a change in the index of playlist items. If we do not remove items from the end, we may end up removing the wrong items from the list, as its index gets modified in each iteration.

Since we have defined this method here, let's add it as a command callback to the right-click delete menu, as follows:

```
def on_remove_selected_context_menu_clicked(self):
  self.remove_selected_files()
```

Adding all files from a directory

The following code uses the `os.walk()` method to recursively walk through all the files looking for `.wav` and `.mp3` files, as follows (see code `5.03—view.py`):

```
def add_all_audio_files_from_directory(self):
  directory_path = tkinter.filedialog.askdirectory()
  if not directory_path: return
  audio_files_in_directory =
```

```
self.get_all_audio_file_from_directory(directory_path)
  for audio_file in audio_files_in_directory:
    self.model.add_to_play_list(audio_file)
    file_path, file_name = os.path.split(audio_file)
    self.list_box.insert(tk.END, file_name)

def get_all_audio_file_from_directory(self, directory_path):
  audio_files_in_directory = []
  for (dirpath, dirnames, filenames) in os.walk(directory_path):
    for audio_file in filenames:
      if audio_file.endswith(".mp3") or audio_file.endswith(".wav"):
        audio_files_in_directory.append(dirpath + "/" + audio_file)
  return audio_files_in_directory
```

Emptying the playlist

The code is as follows (see code 5.03—view.py):

```
def empty_play_list(self):
  self.model.empty_play_list()
  self.list_box.delete(0, END)
```

This completes our third iteration. In this iteration, we saw how to work with the Listbox widget. In particular, we saw how to add items to the Listbox widget, select a particular item from the Listbox widget, and delete one or more items from it.

You now have a playlist where you can add and delete items using the four buttons at the bottom-left corner of the audio player.

Playing audio and adding audio controls

In this iteration, we will code the features marked in the following screenshot:

This includes the play/stop, pause/unpause, next track, previous track, fast forward, rewind, volume change, and mute/unmute features.

Adding the play/stop function

Now that we have a playlist and a `Player` class that can play audio, playing audio is simply about updating the current track index and calling the `play` method.

Accordingly, let's add an attribute, as follows (see code 5.04—`view.py`):

```
current_track_index = 0
```

Furthermore, the **Play** button should act as a toggle between the `play` and `stop` functions. The Python `itertools` module provides the `cycle` method, which is a very convenient way to toggle between two or more values.

Accordingly, import the `itertools` module and define a new attribute, as follows (see code 5.04—`view.py`):

```
toggle_play_stop = itertools.cycle(["play","stop"])
```

Now, every time we call `next(toggle_play_stop)`, the value returned toggles between the `play` and `stop` strings.

> Itertools is a very powerful standard library of Python that can emulate many **iterables** from a functional programming paradigm. An iterable in Python is an interface that implements the `next()` method. Every subsequent call to `next()` is **lazily evaluated**—thereby making them suitable for iterating over large sequences in the most efficient manner. The `cycle()` tool used here is an example of an iterator that can provide infinite sequences of alternating values without the need to define a large data structure.
>
> The following is the documentation of the `itertools` module:
> https://docs.python.org/3/library/itertools.html

Next, modify the `on_play_stop_button_clicked()` method so that it looks like this (see code 5.04—`view.py`):

```
def on_play_stop_button_clicked(self):
  action = next(self.toggle_play_stop)
  if action == 'play':
   try:
     self.current_track_index = self.list_box.curselection()[0]
   except IndexError:
     self.current_track_index = 0
   self.start_play()
```

```
elif action == 'stop':
  self.stop_play()
```

The preceding method simply toggles between calling the `start_play()` and `stop_play()` methods, which are defined as follows:

```
def start_play(self):
  try:
    audio_file = self.model.get_file_to_play(self.current_track_index)
  except IndexError:
    return
  self.play_stop_button.config(image=self.stop_icon)
  self.player.play_media(audio_file)

def stop_play(self):
  self.play_stop_button.config(image=self.play_icon)
  self.player.stop()
```

The preceding code calls the `play` and `stop` methods defined in the `Player` class. It also changes the button image from the *play* icon to the *stop* icon by using the `widget.config(image=new_image_icon)` method.

While we are handling the `play` function, let's modify the command callback so that a user can play a track simply by double-clicking on it. We have already defined a method named `on_play_list_double_clicked` earlier, which is currently empty.

Simply modify it, as follows:

```
def on_play_list_double_clicked(self, event=None):
  self.current_track_index = int(self.list_box.curselection()[0])
  self.start_play()
```

Adding the pause/unpause function

Since we need a single button to toggle between pause and unpause, we will again use the `cycle()` method from the `itertools` module. Define an attribute, as follows (see code 5.04—view.py):

```
toggle_pause_unpause = itertools.cycle(["pause","unpause"])
```

Then, modify the command callback attached to the button, as follows:

```
def on_pause_unpause_button_clicked(self):
  action = next(self.toggle_pause_unpause)
  if action == 'pause':
```

```
    self.player.pause()
  elif action == 'unpause':
    self.player.unpause()
```

This takes care of the pause and unpause features of the program.

Adding the mute/unmute function

This is similar to coding the pause/unpause feature. We need an attribute that can toggle between the `mute` and `unmute` strings. Accordingly, add an attribute, as follows (see code `5.04—view.py`):

```
toggle_mute_unmute = itertools.cycle(["mute","unmute"])
```

Then, modify the command callback to call the `mute` or `unmute` functions from the `player` class, change the button icon to the mute or unmute image, and shift the volume scale accordingly, as follows (see code `5.04—view.py`):

```
def on_mute_unmute_button_clicked(self):
  action = next(self.toggle_mute_unmute)
  if action == 'mute':
    self.volume_at_time_of_mute = self.player.volume
    self.player.mute()
    self.volume_scale.set(0)
    self.mute_unmute_button.config(image=self.mute_icon)
  elif action == 'unmute':
    self.player.unmute(self.volume_at_time_of_mute)
    self.volume_scale.set(self.volume_at_time_of_mute)
    self.mute_unmute_button.config(image=self.unmute_icon)
```

Fast forward/rewind function

The codes for fast forward and rewind are the simplest. We have already defined the methods to handle this in the `Player` class. Now, it's only a matter of connecting them to the concerned command callback, as follows:

```
def on_fast_forward_button_clicked(self):
  self.player.fast_forward()

def on_rewind_button_clicked(self):
  self.player.rewind()
```

Adding the next track/previous track function

While we had defined the code for fast forward and rewind in the Player class, we did not define the method related to next track and previous track there, because this can be handled by the existing play method. All that you need to do is simply increment or decrement the value of current_track and then call the play method. Accordingly, define two methods in the View class, as follows (see code 5.04—view.py):

```
def play_previous_track(self):
    self.current_track_index = max(0, self.current_track_index - 1)
    self.start_play()

def play_next_track(self):
    self.current_track_index = min(self.list_box.size() - 1,
        self.current_track_index + 1)
    self.start_play()
```

Then, simply attach these two methods to the respective command callback, as follows (see code 5.04—view.py):

```
def on_previous_track_button_clicked(self):
    self.play_previous_track()

def on_next_track_button_clicked(self):
    self.play_next_track()
```

Adding the volume change function

We have already defined the volume method in the Player class. Now, all that you need to do is simply get the value of the Volume Scale widget and set the volume in the Player class.

Also, ensure that in case the volume becomes zero, we change the volume button icon to the mute image (see code 5.04—view.py):

```
def on_volume_scale_changed(self, value):
    self.player.volume = self.volume_scale.get()
    if self.volume_scale.get() == 0.0:
        self.mute_unmute_button.config(image=self.mute_icon)
    else:
        self.mute_unmute_button.config(image=self.unmute_icon)
```

This concludes the iteration. The player is now functional enough to be called an audio player. Go ahead and add some music files to the player. Press the play button and enjoy the music! Try out other player controls that we defined in this iteration and they should work as expected.

Creating a seek bar

Now, let's add a seek bar to the audio player. Tkinter offers the Scale widget that we used for the volume scale. The Scale widget could have functioned as a seek bar.

But we want something fancier. Moreover, the Scale widget would look different on different platforms. Instead, we want the seek bar to look uniform on all platforms. This is where we can create our own widget to meet the custom needs of the audio player.

Let's create our own Seekbar widget, as shown in the following screenshot:

The simplest way to create our own widget is to inherit one from an existing widget or the Widget class.

When you look at the source code of Tkinter, you will find that all the widgets inherit from a class named Widget. The Widget class, in turn, inherits from another class called BaseWidget. The BaseWidget class contains the code that is used to handle a widget's destroy() method, but it is not aware of a geometry manager.

Therefore, if we want our custom widget to be aware of and use geometry managers such as pack, grid, or place, we need to inherit from the Widget class or from another Tkinter widget.

Let's assume that we want to create a widget named Wonderwidget. We can do so simply by inheriting from the Widget class, as follows:

```
from tkinter import *

class Wonderwidget(Widget):
  def __init__(self, parent, **options):
    Widget.__init__(self, parent, options)
```

These four lines of code create a widget named Wonderwidget, which can be positioned with geometry managers such as pack, place, or grid.

However, for more practical use cases, we generally inherit from the existing Tkinter widgets, such as Text, Button, Scale, Canvas, and so on. In our case, we will create the Seekbar widget by inheriting from the Canvas class.

Create a new file called seekbar.py (see code 5.05.py). Then, create a new class named Seekbar that inherits from the Canvas widget, as follows:

```
from tkinter import *

class Seekbar(Canvas):
    def __init__(self, parent, called_from, **options):
        Canvas.__init__(self, parent, options)
        self.parent = parent
        self.width = options['width']
        self.red_rectangle = self.create_rectangle(0, 0, 0, 0, fill="red")
        self.seekbar_knob_image = PhotoImage(file="../icons/seekbar_knob.gif")
        self.seekbar_knob = self.create_image(0, 0,
            image=self.seekbar_knob_image)
```

The preceding code calls the __init__ method of the parent Canvas class to initialize the underlying canvas with all the canvas-related options that are passed as an argument.

With as little code as that, let's go back and modify the create_top_display() method in the View class to add this new widget, as follows:

```
self.seek_bar = Seekbar(frame, background="blue", width=SEEKBAR_WIDTH,
height=10)
self.seek_bar.grid(row=2, columnspan=10, sticky='ew', padx=5)
```

Here, SEEKBAR_WIDTH is a constant that we defined as equal to 360 pixels in the program.

If you now run view.py, you will see the Seekbar widget at its place.

The seek bar is not functional, as it does not move when the seek bar knob is clicked.

In order to make the seek bar slide along, we will bind the mouse buttons by defining a new method and calling it from the __init__ method, as follows (see code 5.05—seekbar.py):

```
def bind_mouse_button(self):
    self.bind('<Button-1>', self.on_seekbar_clicked)
    self.bind('<B1-Motion>', self.on_seekbar_clicked)
    self.tag_bind(self.red_rectangle, '<B1-Motion>',
```

```
        self.on_seekbar_clicked)
    self.tag_bind(self.seekbar_knob, '<B1-Motion>',
        self.on_seekbar_clicked)
```

We bind the entire canvas, the red rectangle, and the seek bar knob to a single method named `on_seekbar_clicked`, which can be defined as follows (see code `5.05—seekbar.py`):

```
def on_seekbar_clicked(self, event=None):
    self.slide_to_position(event.x)
```

The preceding method simply calls another method named `slide_to_position`, which is responsible for changing the position of the knob and the size of the red rectangle (see code `5.05—seekbar.py`):

```
def slide_to_position(self, new_position):
    if 0 <= new_position <= self.width:
        self.coords(self.red_rectangle, 0, 0, new_position, new_position)
        self.coords(self.seekbar_knob, new_position, 0)
        self.event_generate("<<SeekbarPositionChanged>>", x=new_position)
```

The preceding code slides the knob to the new position. More importantly, the last line creates a custom event named `SeekbarPositionChanged`. This event will let any code that uses this custom widget handle the event appropriately.

The second argument, `x=new_position`, adds the value of x to `event.x`, making it available to the event handler.

So far, we have only been handling events. Tkinter also lets us create our own events, which are called **virtual events**.

We can specify any name for the event by enclosing the name in double pairs of <<...>>.

In the preceding code, we generated a virtual event named <<SeekbarPositionChanged>>.

We then bound it to the appropriate event handler in the `View` class, as follows:

```
self.root.bind("<<SeekbarPositionChanged>>", self.seek_new_position)
```

That's all that there is to the custom `Seekbar` widget. We can write a small test in `seekbar.py` that will check whether the `Seekbar` widget works as expected:

```
class TestSeekBar :
  def __init__(self):
    root = tk.Tk()
    root.bind("<<SeekbarPositionChanged>>", self.seek_new_position)
    frame = tk.Frame(root)
    frame.grid(row=1, pady=10, padx=10)
    c = Seekbar(frame, background="blue", width=360, height=10)
    c.grid(row=2, columnspan=10, sticky='ew', padx=5)
    root.mainloop()

  def seek_new_position(self, event):
    print("Dragged to x:", event.x)

if __name__ == '__main__':
  TestSeekBar()
```

Go ahead and run the `5.05—seekbar.py` program; it should produce a seek bar. The seek bar should slide when you drag the seek bar knob or click at various places on the canvas.

This concludes the iteration. We will make the audio player's seek bar functional in the next iteration.

One-time updates during audio playback

The audio program must update some information as soon as an audio track starts playing. Broadly speaking, there are two kinds of updates that the program needs to monitor and update:

- **One-time updates**: Examples of this include the name of the track and the total length of the track.
- **Continuous updates**: Examples of this include the position of the seek bar knob and the elapsed play duration. We also need to check continuously whether a track has ended either to play the next track, play the current track again, or stop playing, depending on the loop choice made by the user.

These two kinds of updates will affect sections of the audio player, as shown in the following screenshot:

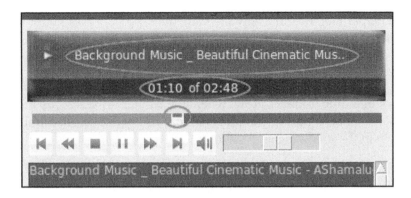

Let's start with the one-time updates, as they are relatively simple to implement.

Since these updates must occur when the playback starts, let's define a method named `manage_one_time_updates()` and call it from within the `start_play()` method of the `View` class, as follows (see code 5.06—`view.py`):

```
def manage_one_time_track_updates_on_play_start(self):
  self.update_now_playing_text()
  self.display_track_duration()
```

Next, define all the methods called from within the preceding method, as follows:

```
def update_now_playing_text(self):
  current_track = self.model.play_list[self.current_track_index]
  file_path, file_name = os.path.split(current_track)
  truncated_track_name = truncate_text(file_name, 40)
  self.canvas.itemconfig(self.track_name, text=truncated_track_name)

def display_track_duration(self):
  self.track_length = self.player.track_length
  minutes, seconds = get_time_in_minute_seconds(self.track_length)
  track_length_string = 'of {0:02d}:{1:02d}'.format(minutes, seconds)
  self.canvas.itemconfig(self.track_length_text, text=track_length_string)
```

These two methods simply find out the track name and track duration and update the related canvas text by using a call to `canvas.itemconfig`.

Just like we use `config` to change the value of widget-related options, the `Canvas` widget uses `itemconfig` to change the options for individual items within the canvas. The format for `itemconfig` is as follows:

```
canvas.itemconfig(itemid, **options).
```

Let's define two helper methods in a new file named `helpers.py` and import the methods in the view namespace. The two methods are `truncate_text` and `get_time_in_minutes_seconds`. The code for this can be found in the `5.06—helpers.py` file.

That takes care of one-time updates. Now, when you run `5.06—view.py` and play some audio file, the player should update the track name, and the total track duration in the top console, as shown in the following screenshot:

We will take care of periodic updates in the next iteration.

Managing continuous updates

Next, we will update the position of the seek bar knob and the elapsed play duration, as shown in the following screenshot:

This is nothing but a simple form of Tkinter-based animation.

The most common pattern of animating with Tkinter involves drawing a single frame and then calling the same method using the after method of Tkinter, as follows:

```
def animate(self):
  self.draw_frame()
  self.after(500, self.animate)
```

Take a note of the `self.after` method, which calls the `animate` method in a loop. Once called, this function will keep updating frames once every `500` milliseconds. You can also add some conditions to break out of the animation loop. This is generally how all animations are handled in Tkinter. We will use this technique over and over again in several upcoming examples.

Now that we know how to manage animations in Tkinter, let's use the pattern to define a method that takes care of these periodic updates.

Define a method named `manage_periodic_updates_during_play`, which calls itself every 1 second to update the timer and the seek bar, as follows (see code `5.07—view.py`):

```
def manage_periodic_updates_during_play(self):
  self.update_clock()
  self.update_seek_bar()
  self.root.after(1000, self.manage_periodic_updates_during_play)
```

Then, define two methods named `update_clock` and `update_seek_bar`, which update the sections highlighted in the preceding screenshot.

The `update_clock` method gets the elapsed duration in seconds from the `Player` class, converts it into minutes and seconds, and updates the canvas text using `canvas.itemconfig`, as follows (see code `5.07—view.py`):

```
def update_clock(self):
    self.elapsed_play_duration = self.player.elapsed_play_duration
    minutes, seconds = get_time_in_minute_seconds(self.elapsed_play_duration)
    current_time_string = '{0:02d}:{1:02d}'.format(minutes, seconds)
    self.canvas.itemconfig(self.clock, text=current_time_string)
```

You may recall that we had previously defined a `slide_to_position` method in the `Seekbar` class. The `update_seek_bar` method simply calculates the proportionate position of the seek bar and then calls the `slide_to_position` method to slide the knob of the seekbar, as follows (see code `5.07—view.py`):

```
def update_seek_bar(self):
    seek_bar_position = SEEKBAR_WIDTH *
    self.player.elapsed_play_duration /self.track_length
    self.seek_bar.slide_to_position(seek_bar_position)
```

Now, if you run `5.07-view.py`, add an audio file, and play it, the elapsed duration should be updated continuously in the top display. The seek bar should also move forward as the play progresses.

That's great, but there is still one small detail missing. We want that when a user clicks somewhere on the seek bar, the playing audio seeks the new position. The code for seeking a new position is simple (see code `5.07-view.py`):

```
def seek_new_position(self, event=None):
  time = self.player.track_length * event.x /SEEKBAR_WIDTH
  self.player.seek(time)
```

However, the preceding method needs to be called whenever the seek bar position is changed. Let's do this by adding a binding to the virtual event from within `5.07-view.py`, as follows:

```
self.root.bind("<<SeekbarPositionChanged>>", self.seek_new_position)
```

Now, when you run `5.07-view.py`, play an audio file and click on the seek bar; the audio should start playing from the new position.

This concludes the iteration. We will look at how to loop over tracks in the next iteration.

Looping over tracks

Let's add the feature that allows users to loop over tracks. We have already defined radio buttons to allow three choices, as shown in the following screenshot:

In essence, the player should provide a choice from the following three options:

- **No Loop**: Play a track and end there
- **Loop Current**: Play a single track repeatedly
- **Loop All**: Looping through the entire playlist, one after another

The decision to follow one of these three options needs to be taken immediately after a particular track ends playing. The best place to judge whether a track has come to its end is from within the periodic updates loop that we created earlier.

Therefore, modify the `manage_periodic_updates_during_play()` method to add the following two lines of highlighted code (see code `5.08`—`view.py`):

```
def manage_periodic_updates_during_play(self):
  self.update_clock()
  self.update_seek_bar()
  if not self.player.is_playing():
    if self.not_to_loop(): return
  self.root.after(1000, self.manage_periodic_updates_during_play)
```

This in effect means that the looping decision is checked only when the currently playing track ends. Then, define the `not_to_loop()` method, as follows (see code `5.09`—`view.py`):

```
def not_to_loop(self):
  selected_loop_choice = self.loop_value.get()
  if selected_loop_choice == 1: # no loop
    return True
  elif selected_loop_choice == 2: # loop current
    self.start_play()
    return False
  elif selected_loop_choice == 3: #loop all
    self.play_next_track()
  return True
```

The code first checks the value of the selected radio button and, based on the selected choice, makes the looping choice:

- If the selected loop value is 1 (No Loop), it does nothing and returns `True`, breaking out of the continuous update loop.
- If the selected loop value is 2 (loop over the current song), it again calls the `start_play` method and returns `False`. Thus, we do not break out of the update loop.
- If the loop value is 3 (Loop All), it calls the `play_next_track` method and returns `True`. Thus, we break out of the previous update loop.

The audio player can now loop over the playlist based on the looping preference set by the user.

Let's conclude this iteration by overriding the close button so that the audio player properly deletes the player object when the user decides to close the player while it is playing.

To override the destroy method, first add a protocol override command to the `View` __init__ method, as follows (see code 5.08—view.py):

```
self.root.protocol('WM_DELETE_WINDOW', self.close_player)
```

Finally, define the `close_player` method, as follows:

```
def close_player(self):
  self.player.stop()
  self.root.destroy()
```

This concludes the iteration. We coded the logic required to loop over tracks and then overrode the close button to ensure that a playing track is stopped before we exit the player.

Adding a tooltip

In this final iteration, we will add a tooltip named the **Balloon widget** to all the buttons in our player.

A tooltip is a small **popup** that shows up when you hover your mouse over the Bound widget (buttons, in our case). A typical tooltip for the application will look as follows:

Although core Tkinter has many useful widgets, it is far from complete. For us, the tooltip or Balloon widget is not provided as a core Tkinter widget. Therefore, we look for these widgets in what are called **Tkinter extensions**.

These extensions are nothing but a collection of extended Tkinter widgets, just like the custom seek bar that we created.

There are literally hundreds of Tkinter extensions. In fact, we just wrote our own Tkinter extension in this chapter.

However, the following are some of the popular Tkinter extensions:

- **Pmw**: (http://pmw.sourceforge.net)
- **Tix**: (http://wiki.Python.org/moin/Tix)

- **TkZinc**: (`http://wiki.Python.org/moin/TkZinc`)
- **Widget Construction Kit (WCK)**: (`http://effbot.org/zone/wck.htm`)

Pmw list of extensions

Talking about Pmw, here is a quick list of widget extensions and dialogs from the package.

Widgets

The following table shows a list of widget extensions:

ButtonBox	ComboBox	Counter	EntryField
Group	HistoryText	LabeledWidget	MainMenuBar
MenuBar	MessageBar	NoteBook	OptionMenu
PanedWidget	RadioSelect	ScrolledCanvas	ScrolledField
ScrolledFrame	ScrolledListBox	ScrolledText	TimeCounter

Dialogs

The following table shows a list of widget dialogs:

AboutDialog	ComboBoxDialog	CounterDialog	Dialog
MessageDialog	PromptDialog	SelectionDialog	TextDialog

Miscellaneous

The following is a list of miscellaneous widgets offered by Pmw:

- `Balloon`
- `Blt` (used for graph generation)
- The `Color Module` functions

Pmw offers a large list of extended widgets. For a demonstration of all these widgets, browse the Pmw package that you installed earlier and look for a directory named demo. Within demo, look for a file named All.py, which demonstrates all of these Pmw extensions with a sample working code.

Pmw provides the Balloon widget implementation, which will be used in the current example. Begin by importing Pmw into the namespace, as follows (see code 5.09—view.py):

```
import Pmw
```

Next, instantiate the Balloon widget within the create_gui method, as follows:

```
self.balloon = Pmw.Balloon(self.root)
```

Finally, bind the Balloon widget to each button widget in the audio player. We will not reproduce the code for each button. However, the format is as follows:

```
balloon.bind(name of widget, 'Description for the balloon')
```

Thus, the **Add File** button will have a balloon binding, as follows:

```
self.balloon.bind(add_file_button, 'Add New File')
```

Add similar code for each button in 5.09—view.py.

This completes the iteration. We added Balloon tooltips to the audio player's buttons using the Pmw Tkinter extension. Most importantly, we got to know about the Tkinter extensions and when to use them.

 When you need a widget implementation that is not available as a core widget, try looking for its implementations in Pmw or TIX. If you don't find one that suits your needs, search the internet for some other Tkinter extension. If you still don't find your desired implementation, it's time to build one.

This brings us to the end of this chapter. The audio player is ready!

Summary

Let's recap the things that we touched upon in this chapter.

In addition to reinforcing a lot of GUI programming techniques that we discussed in the previous chapters, you learned how to work with more widgets such as Listbox, ttk Scale, and Radiobutton. We looked deeper into the features of the Canvas widget.

Most importantly, we learned how to create our custom widgets, thereby extending Tkinter's core widgets. This is a really powerful technique that can be applied to build all sorts of features into programs.

We saw how to generate and handle virtual events.

We saw the most common technique for applying animation in Tkinter programs. This technique can also be used to build all sorts of interesting games.

Finally, we got to know about some common Tkinter extensions, such as Pmw, WCK, TIX, and so on.

Now, let's lose ourselves in some music!

QA section

Before you proceed to the next chapter, make sure you can answer these questions to your satisfaction:

- How can we create our own custom widgets in Tkinter?
- How do you create animations with Tkinter?
- What are virtual events? When and how do we use them?
- What are Tkinter extensions? What are the most popular ones?

Further reading

Look at the documentation for popular Tkinter extensions such as Pmw, Tix, WCK, and others. Take a note of the commonly available widgets in these extensions.

6
Paint Application

We used the Canvas widget to define a custom widget in Chapter 5, *Building an Audio Player*. The Canvas widget is truly one of Tkinter's highlights. It is an incredibly powerful and flexible widget. Let's, therefore, devote most of this chapter to looking at the Canvas widget in detail.

We will now develop a paint application. The application will let the user draw freehand lines, straight lines, circles, rectangles, arcs, and other polygons. It will also let the user define new complex shapes.

In addition to exploring the Canvas widget, we will also develop a tiny GUI framework on top of the Tkinter interface. As you will see, frameworks are a great way to maximize code reuse. This makes them a powerful tool for **Rapid Application Development (RAD)**.

Some of the key learning objectives for this chapter are as follows:

- Master the Canvas widget API
- Learn to build and use custom GUI frameworks for maximum code reuse and rapid application development
- Learn to use the colorchooser module of Tkinter
- Learn to use the ttk ComboBox widget
- Get to know available widget methods
- Reinforce things that we have learned in previous projects

Overview of the application

In its final form, our paint application would look as follows:

 There are no external library requirements for this chapter, so let's dive into the code.

Creating a tiny framework

So why do we need another framework on top of Tkinter? If we need to build just a single program, we need not build a framework. However, if we find ourselves writing the same boilerplate code over and over again, a framework is what we need. That is, a framework is a tool that lets us easily generate generic and often-used patterns with ease.

Consider, for example, menus used in programs. A menu is such a common element in most programs, yet we need to handcraft each menu item every time we sit down to write a program. What if we could further abstract to simplify menu generation?

This is where frameworks come in handy.

Say you have a program that has 10 different top-level menus. Say each of the top-level menus has five menu items. We will have to then write 50 lines of code simply to display these 50 menu items. You have to link each of them manually to other commands besides having to set tons of options for each of them.

If we keep doing this for all our widgets, our GUI programming becomes an exercise in typing. Every extra line of code that you write adds to the program complexity, making it more difficult for someone else to read, maintain, modify, and/or debug the code.

This is where using a custom framework comes to our aid. Let's develop a tiny framework that makes menu generation easy for us.

We create a file, `framework.py`, and create a new class, `Framework`, to the file. Every class that uses this framework must inherit from this class and should pass the root window as an argument to this class by calling the super method as follows:

```
super().__init__(root)
```

This will make all methods defined in the `Framework` class available to the inheriting class.

We will now define a method, `build_menu`, which takes a tuple in an expected format as input and automatically creates the menu for us. Let's define an arbitrary rule that each group of menu items must be represented by a single entry in a tuple.

Furthermore, we come up with a rule that each item in the tuple must be presented in the following format:

```
'Top Level Menu Name – Menu Item Name / Accelrator
/Commandcallback/Underlinenumber'
```

`MenuSeparator` is denoted by a string `'sep'`.

An alternative representation of menu definition could be specifying it as a tuple instead of a string definition, which is like asking the user to already split the definition rather than us having to extract the menu definition from a string.

For instance, passing this tuple as an argument to the build_menu method should generate three menus as shown in the following code:

```
menu_items = (
'File - &New/Ctrl+N/self.new_file, &Open/Ctrl+O/self.open_file',
'Edit - Undo/Ctrl+Z/self.undo',
'sep',
'Options/Ctrl+T/self.options',
'About - About//self.about'
)
```

Take a look at the following screenshot:

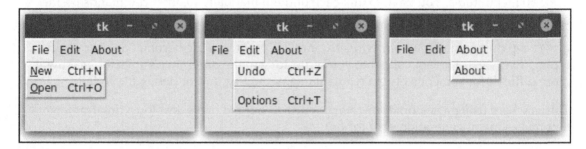

The first item of the string (before dash (–)) represents the top-level menu button. Each subsequent part of the string separated by a forward slash (/) represents one menu item, its accelerator key, and the attached command callback.
The position of the ampersand symbol (&) represents the position of the shortcut key to be underlined. If we encounter the string sep, we add a menu separator.

Now that we have defined the rules, the code for build_menu is as follows: (see the framework.py code):

```
def build_menu(self, menu_definition):
    menu_bar = tk.Menu(self.root)
    for definition in menu_definition:
        menu = tk.Menu(menu_bar, tearoff=0)
        top_level_menu, pull_down_menus = definition.split('-')
        menu_items = map(str.strip, pull_down_menus.split(','))
        for item in menu_items:
            self._add_menu_command(menu, item)
        menu_bar.add_cascade(label=top_level_menu, menu=menu)
```

```
    self.root.config(menu=menu_bar)

def _add_menu_command(self, menu, item):
  if item == 'sep':
    menu.add_separator()
  else:
    menu_label, accelrator_key, command_callback =item.split('/')
    try:
      underline = menu_label.index('&')
      menu_label = menu_label.replace('&', '', 1)
    except ValueError:
      underline = None
    menu.add_command(label=menu_label,underline=underline,
      accelerator=accelrator_key,
        command=eval(command_callback))
```

The description of the code is as follows:

- The method, build_menu, operates on a tuple by the name
  menu_definition, which must specify all desired menus and menu items in the
  exact format, as previously discussed.
- It iterates through each item in the tuple, splitting the item based on the dash (–)
  delimiter, building the top-menu button for each item left to the dash (–)
  delimiter.
- It then splits the second part of the string based on the comma (,) delimiter.
- It then iterates through this second part, creating menu items for each of the
  parts, adding the accelerator key, command callback, and underline key using
  another method, _add_menu_command.
- The _add_menu_command method iterates through the string and adds
  a separator if it finds the string sep. If not, it next searches for an ampersand (&)
  in the string. If it finds one, it calculates its index position and assigns it to the
  underline variable. It then replaces the ampersand value with an empty string,
  because we do not want to display the ampersand in our menu item.
- If an ampersand is not found in a string, the code assigns None to the underline
  variable.
- Finally, the code adds a command callback, accelerator key, and underline value
  to the menu item. Note that our framework adds only the accelerator key label. It
  is the developer's responsibility to bind events to the bound keys.

Our demonstration of making GUI frameworks ends here. We can now use this method to define literally hundreds of menus simply by adding one new line for each group of menus.

However, this is a rather rudimentary framework. The rules for defining items are completely arbitrary. The choice of delimiters means that we can no longer use the dash (–), slash (/), and ampersand (&) characters that we have used as delimiters in any menus that we define using this framework.

Our framework does not lay down rules for any other widgets. In fact, this definition is not even sufficient to generate other types of menu such as cascading menus, check button menus, or radio button menus. We will, however, not extend the framework further, as it is sufficient to have developed the concept behind framework design and usage and that is all we need to use in our paint application.

We have also included a small test in the `framework.py` file. If you execute the file as a standalone program, it should pop up a window and define some menus for testing.

 Fully-fledged frameworks use more **structured markup languages** to represent rules. **XML** is one of the most popular choices for writing GUI frameworks. You can find an example of a full-blown XML-based **Tkinter RAD (tkRAD)** framework here: `https://github.com/muxuezi/tkRAD`. A simple menu implementation using the preceding framework can be seen here: `https://github.com/muxuezi/tkRAD/blob/master/xml/rad_xml_menu.py`.

Using a framework for smaller programs may be overkill, but they are invaluable assets for large programs. Hopefully, you should now be able to appreciate the benefits of using frameworks for larger programs.

Now that we have the code for `build_menu`, we can extend it to add as many menu items as required without having to write repetitive and similar code for each of them.

This ends our first iteration. We will use this tiny framework to define the menu for our drawing program in the next step.

Setting up a broad GUI structure

Let's now set up the broad GUI elements of our program. We will create a `PaintApplication` class in `6.01.py`. Since we want to draw the menu using our framework, we import the framework into our file and inherit from the `Framework` class as follows:

```
import framework

class PaintApplication(framework.Framework):
    def __init__(self, root):
        super().__init__(root)
        self.create_gui()
```

The __init__ method calls another method, create_gui, which is responsible for creating the basic GUI structure for our program.

The create_gui method simply delegates the task to five separate methods, each being responsible for creating one section of the GUI as follows (see code 6.01.py):

```
def create_gui(self):
    self.create_menu()
    self.create_top_bar()
    self.create_tool_bar()
    self.create_drawing_canvas()
    self.bind_menu_accelrator_keys()
```

These five methods together build a structure as shown in the following screenshot (see code 6.01.py):

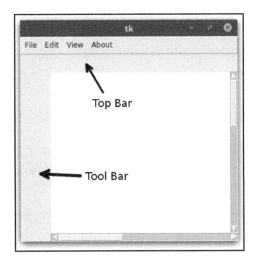

We have written similar code in all previous chapters, hence we will not reproduce the code for these five methods here. Note, however, a few things about the code in 6.01.py:

- Since we want to use the framework, we inherit from the Framework class and call its __init__ method using super()

- The `create_menu` method specifies the tuple for our menu definition and calls the `build_menu` method defined earlier in our framework

We define a lot of empty methods that will be implemented later. Each empty method is added as a command callback to individual menu items. The empty methods defined here are:

```
on_new_file_menu_clicked()
on_save_menu_clicked()
on_save_as_menu_clicked()
on_close_menu_clicked()
on_canvas_zoom_out_menu_clicked()
on_canvas_zoom_in_menu_clicked()
on_undo_menu_clicked()
on_about_menu_clicked()
```

This gives us a broad GUI structure for our program. Next, we will look at interacting with the drawing canvas.

Dealing with mouse events

When we draw in a paint program, we use a mouse as the primary input device.

There are primarily two kinds of mouse event that cause changes on the drawing canvas and are therefore of interest:

- Click and release
- Click, drag, and release

There is also a third event in which we have limited interest—the mouse movements with no buttons clicked. Our interest is limited there since an unclicked motion normally does not cause any changes on the canvas.

We ignore right-click and wheel-scroll as we will not be using them in our program.

In both the preceding cases, we need to know where the mouse was first clicked and where it was released. For click and release, this could be the same location. For click, drag, and release this will normally be different locations.

Accordingly, we define four attributes to keep track of the coordinates for these two locations (see code `6.02.py`):

```
start_x, start_y = 0, 0
end_x, end_y = 0, 0
```

Our immediate goal then is to bind our mouse events in such a way that any click or drag gives us the value of these four start and end coordinates.

The coordinates of the Canvas widget begin at the top-left corner ((0, 0) is the top-corner).

The Canvas widget uses two coordinate systems:

- The **window coordinate system**, which is always 0, 0 for the leftmost corner, no matter where you scroll down or up the canvas
- The **canvas coordinate system**, which specifies where the items are actually drawn on the canvas

We will mostly be interested in the canvas coordinate system, but mouse events emit data on the window coordinate system. To convert from the window coordinate system to the canvas coordinate system we can use the following methods:

```
canvas_x = canvas.canvasx(event.x)
canvas_y = canvas.canvasy(event.y)
```

Let's now modify our __init__ method to also call a method, `bind_mouse`. We define the `bind_mouse` method as follows (see code `6.02.py`):

```
def bind_mouse(self):
    self.canvas.bind("<Button-1>", self.on_mouse_button_pressed)
    self.canvas.bind( "<Button1-Motion>",
                      self.on_mouse_button_pressed_motion)
    self.canvas.bind( "<Button1-ButtonRelease>",
      self.on_mouse_button_released)
    self.canvas.bind("<Motion>", self.on_mouse_unpressed_motion)
```

We then define the first three methods that were bound just now. We ignore the unpressed motion for now by making an empty method. Remember that we are interested in getting the start and end coordinates, which are acquired as follows (see code `6.02.py`):

```
def on_mouse_button_pressed(self, event):
    self.start_x = self.end_x = self.canvas.canvasx(event.x)
    self.start_y = self.end_y = self.canvas.canvasy(event.y)
    print("start_x, start_y = ", self.start_x, self.start_y)
```

```
def on_mouse_button_pressed_motion(self, event):
    self.end_x = self.canvas.canvasx(event.x)
    self.end_y = self.canvas.canvasy(event.y)
def on_mouse_button_released(self, event):
    self.end_x = self.canvas.canvasx(event.x)
    self.end_y = self.canvas.canvasy(event.y)
    print("end_x, end_y = ", self.end_x, self.end_y)
```

We have temporarily added two `print` statements to show these four values on the console (see code `6.02.py`).

Now that we have the location of the start and end mouse events, we can act upon those events to do all kinds of activities on the canvas.

Adding toolbar buttons

Next, we need to add 16 buttons to the left toolbar. Furthermore, depending on which button is clicked, different options would show up in the top bar as shown here:

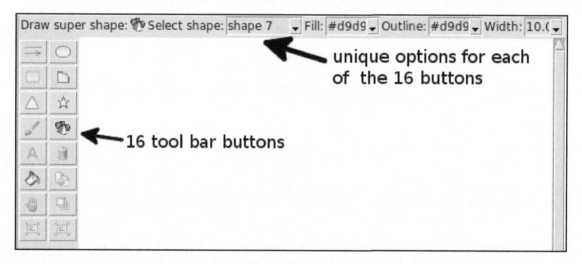

We do not want our code structure to be too bloated by conditional logic to switch among these 16 functions. Therefore, we will call these methods dynamically.

We first begin by defining a tuple of all 16 function names (see code `6.01.py`):

```
tool_bar_functions = (
  "draw_line", "draw_oval", "draw_rectangle", "draw_arc",
  "draw_triangle", "draw_star", "draw_irregular_line",
```

```
"draw_super_shape", "draw_text", "delete_item",
"fill_item", "duplicate_item", "move_to_top",
"drag_item", "enlarge_item_size", "reduce_item_size"
)
```

Doing so ensures that we do not have to call each method explicitly from our code. We can instead use the index of the tuple to retrieve the method name and call it dynamically using the following:

```
getattr(self, self.toolbar_functions[index])
```

This makes sense here because we would eventually add more features to our drawing program by simply extending the `toolbar_functions` tuple.

We further define an attribute, `selected_tool_bar_function`, which will keep track of which button was last clicked. We initialize it to the first button (`draw_line`) as follows:

```
selected_tool_bar_function = tool_bar_functions[0]
```

Next, we create a folder named `icons` and add icons for all these 16 toolbar buttons. The icons have been named the same as the corresponding function name.

Maintaining this consistency allows us to use the same tuple to loop over and build our toolbar buttons. This style of programming is what you could call programming using **conventions over configuration**.

We next create the method that makes the actual buttons (see code `6.03.py`):

```
def create_tool_bar_buttons(self):
    for index, name in enumerate(self.tool_bar_functions):
        icon = tk.PhotoImage(file='icons/' + name + '.gif')
        self.button = tk.Button(self.tool_bar, image=icon, command=lambda
                    index=index: self.on_tool_bar_button_clicked(index))
        self.button.grid(row=index // 2, column=1 + index % 2, sticky='nsew')
        self.button.image = icon
```

The preceding code creates all the buttons and adds command callbacks to the buttons as highlighted. We accordingly define the command callback as follows (see code `6.03.py`):

```
def on_tool_bar_button_clicked(self, button_index):
    self.selected_tool_bar_function = self.tool_bar_functions[button_index]
    self.remove_options_from_top_bar()
    self.display_options_in_the_top_bar()
```

The preceding method sets the value of `selected_tool_bar_function`. Next, it calls two methods that are defined as follows (see code 6.03.py):

```
def remove_options_from_top_bar(self):
    for child in self.top_bar.winfo_children():
        child.destroy()
```

We need to remove any existing options currently displaying in the top bar before we can display options for the newly selected button. The `winfo_children` method used just now returns a list of all widgets that are children of this widget.

Now that we have removed all items from the top bar, we define the selected tool icon on the top bar:

```
def display_options_in_the_top_bar(self):
    self.show_selected_tool_icon_in_top_bar(self.selected_tool_bar_function)
```

Currently, this method only calls one other method to display the selected tool icon in the top bar. We will, however, use this method as the central place for adding options to the top bar later in the chapter.

We do not discuss the `show_selected_tool_icon_in_top_bar` method here as it simply adds a label with an icon to the top bar (see code 6.03.py):

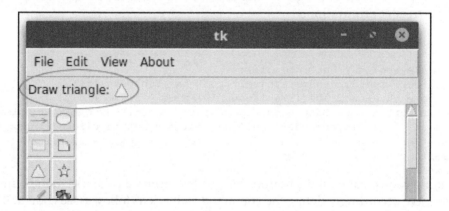

Now, if you go and run the code 6.03.py, it should display all 16 buttons in the left toolbar. Furthermore, clicking on any one of the buttons should display the selected button in the top bar, as shown in the preceding screenshot.

The `winfo_children()` method used earlier is an example of widget methods that are available to be called on all widgets. Several useful widget methods are defined in Tkinter.

In addition to the widget methods that are available on all widgets, some methods are only available on the top-level window. You can get a list of all such available methods and their descriptions by typing the following in your Python 3 console:

- `>>> import tkinter`
- `>>> help (tkinter.Misc)`
- `>>> help (tkinter.Wm)`

These are available online at `http://effbot.org/tkinterbook/widget. htm` and at `http://effbot.org/tkinterbook/wm.htm`.
You are encouraged to take a look at all these available methods.

Next, we will extend our program to actually draw items on the canvas.

Drawing items on the canvas

Objects added to the canvas are called **items**. New items are added to the canvas using different create methods such as `create_line`, `create_arc`, `create_oval`, `create_rectangle`, `create_polygon`, `create_text`, `create_bitmap`, and `create_image`.

Items added to the canvas are placed in a stack. New items are added on top of items already on the canvas. Every time you add an item using one of the various create methods, it returns a unique item handle or an item ID that is a unique integer. This item handle can be used to refer to and manipulate the added item.

In addition to an item handle, items can have the following item specifiers:

- `tags` are specifiers that we can add to one or more items
- ALL (or the string all) matches all items on the canvas
- CURRENT (or `current`) matches the item under the mouse pointer if any

We can use any of the preceding item specifiers for methods that act on canvas items.

To add a tag to an item, you specify the tag (which is a string) as its configurable option, either at the time of creating the object or later using the `itemconfig` method or the `addtag_withtag` method, as follows:

```
canvas.create_rectangle(10, 10, 50, 50, tags="foo")
canvas.itemconfig(item_specifier, tags="spam")
canvas.addtag_withtag("spam", "baz")
```

You can add multiple tags to an item at once by passing in the tags as a tuple of strings, as follows:

```
canvas.itemconfig(item_specifier, tags=("tag_A", "tag_B"))
```

To get all tags associated with an item handle, use `gettags` as follows:

```
canvas.gettags(item_handle)
```

This returns a tuple of all tags associated with that item handle.

To get the item handles for all items that have a given tag, use `find_withtag`:

```
canvas.find_withtag("spam")
```

This returns a tuple of item handles for all items with a tag of spam.

Given this information, let's code the functionality for the first six buttons, as shown in the following screenshot:

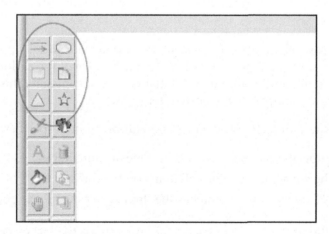

More specifically, we will code the functionality for the following function names that we have already defined earlier in the tuple `tool_bar_functions`: `"draw_line"`, `"draw_oval"`, `"draw_rectangle"`, `"draw_arc"`, and `"draw_triangle"`, `"draw_star"`

Here's the code for `draw_ line` (see code `6.04.py`):

```
def draw_line(self):
    self.current_item = self.canvas.create_line(self.start_x,
        self.start_y, self.end_x,
            self.end_y, fill=self.fill, width=self.width, arrow=self.arrow,
                dash=self.dash)
```

This uses the `create_line` method and draws a line from the start *x, y* coordinates to the end *x, y* coordinates. We have defined four new attributes for handling four different properties of the line:

- `fill`: Line color. Default is `black`, initialized as red in our program.

- `width`: Default is 1, initialized as 2 in our program.

- `arrow`: Default is `None`. The available choices are: `None`, `First`, `Last`, `Both`.

- `dash`: A `dash` pattern, which is a list of segment lengths. Only the odd segments are drawn.

We will later provide options for changing these four values from the top bar and hence these have been added as class attributes.

Also note that since `create_line` (and all create methods) return the item handle for the created item, we store it in an attribute named `current_item`. This gives us access to the last created item, which we will soon put to good use.

Next, here's the code for `draw_ oval` (see code `6.04.py`):

```
def draw_oval(self):
    self.current_item = self.canvas.create_oval(self.start_x,
        self.start_y, self.end_x,
            self.end_y, outline=self.outline, fill=self.fill,width=self.width)
```

This is identical to the code for `draw_line`, except that we added a new attribute named outline that takes care of the outline color.

We will not discuss the code for `create_rectangle` and `create_arc`, which are almost identical to the code of `draw_oval` discussed here (see code `6.04.py`).

Let's now discuss the `create_polygon` method. This method can be used to create all sorts of interesting shapes. Let's begin with the simple case of drawing an equilateral triangle (see code `6.04.py`):

```
def draw_triangle(self):
    dx = self.end_x - self.start_x
    dy = self.end_y - self.start_y
    z = complex(dx, dy)
    radius, angle0 = cmath.polar(z)
    edges = 3
    points = list()
    for edge in range(edges):
        angle = angle0 + edge * (2 * math.pi) / edges
        points.append(self.start_x + radius * math.cos(angle))
        points.append(self.start_y + radius * math.sin(angle))
    self.current_item = self.canvas.create_polygon(points,
        outline=self.outline,
            fill=self.fill, width=self.width)
```

The preceding code first converts the changes in the *x, y* coordinates from the Cartesian coordinate system to the polar coordinates represented by an angle and a radius. It then calculates the *x, y* coordinates for all three edges of the triangle using the following formula:

```
x = r*cosσ and y = r*sinσ
```

Once we have the x, y coordinates for all three vertices of the triangle, we call the `create_polygon` method to draw the triangle.

Let's now use the `create_polygon` method to make stars. A star (and many other polygons) can be thought of as a collection of points or spokes on two concentric circles, as shown in the following figure:

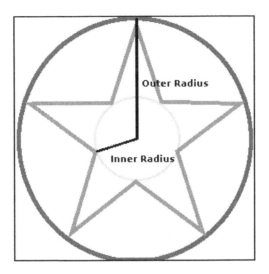

The star shown in the preceding figure has five spokes. We will later allow the user to change the number of spokes. Therefore, let's start by defining a class attribute as follows:

```
number_of_spokes = 5
```

The shape of the star is also determined by the ratio of the radius of the inner circle to the radius of the outer circle, as in the preceding figure. This is called the **spoke ratio**. This ratio is 2 for a standard star. Changing this ratio can also produce all sorts of interesting star shapes. However, we will keep it at 2 for our example. Given these rules, the code for draw_star is defined as follows (see code 6.04.py):

```python
def draw_star(self):
    dx = self.end_x - self.start_x
    dy = self.end_y - self.start_y
    z = complex(dx, dy)
    radius_out, angle0 = cmath.polar(z)
    radius_in = radius_out / 2 # this is the spoke ratio
    points = list()
    for edge in range(self.number_of_spokes):
        # outer circle angle
        angle = angle0 + edge * (2 * math.pi) / self.number_of_spokes
        # x coordinate (outer circle)
        points.append(self.start_x + radius_out * math.cos(angle))
        # y coordinate (outer circle)
        points.append(self.start_y + radius_out * math.sin(angle))
        # inner circle angle
        angle += math.pi / self.number_of_spokes
        # x coordinate (inner circle)
```

```
        points.append(self.start_x + radius_in * math.cos(angle))
        # y coordinate (inner circle)
        points.append(self.start_y + radius_in * math.sin(angle))
    self.current_item = self.canvas.create_polygon(points,
outline=self.outline, fill=self.fill, width=self.width)
```

The preceding code is heavily commented for you to understand. This is very similar to the code we used to draw triangles.

Now, instead of having points on one circle (as for triangles), we have points on two circles. We again use the same technique to first convert the *x, y* coordinates from mouse events to polar coordinates. Once we have the polar coordinates, it is easy to move the points in the circle.

We then move the points by a given angle and change back to Cartesian coordinates. We keep appending all the points to an empty list called **points**. Once we have all the points, the last line calls the `create_polygon` method of the canvas object to draw the star. Now we have all the methods to create these six shapes. But they need to be called from somewhere for the drawing to happen. And we have already decided that they would be called dynamically.

Accordingly, we define a method, `execute_selected_method`, which takes the string for the selected toolbar function, converts the string into a callable function, and executes it dynamically.

The code is as follows (see code `6.04.py`):

```
def execute_selected_method(self):
    self.current_item = None
    func = getattr(self, self.selected_tool_bar_function,
        self.function_not_defined)
    func()
```

This method, `getattr`, provides a reference to a method from the given string at runtime. A second argument provides a fallback mechanism whereby if the method object from the first argument is not found, a reference to the second method is provided.

This helps us gracefully handle situations where a dynamically created method does not exist. We simply define the fallback method as an empty method to handle those cases (see code `6.04.py`):

```
def function_not_defined(self):
    pass
```

So now we have a method to execute the selected method dynamically. Where do we plug in this method?

Since the drawing must begin when the mouse is clicked, we call the execute_selected_method method once from the on_mouse_button_pressed method.

The drawing must continue while the mouse is dragged in a clicked position. So we call this method again from the on_mouse_button_pressed_motion method.

However, although we want to keep the last drawn object during the mouse motion, we want to remove all other items except for the last drawn item. We therefore modify on_mouse_button_pressed_motion as follows (see code 6.04.py):

```
def on_mouse_button_pressed_motion(self, event):
    self.end_x = self.canvas.canvasx(event.x)
    self.end_y = self.canvas.canvasy(event.y)
    self.canvas.delete(self.current_item)
    self.execute_selected_method()
```

Now, if you run 6.04.py, the top six buttons on the toolbar should function as shown in the following screenshot:

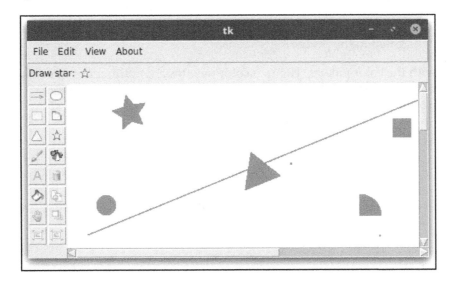

Adding a color palette

We can now draw basic shapes in our paint program. However, we still cannot change the colors of these shapes. Before we allow users to change colors, we must provide a way for them to select colors.

We will, therefore, provide a color chooser, letting the user select two different colors: the foreground color and the background color.

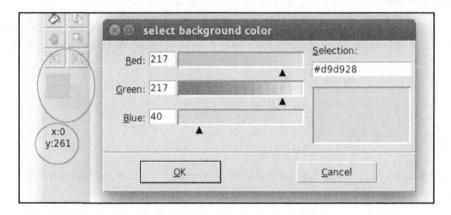

While we are at it, let's also add a label showing the *x*, *y* coordinate of the mouse over the canvas, as highlighted in the preceding screenshot.

Let's begin with the color palette. The two color palettes are nothing but two small rectangle items placed on a canvas. To show these two rectangles, we define a method, `create_color_palette` and call it from the existing `create_gui` method.

The code for `create_color_palette` is as follows (see code `6.05.py`):

```
def create_color_palette(self):
    self.color_palette = Canvas(self.tool_bar, height=55, width=55)
    self.color_palette.grid(row=10, column=1, columnspan=2, pady=5, padx=3)
    self.background_palette = self.color_palette.create_rectangle( 15,
        15, 48, 48,
        outline=self.background, fill=self.background)
    self.foreground_palette = self.color_palette.create_rectangle(
        1, 1, 33, 33, outline=self.foreground, fill=self.foreground)
    self.bind_color_palette()
```

The method ends by calling a method named `bind_color_palette`, which is defined as follows (see code `6.05.py`):

```
def bind_color_palette(self):
    self.color_palette.tag_bind(self.background_palette,
                        "<Button-1>", self.set_background_color)
    self.color_palette.tag_bind(self.foreground_palette,
                        "<Button-1>", self.set_foreground_color)
```

The preceding code simply binds the mouse click to two not yet defined methods, `set_background_color`, and `set_foreground_color`, using the `tag_bind` method of the Canvas widget.

Here's the signature of the `tag_bind` method:

```
tag_bind(item, event=None, callback, add=None)
```

The method adds an event binding to all matching items. Note that the bindings apply to the items, not the tag. For example, if you add the existing tag to new items after a call to `tag_bind`, the new items will not automatically bind to the event.

Next, let's define the method that actually opens a color picker and sets the foreground and background colors based on user-selected colors.

Tkinter comes with a built-in `colorchooser` module that we import into our namespace as follows (see code `6.06.py`):

```
from tkinter import colorchooser
```

To open a color chooser, we need to call its `askcolor` method, as shown here:

```
def get_color_from_chooser(self, initial_color, color_type="a"):
    color = colorchooser.askcolor(color=initial_color, title="select {}
                            color".format(color_type))[-1]
    if color:
        return color
    else:  # dialog has been cancelled
        return initial_color
```

Upon clicking **OK**, the color chooser returns a tuple of the form:

```
((217.84765625, 12.046875, 217.84765625), '#d90cd9')
```

Where the first item of the tuple is another tuple comprising the RGB values of the chosen color and the last item of the tuple represents the hexadecimal color code of the chosen color, if the **Cancel** button is clicked, it returns `None`.

We then use the preceding method to set the foreground and background colors as follows:

```
def set_foreground_color(self, event=None):
    self.foreground = self.get_color_from_chooser(self.foreground,
        "foreground")
    self.color_palette.itemconfig(self.foreground_palette, width=0,
        fill=self.foreground)

def set_background_color(self, event=None):
    self.background = self.get_color_from_chooser( self.background,
        "background")
    self.color_palette.itemconfig(self.background_palette, width=0,
        fill=self.background)
```

This concludes coding the color chooser for our paint program. However, note that the colors you choose will simply change the value of the foreground and background attributes. It will not change the color of items drawn on the canvas. We will do that in a separate iteration.

Finally, let's define the methods that show the current mouse position in a label.

We create two new methods (see code 6.05.py):

```
def create_current_coordinate_label(self):
    self.current_coordinate_label = Label(self.tool_bar, text='x:0\ny: 0 ')
    self.current_coordinate_label.grid( row=13, column=1, columnspan=2,
        pady=5, padx=1, sticky='w')

def show_current_coordinates(self, event=None):
    x_coordinate = event.x
    y_coordinate = event.y
    coordinate_string = "x:{0}\ny:{1}".format(x_coordinate, y_coordinate)
    self.current_coordinate_label.config(text=coordinate_string)
```

And we call the show_current_coordinates from our existing on_mouse_unpressed_motion method as follows (see code 6.05.py):

```
def on_mouse_unpressed_motion(self, event):
    self.show_current_coordinates(event)
```

Adding top bar options for draw methods

Each of the 16 toolbar buttons can have its own option. Just like we called the functions related to the toolbar buttons dynamically, we will again call methods to display options for the top bar dynamically.

So we decide that the method for handling the top bar options would be named by appending the string _options to the existing method.

Suppose we want to display the options for the draw_line method, it would be defined in the method called draw_line_options. Similarly, we have to define methods such as draw_arc_options, draw_star_options, and others.

We achieve this dynamic call in the display_options_in_the_top_bar method as follows (see code 6.06.py):

```
def display_options_in_the_top_bar(self):
    self.show_selected_tool_icon_in_top_bar(self.selected_tool_bar_function)
    options_function_name =
      "{}_options".format(self.selected_tool_bar_function)
    func = getattr(self, options_function_name, self.function_not_defined)
    func()
```

Now, with that code in place, every time a toolbar button is clicked the program will look for a method named by appending the _options string to the current method related to the button. If it finds one, it will be executed. If not found, the fallback function function_not_defined will be called, which is an empty method to silently ignore the absence of a method.

The Canvas widget lets you specify the fill color, outline color, and border width for most shapes as their configurable options.

In addition to these, the Canvas widget also has several other configurable options for many of these basic shapes. For instance, for a line, you can specify whether it will have an arrowhead shape at the end or it will be dashed.

We need to display the following top options for the first six buttons:

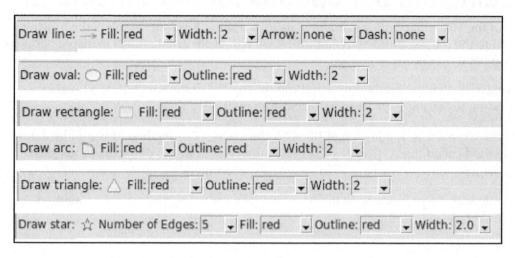

As can be seen, we need to create Combobox widgets for fill, outline, width, arrow, and dash. We first import the `ttk` module into our namespace and then create the Combobox widget as shown in the following code (see code 6.06.py):

```
def create_fill_options_combobox(self):
    Label(self.top_bar, text='Fill:').pack(side="left")
    self.fill_combobox = ttk.Combobox(self.top_bar, state='readonly',
        width=5)
    self.fill_combobox.pack(side="left")
    self.fill_combobox['values'] = ('none', 'fg', 'bg', 'black', 'white')
    self.fill_combobox.bind('<<ComboboxSelected>>', self.set_fill)
    self.fill_combobox.set(self.fill)
```

The ttk Combobox widget binds to another method called `set_fill`, which is defined as follows (6.06.py):

```
def set_fill(self, event=None):
    fill_color = self.fill_combobox.get()
    if fill_color == 'none':
        self.fill = '' # transparent
    elif fill_color == 'fg':
        self.fill = self.foreground
    elif fill_color == 'bg':
        self.fill = self.background
    else:
        self.fill = fill_color
```

We define a similar `combobox` for the `width`, `outline`, `arrow`, and `dash` properties. We also define a `combobox` to allow the user to change the number of spokes in the star.

Since the code for all these methods is pretty similar to the code we have just discussed, we do not explore it here (`6.06.py`).

Finally, we add the required comboboxes to each of the six options methods as follows:

```
def draw_line_options(self):
  self.create_fill_options_combobox()
  self.create_width_options_combobox()
  self.create_arrow_options_combobox()
  self.create_dash_options_combobox()
```

There's similar code for all the other five toolbar buttons (see code `6.06.py`).

Now, if you run code `6.06.py`, it should display options for the first six buttons.

When you change the options, the change is reflected in all subsequent drawings on the canvas.

However, there is a small bug in our code. What if someone has chosen the fill color as the foreground color? And then they change the foreground color from the color palette. Although this changes the value of the foreground attribute, it does not change the value of the fill attribute. Our program will keep using the old foreground value for fill.

In order to fix this bug, we modify the code for `set_background_color` and `set_foreground_color` to call two new methods:

```
def try_to_set_fill_after_palette_change(self):
  try:
    self.set_fill()
  except:
    pass

def try_to_set_outline_after_palette_change(self):
  try:
    self.set_outline()
  except:
    pass
```

The two methods are kept in a `try…except` block because not every toolbar button will have a fill and outline options `combobox`. Even if a toolbar button has the fill or outline `combobox`, it may not be selected to use the foreground or background color.

Lastly, since we want the `draw_line` options to populate the top bar immediately when the program starts, we add the following two lines to the `create_gui` method (see the `6.06.py` code):

```
self.show_selected_tool_icon_in_top_bar("draw_line")
self.draw_line_options()
```

This concludes this iteration. We will add functionality to a few other toolbar buttons in the next iteration.

Drawing irregular lines and super shapes

Let's now add the capability to draw irregular or continuous free-flowing lines. We will also add the ability to draw a variety of interesting shapes on the drawing canvas, as shown here:

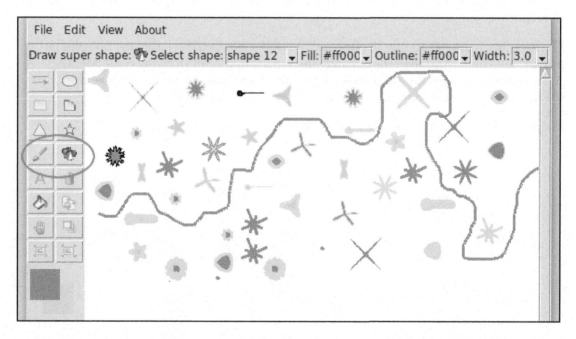

As a reminder, all our buttons are linked to dynamically call functions defined in our `tool_bar_functions` tuple. Furthermore, we can specify unique options for a given function by adding the `_options` string to the function name.

Drawing irregular lines

To add the capability to draw irregular lines, we just need to define the method named `draw_irregular_line`. To specify options that appear in the top bar, we need to define the method named `draw_irregular_line_options`.

We define the `draw_irregular_line` method as follows (see code `6.07.py`):

```
def draw_irregular_line(self):
  self.current_item = self.canvas.create_line(
    self.start_x, self.start_y, self.end_x, self.end_y, fill=self.fill,
      width=self.width)
  self.canvas.bind("<B1-Motion>", self.draw_irregular_line_update_x_y)

def draw_irregular_line_update_x_y(self, event=None):
  self.start_x, self.start_y = self.end_x, self.end_y
  self.end_x, self.end_y = event.x, event.y
  self.draw_irregular_line()
```

The preceding code is similar to the code for `draw_line`, except that it adds an extra line that binds mouse-clicked movements to a new method that replaces the start *x, y* coordinates with the end *x, y* coordinates and again calls back the `draw_irregular_line` method, thereby drawing in a continuous manner.

The options that show in the top bar are defined using the following method (see code `6.07.py`):

```
def draw_irregular_line_options(self):
  self.create_fill_options_combobox()
  self.create_width_options_combobox()
```

Now we can draw irregular lines on the canvas. However, since we have modified the mouse binding, all other methods will also start to draw in a continuous manner.

We, therefore, need to rebind the buttons back to their original bindings. We do that by modifying `on_tool_bar_button_clicked` to call `bind_mouse`, which then restores the mouse binding to its original behavior.

Adding an event binding to more than one method wipes away the previous binding, whereby the new binding replaces any existing binding. Alternatively, you can use `add="+"` as an additional argument to keep more than one binding to the same event, as follows:
```
mywidget.bind("<SomeEvent>", method1, add="+")
mywidget.bind("<SameEvent>", method2, add="+")
```

This will bind the same event to `method1` and `method2`.

Drawing super shapes

We call these shapes super shapes because we can build many interesting shapes using a single mathematical formula called **Super Formula**. See `https://en.wikipedia.org/wiki/Superformula` for more details on the formula.

The super formula takes six input arguments: a, b, m, n1, n2, and n3. Varying these five arguments produces varied shapes found in nature such as the shapes of shells, starfish, flowers, and more.

We do not get into why or how this formula works. All we do is write a method that, given these five arguments, returns the coordinates for unique shapes. We then pass these coordinates to our `create_polygon` method to create these shapes on the canvas. The method that returns these points is defined as follows (see code `6.07.py`):

```python
def get_super_shape_points(self, a, b, m, n1, n2, n3):
    # https://en.wikipedia.org/wiki/Superformula
    points = []
    for i in self.float_range(0, 2 * math.pi, 0.01):
     raux = (abs(1 / a * abs(math.cos(m * i / 4))) ** n2 + \
            abs(1 / b * abs(math.sin(m * i / 4))) ** n3)
     r = abs(raux) ** (-1 / n1)
     x = self.end_x + r * math.cos(i)
     y = self.end_y + r * math.sin(i)
     points.extend((x, y))
    return points
```

The method uses a custom-defined `float_range` method, since Python's built-in range method does not allow for float step sizes. The `float_range` generator method is defined as follows:

```python
def float_range(self, x, y, step):
    while x < y:
     yield x
     x += step
```

Next, we define the `draw_super_shape` method, which creates a polygon with the calculated points (see code `6.07.py`):

```python
def draw_super_shape(self):
    points = self.get_super_shape_points
        (*super_shapes[self.selected_super_shape])
```

```
self.current_item = self.canvas.create_polygon(points,
    outline=self.outline,
      fill=self.fill, width=self.width)
```

Now we want to provide a different set of five parameters to the super formula. We define a new file named `supershapes.py` with a dictionary named `super_shapes` *with* different shapes represented by a shape name and five parameters as follows:

```
super_shapes = {
 "shape A": (1.5, 1.5, 5, 2, 7, 7),
 "shape B": (1.5, 1.5, 3, 5, 18, 18),
 "shape C": (1.4, 1.4, 4, 2, 4, 13),
 "shape D": (1.6, 1.6, 7, 3, 4, 17),
 "shape E": (1.9, 1.9, 7, 3, 6, 6),
 "shape F": (4, 4, 19, 9, 14, 11),
 "shape G": (12, 12, 1, 15, 20, 3),
 "shape H": (1.5, 1.5, 8, 1, 1, 8),
 "shape I": (1.2, 1.2, 8, 1, 5, 8),
 "shape J": (8, 8, 3, 6, 6, 6),
 "shape K": (8, 8, 2, 1, 1, 1),
 "shape L": (1.1, 1.1, 16, 0.5, 0.5, 16)
 }
```

We also define an attribute (see code `6.07.py`):

```
selected_super_shape = "shape A"
```

Next, we define a `combobox` to let the user select from among the shapes defined previously (`6.07.py`):

```
def create_super_shapes_options_combobox(self):
  Label(self.top_bar, text='Select shape:').pack(side="left")
  self.super_shape_combobox = ttk.Combobox(self.top_bar,
    state='readonly', width=8)
  self.super_shape_combobox.pack(side="left")
  self.super_shape_combobox['values'] = sorted(tuple(shape for shape in
    super_shapes.keys()))
  self.super_shape_combobox.bind('<<ComboboxSelected>>',
    self.set_selected_super_shape)
  self.super_shape_combobox.set(self.selected_super_shape)
```

And we define a method that sets the selected shape for the value of `selected_super_shape` (see code `6.07.py`):

```
def set_selected_super_shape(self, event=None):
  self.selected_super_shape = self.super_shape_combobox.get()
```

Finally, we define the `draw_super_shapes_options` that shows all of the options we want to show in the top option bar (see code `6.07.py`):

```
def draw_super_shape_options(self):
    self.create_super_shapes_options_combobox()
    self.create_fill_options_combobox()
    self.create_outline_options_combobox()
    self.create_width_options_combobox()
```

This concludes the iteration. You can now run `6.07.py` and draw irregular lines as well as all of the super shapes that we have defined in the `supershapes.py` file. In fact, you can extend the `super_shapes` dictionary to add many more shapes simply by changing the values for the five parameters. You can look at `https://en.wikipedia.org/wiki/Superformula` for values of parameters that create interesting shapes.

Adding functionality to the remaining buttons

We will now code the features related to the remaining toolbar buttons:

Specifically, we will code the following functions: `draw_text`, `delete_item`, `fill_item`, `duplicate_item`, `move_to_top`, `drag_item`, `enlarge_item_size`, and `reduce_item_size`.

Let's start with the code for `draw_text`. When a user clicks on the `draw_text` button, we want to show the following options in the top bar:

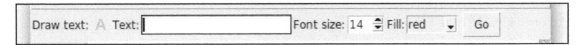

The user can enter text in the textbox and specify its font size and fill color. Once the user presses the **Go** button, the text appears on the center of the canvas.

Let us, therefore, define the `draw_text_options` method as follows (see code `6.08.py`):

```
def draw_text_options(self):
    Label(self.top_bar, text='Text:').pack(side="left")
    self.text_entry_widget = Entry(self.top_bar, width=20)
    self.text_entry_widget.pack(side="left")
    Label(self.top_bar, text='Font size:').pack(side="left")
    self.font_size_spinbox = Spinbox(self.top_bar, from_=14, to=100, width=3)
    self.font_size_spinbox.pack(side="left")
    self.create_fill_options_combobox()
    self.create_text_button = Button(self.top_bar,
        text="Go", command=self.on_create_text_button_clicked)
    self.create_text_button.pack(side="left", padx=5)
```

The preceding code is self-explanatory. The **Go** button is attached to a command callback named `on_create_text_button_clicked`, which is defined as follows (see code `6.08.py`):

```
def on_create_text_button_clicked(self):
    entered_text = self.text_entry_widget.get()
    center_x = self.canvas.winfo_width()/2
    center_y = self.canvas.winfo_height()/2
    font_size = self.font_size_spinbox.get()
    self.canvas.create_text(center_x, center_y, font=("", font_size),
        text=entered_text, fill=self.fill)
```

Our `draw_text` method is now functional. Next, let's code the `delete_item` method.

The operations that we want to do now are slightly different from their predecessors. Earlier, we were creating items on the canvas. Now we have to target items already present on the canvas.

The item that needs to be targeted is the one on which the user clicks with their mouse. Fortunately, getting the item handle for the item under the mouse is very easy using the current tag.

Accordingly, the code for delete_item is as follows (see code 6.08.py):

```
def delete_item(self):
    self.current_item = None
    self.canvas.delete("current")
```

Now, if you select the **Delete** button from the toolbar and click on any item on the canvas, that item is deleted.

Next, let's code the fill_item and fill_item_options methods (see code 6.08.py):

```
def fill_item(self):
    try:
        self.canvas.itemconfig("current", fill=self.fill, outline=self.outline)
    except TclError:
        self.canvas.itemconfig("current", fill=self.fill)
```

We had to use a try...except block because some canvas items such as lines and text do not have an outline option:

```
def fill_item_options(self):
    self.create_fill_options_combobox()
    self.create_outline_options_combobox()
```

Next, we code the duplicate_item method. In order to duplicate an item we need to know three things:

- Type of item—if the item is a line, oval, arc, rectangle, or polygon
- The coordinates for the item
- The configurations of the item

We can get the type of item as a string using the type method as follows:
canvas.type(item_specifier)

This returns a string such as line, oval, arc, rectangle, or polygon. In order to recreate an item of the same type, we need to append the string create_ to the returned type and call the method.

The coordinates of a given item can be obtained by calling the coordinates method as follows:

```
coordinates = canvas.coords("item_specifier")
```

The configurations for an item can be obtained as a dictionary using the following command:

```
canvas.itemconfig(item_specifier)
```

This returns all the configurations for an item, whether specified or not specified.

For example, here's a sample of a dictionary returned by calling the preceding method on a canvas item:

```
{'outline': ('outline', '', '', 'black', 'red'), 'outlinestipple':
 ('outlinestipple', '', '', '', ''), 'activestipple':
 ('activestipple', '', '', '', ''), 'state': ('state', '', '',
 '', ''), 'offset': ('offset', '', '', '0,0', '0,0'),
 'activefill': ('activefill', '', '', '', ''), 'disabledwidth':
 ('disabledwidth', '', '', '0.0', '0'), 'disabledoutlinestipple':
 ('disabledoutlinestipple', '', '', '', ''), 'outlineoffset':
 ('outlineoffset', '', '', '0,0', '0,0'), 'width': ('width', '',
 '', '1.0', '2.0'), 'disabledfill': ('disabledfill', '', '', '',
 ''), 'disabledoutline': ('disabledoutline', '', '', '', ''),
 'dash': ('dash', '', '', '', ''), 'disableddash':
 ('disableddash', '', '', '', ''), 'disabledstipple':
 ('disabledstipple', '', '', '', ''), 'tags': ('tags', '', '',
 '', 'current'), 'stipple': ('stipple', '', '', '', ''),
 'activewidth': ('activewidth', '', '', '0.0', '0.0'),
 'activedash': ('activedash', '', '', '', ''), 'dashoffset':
 ('dashoffset', '', '', '0', '0'), 'activeoutlinestipple':
 ('activeoutlinestipple', '', '', '', ''), 'activeoutline':
 ('activeoutline', '', '', '', ''), 'fill': ('fill', '', '', '',
 'red')}
```

Clearly, we do not require those configuration values that are empty or zero. We, therefore, write a method that filters out all unnecessary configurations:

```
def get_all_configurations_for_item(self):
    configuration_dict = {}
    for key, value in self.canvas.itemconfig("current").items():
        if value[-1] and value[-1] not in ["0", "0.0", "0,0", "current"]:
            configuration_dict[key] = value[-1]
    return configuration_dict
```

Now that we know how to fetch all required elements to duplicate a canvas item, here's the code for `duplicate_item` (see code `6.08.py`):

```
def duplicate_item(self):
  try:
     function_name = "create_" + self.canvas.type("current")
  except TypeError:
     return
  coordinates = tuple(map(lambda i: i+10, self.canvas.coords("current")))
  configurations = self.get_all_configurations_for_item()
   self.canvas_function_wrapper(function_name, coordinates, configurations)
```

Finally, the last line calls a `wrapper` function that actually runs the function that duplicates the canvas item (see code `6.08.py`):

```
def canvas_function_wrapper(self, function_name, *arg, **kwargs):
  func = getattr(self.canvas, function_name)
  func(*arg, **kwargs)
```

Now, if you create an item, select the **duplicate item** button, and click on the item, a duplicate item is created. However, since we do not want the duplicate item to be created exactly on top of the existing item, we offset its coordinates by 10 pixels from the coordinates of the item being duplicated. This offsetting is done in the line:

```
coordinates = tuple(map(lambda i: i+10, self.canvas.coords("current")))
```

Now, if you create an item on the canvas, select the **duplicate item** button, and click on the item, its duplicate is created at an offset of 10 pixels from the original item.

Next, we code the `move_to_top` method. We have already discussed that items added to the canvas are added on top of each other. What if we want to move an item previously added to the canvas? The following figure shows what it means to move an item on top of another:

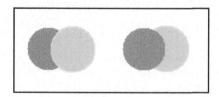

We use the `tag_raise` and `tag_lower` methods to move items higher and lower in the stack. We use `tag_raise` to define the `move_to_top` method as follows (see code `6.08.py`):

```
def move_to_top(self):
    self.current_item = None
    self.canvas.tag_raise("current")
```

The preceding code raises the clicked item highest up in the item's stack.

When you draw multiple items on the canvas, the items are placed in a stack. By default, new items get added on top of items previously drawn on the canvas. You can, however, change the stacking order using: `canvas.tag_raise(item)`.
If multiple items match, they are all moved, with their relative order preserved. However, this method will not change the stacking order for any new window item that you draw within the canvas.
Then there are the `find_above` and `find_below` methods that you can use to find items above or below an item in the canvas stacking order.

Next, we will define the `drag_item` method. This method uses the move method to change the coordinates of a given item (see code `6.08.py`):

```
def drag_item(self):
    self.canvas.move("current", self.end_x - self.start_x, self.end_y -
self.start_y)
    self.canvas.bind("<B1-Motion>", self.drag_item_update_x_y)

def drag_item_update_x_y(self, event):
    self.start_x, self.start_y = self.end_x, self.end_y
    self.end_x, self.end_y = event.x, event.y
    self.drag_item()
```

Since we want the drag to occur continuously and not as a jump from one place to another, we temporarily bind the mouse binding to update the start and end coordinates like we did when we defined the `draw_irregular_line` method.

Finally, we define two methods to enlarge and reduce item size. We will use the `canvas.scale` method to increase and reduce item size by 20%:

```
def enlarge_item_size(self):
    self.current_item = None
    if self.canvas.find_withtag("current"):
        self.canvas.scale("current", self.end_x, self.end_y, 1.2, 1.2)
        self.canvas.config(scrollregion=self.canvas.bbox(tk.ALL))
```

```
def reduce_item_size(self):
  self.current_item = None
  if self.canvas.find_withtag("current"):
    self.canvas.scale("current", self.end_x, self.end_y, .8, .8)
    self.canvas.config(scrollregion=self.canvas.bbox(tk.ALL))
```

Note that, immediately upon item resize, we reconfigure the scroll region option to update the scroll bar.

 The bbox method returns the bounding box for an item. The syntax is: .canvas.bbox(item_specifier). This returns the bounding box as a tuple of length 4. If the item-specifier is omitted, the bounding box for all items is returned.

Note that bounding box values are approximate and may differ from the real value by a few pixels.

This concludes the iteration. All the buttons in the left toolbar are now functional (see code 6.08.py).

Adding functionality to menu items

Recall that, at the time of creating our menu using the Framework class, we created empty methods that were linked to our menu items. We will now modify those empty methods to make them functional (see code 6.09.py)

File | New Menu:

The canvas delete method can be used to delete an item, given an item-specifier. Here we use ALL to delete all items from the canvas:

```
def on_new_file_menu_clicked(self, event=None):
  self.start_new_project()

def start_new_project(self):
  self.canvas.delete(ALL)
  self.canvas.config(bg="#ffffff")
  self.root.title('untitled')
```

File | Save, File | Save As:

Tkinter lets you save canvas objects as a postscript file using the command `postscript()`. Note, however, that the resulting postscript file cannot save images or any widgets embedded on the canvas. Furthermore, note that the pickling of Tkinter widgets or saving to `.jpg` or `.png` formats is not possible. This is one of the major limitations of Tkinter.

Here's the code for the save and save as features (see code `6.09.py`):

```
def actual_save(self):
    self.canvas.postscript(file=self.file_name, colormode='color')
    self.root.title(self.file_name)
```

We do not discuss the **Close** and **About** menu as we have coded similar menus in all our previous projects (see code `6.09.py`).

Edit | Undo:

Recall that all items added to the canvas are stored in a stack. We can access the stack using the canvas command:

```
canvas.find("all")
```

Using this, we implement a very basic undo operation, which lets us delete the last drawn item on the canvas.

Accordingly, the code for adding the undo feature is as follows (see code `6.09.py`):

```
def on_undo_menu_clicked(self, event=None):
    self.undo()

def undo(self):
    items_stack = list(self.canvas.find("all"))
    try:
        last_item_id = items_stack.pop()
    except IndexError:
        return
    self.canvas.delete(last_item_id)
```

Note that this will not undo any styling changes such as changes in color, width, outline, and so on. In fact, it will only be able to delete the last item from the stack.

We can implement a fully-fledged undo stack by saving all actions in a suitable data structure, but that would be an exercise worth its own chapter.

In addition to the find method we used here, the Canvas widget has a method named:

```
find_closest(x, y, halo=None, start=None)
```

It returns the item handle for the item closest to the given position on the canvas. This means that if there is only one item on the canvas, it will be selected regardless of how near or how far you click from it.

If, on the other hand, you want objects only within a certain area, you can use:

```
find_overlapping(x1, y1, x2, y2)
```

This returns all items that overlap the given rectangle, or that are completely enclosed by it.

Now that we have a hold on the item to be manipulated, we can proceed to do whatever we want with the item.

For a complete list of canvas methods, please see http://infohost.nmt.edu/tcc/help/ pubs/tkinter/web/canvas-methods.html.

View | Zoom in, View | Zoom out:

Finally, we define these two methods using the canvas.scale method. We have already used the scale methods earlier to enlarge and reduce individual items. Here, we simply use the method on the ALL item-specifier, as in the following code (see code 6.09.py):

```
def canvas_zoom_in(self):
    self.canvas.scale("all", 0, 0, 1.2, 1.2)
    self.canvas.config(scrollregion=self.canvas.bbox(ALL))
```

That concludes the iteration and the chapter.

Summary

To summarize, in this chapter, we began by creating a custom GUI framework on top of Tkinter.

We saw how GUI frameworks can be used to generate boilerplate code for our programs, thereby ensuring maximum code reuse and rapid application development.

Next, we explored the Canvas widget in detail. We saw how to create various canvas items. Then, we saw how we could manipulate the attributes of these canvas items using tag or ID.

We saw the `colorchooser` module of Tkinter in action. We worked with the ttk Combobox widget. We also looked at common methods that are available on all Tkinter widgets.

We also saw the benefits of writing programs that use convention over configuration to ease the logical flow of the program.

QA section

Before you proceed to the next chapter, make sure you can answer these questions to your satisfaction:

- What are software frameworks? Why are they used?
- When is it beneficial to use software frameworks instead of writing code from scratch?
- What is a structured markup language? Can you a list a few of them?
- What is the convention over configuration software design paradigm?
- What are tags used for in the context of Tkinter's Canvas widget?

Further reading

Read the complete documentation for the Tkinter Canvas widget. You can find the documentation by typing the following command in a Python command shell:

```
>>> import tkinter
>>>  help(tkinter.Canvas)
```

7
Piano Tutor

In the last chapter, we explored most of the common options available for the Canvas widget. Let's now see the PhotoImage widget in action.

Let's build a program called *Piano Tutor*. This program will help new piano players identify musical scales, chords, and chord progressions. It will also help piano learners learn and identify music written on music sheets. People with some musical knowledge will feel right at home, but do not worry if you know nothing about piano or musical terms such as scales, chords, and chord progressions. We will cover the bare minimum of musical know-how as we progress.

In its final form, the program looks as follows:

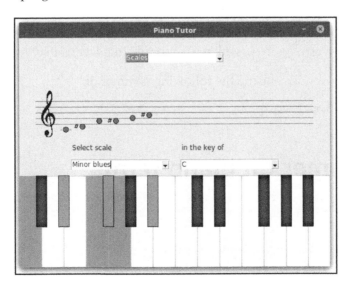

The **Piano Tutor** will have *three broad sections* that can be selected from the topmost drop-down menu. They are as follows:

- Scale Finder
- Chord Finder
- Chord Progression Builder

Some of the key objectives of this chapter are:

- Getting to understand some important methods defined on the root window
- Using the PhotoImage widget class
- Practical applications of the Place geometry manager
- Understanding grid weights
- Learning how to work with seemingly complex ideas such as representing musical knowledge in a fashion that computers can understand
- Using JSON to store data

Technical requirements

Besides Tkinter, we will use a few standard Python libraries. The next import should execute without any error as they are built-in in most Python distributions:

```
import json, collections, functools, math
```

In addition, we use `simpleaudio`, which is a module that lets us play notes on the piano.

You can install `simpleaudio` using the following command:

```
pip3 install simpleaudio
```

A brief primer on piano terms

Since this is a piano-related program, a brief understanding of some of the common terms used in this context is required.

In this section, we will use this figure as a reference:

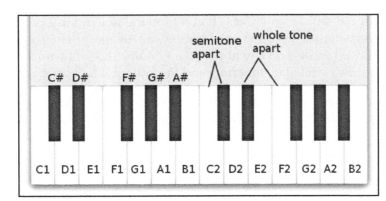

The keyboard of a piano comprises a set of 12 keys (seven white and five black keys), which forms what is called a **chromatic scale**. This pattern of 12 keys repeats over and over again totaling up to 88 keys on a standard piano. The pattern repeats twice in the preceding image (*C1* to *B1* and then *C2* to *B2*).

The distance between any two adjacent keys is called a **semitone**. Please take note of this term as we will define all piano-related rules using semitones—a measure of distance between keys. An interval of two semitones is called a **whole tone**. We will not bother with whole tones as far as our program is concerned.

The white keys of the piano are labeled by note names *A* to *G*. However, as per convention the counting of notes begins at *C*. *C* is the first white key just before the set of two black keys. The names of white keys are marked on the keys and the names of black keys are marked above them.

Since there are multiple sets of 12 keys they are differentiated among themselves by appending a number after them. For example, *C1* is the first white key, while *C2* is the key at the same position, but an octave higher. The black key just next to *C* is called **C sharp** (**C#**). Since it is also just before the key **D** it has another name—*D* flat (D♭). We will, however, stick with calling all black keys by using the sharp symbol (#). Since the notes *E* and *B* do not have any sharp keys they are not immediately followed by any black key.

Learning about scales

A **scale** is an organized sequence of notes chosen from the 12 notes in a particular pattern, which gives it a characteristic feel, perhaps a happy, sad, exotic, oriental, enigmatic, or rebellious feel. A scale can start on any note of the 12 notes and follows a definite pattern. The first note of a scale is called its **root note** and the pattern it follows gives it a scale type.

One particular scale of relevance to us is called the **Major scale**. Starting at any key, the Major scale follows the following pattern:

W W S W W W S

where *W* stands for whole tone (jump of two keys) and *S* stands for semitones (jump of one key).

For example, if you play the notes *C1, D1, E1, F1, G1, A1, B1, C2*, and back, one-by-one, you have played a *C* Major scale. A Major scale sounds uplifting while another scale named minor can sound a bit sad. Don't worry about names—there are hundreds of scales and we just need to know that scales are a *sequence* of notes played together following a certain set of rules.

Learning about chords

In contrast, a **chord** is when you play two or more notes simultaneously. For example, if I play three notes C, F, and G altogether; it's a chord. Chords generally provide the bass section to a music.

If you keep playing the same chord over and over again it will sound monotonous—so you jump from one chord—again following a rule. This is called **chord progression**. More simply, an ordered series of chords is called a chord progression.

The musical notes can be written on a music sheet or **score sheet** that comprises of five lines. The notes are represented by black dots, which can lie on the line or in spaces between them. The names of notes for two octaves are shown on the following score sheet. The icon marked as **treble clef** means that these notes are to be played with the right hand:

Do not worry, we are not required to memorize the music notation for completing our program. We will, however, use it as a reference when drawing the score sheet.

We are now equipped with all the musical knowledge required to write this program. Let's start coding.

Building the broad GUI structure

We start as usual by building the root window (7.01/view.py):

```
root = Tk()
SCREEN_WIDTH = root.winfo_screenwidth()
SCREEN_HEIGHT = root.winfo_screenheight()
SCREEN_X_CENTER = (SCREEN_WIDTH - WINDOW_WIDTH) / 2
SCREEN_Y_CENTER = (SCREEN_HEIGHT - WINDOW_HEIGHT) / 2
root.geometry('%dx%d+%d+%d' % (WINDOW_WIDTH, WINDOW_HEIGHT,
SCREEN_X_CENTER,  SCREEN_Y_CENTER))
root.resizable(False, False)
PianoTutor(root)
root.mainloop()
```

We also create a new file named constants.py(7.01), which currently holds the height parameters for the window.

We use two root window methods, root.winfo_screenwidth() and root_winfo_screenheight(), to obtain the screen width and height, respectively. We define two constants, WINDOW_WIDTH and WINDOW_HEIGHT, and then place the window on the *x*, *y* center of the computer screen.

Notice the line root.resizable(False, False). This root window method takes two Boolean arguments to decide if the window is resizable in the *x* and *y* directions. Setting both arguments to False makes our window fixed in size.

The root window is then passed as an argument to a new class, PianoTutor, which takes care of building the internals of the program. This class is defined next.

The GUI for this program is divided into four broad rows:

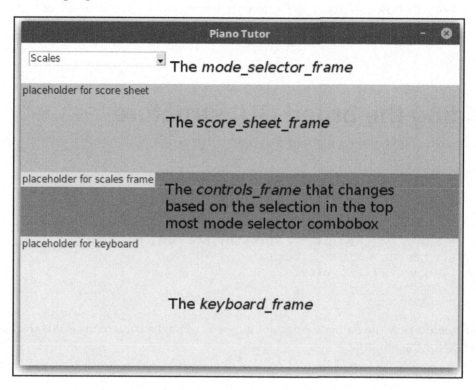

The topmost row is built in a `Frame` named `mode_selector_frame` and has a `combobox` that lets the user select from one of three options—scales, chords, and chord progressions.

The second row is a placeholder for placing the music score sheet and is accordingly called the `score_sheet_frame`.

The third row requires a bit of attention. Depending on what is selected in the topmost `combobox`, the contents of this row change. In our code so far, (`7.01/view.py`), it displays three different colored frames for the three different choices one can make using the topmost `combobox`. Since we will place controls on this frame, we decided to call it a `controls_frame` for want of a better name.

The fourth row shows the piano keyboard and the frame is named `keyboard_frame`, the implementation of which will be discussed in the section entitled *Making the Piano Keyboard*.

Putting up the skeleton structure

To start, we build a class `PianoTutor` (`7.01/view.py`), the `__init__` method of which is defined as follows:

```
class PianoTutor:
  def __init__(self, root):
    self.root = root
    self.root.title('Piano Tutor')
    self.build_mode_selector_frame()
    self.build_score_sheet_frame()
    self.build_controls_frame()
    self.build_keyboard_frame()
    self.build_chords_frame()
    self.build_progressions_frame()
    self.build_scales_frame()
```

In the preceding code, we are simply defining method calls to build multiple Frame widgets of predefined heights. We won't elaborate much upon the preceding code as we wrote similar code in all of the previous chapters.

Let's look at one example of frame creation. All other frames follow a similar pattern (`7.01 /view.py`) and will not be discussed here:

```
def build_score_sheet_frame(self):
  self.score_sheet_frame = Frame(self.root, width=WINDOW_WIDTH, height=
                  SCORE_DISPLAY_HEIGHT, background='SteelBlue1')
  self.score_sheet_frame.grid_propagate(False)
  Label(self.score_sheet_frame, text='placeholder for score sheet',
              background='SteelBlue1').grid(row=1, column=1)
  self.score_sheet_frame.grid(row=1, column=0)
```

This is simple `Frame` creation using the `grid` geometry manager. However, take a note of the line `self.score_sheet_frame.grid_propagate(False)`.

In Tkinter, the container window (Frame in the previous example) is designed to *shrink to fit* around its contents.

Even though we have explicitly added a width or height to the frame, if we comment the `grid_propagate(false)` line, you will notice that the width and height parameters given by us are simply ignored and the frame will shrink to exactly fit its children—the Label widgets height in our case. We do not want to allow this shrinking of Frames and `grid_propagate(False)` lets us achieve that.

If we were using pack manager, we would have used `frame.pack_propagate(False)` instead to achieve the same result.

Next, our topmost mode selector `combobox` is bound to the following callback (`7.01/view.py`):

```
self.mode_selector.bind("<<ComboboxSelected>>", self.on_mode_changed)
```

Here's how we define the `on_mode_changed` method (`7.01/view.py`):

```
def on_mode_changed(self, event):
    selected_mode = self.mode_selector.get()
    if selected_mode == 'Scales':
        self.show_scales_frame()
    elif selected_mode == 'Chords':
        self.show_chords_frame()
    elif selected_mode == 'Chord Progressions':
        self.show_progressions_frame()

def show_scales_frame(self):
    self.chords_frame.grid_remove()
    self.progressions_frame.grid_remove()
    self.scales_frame.grid()

def show_chords_frame(self):
    self.chords_frame.grid()
    self.progressions_frame.grid_remove()
    self.scales_frame.grid_remove()

def show_progressions_frame(self):
    self.chords_frame.grid_remove()
    self.progressions_frame.grid()
    self.scales_frame.grid_remove()
```

Take a note of the `grid_remove()` method mentioned previously. This method removes the widget from the grid manager, thereby making it invisible. You can make it visible again by using `grid()` on it. So effectively, whenever a user selects one of the three options (`Scales`, `Chords`, and `Chord Progression`) from the topmost `combobox`, the other two frames are hidden using `grid_remove` and the frame for the selected option is made visible using `grid`.

This completes the first iteration where we defined the broad GUI structure with the capability to switch between scales, chords, and chord progression frames based on choices made in the topmost combobox.

Making the piano keyboard

Let's now build the piano keyboard. All keys on the keyboard will be made using the Label widget. We will superimpose the label widget with an image of black and white keys using Tkinter's `PhotoImage` class.

The `PhotoImage` class is used to display images in label, text, button, and canvas widgets. We used it in Chapter 2, *Making a Text Editor* to add icons to buttons. Since this class can only handle `.gif` or `.bpm` format images, we add four `.gif` images to a folder named `pictures`. These four images are `black_key.gif`, `white_key.gif`, `black_key_pressed.gif`, and `white_key_pressed.gif`.

Since we will refer to these images over and over again, we add their reference to 7.02 `constants.py`:

```
WHITE_KEY_IMAGE = '../pictures/white_key.gif'
WHITE_KEY_PRESSED_IMAGE = '../pictures/white_key_pressed.gif'
BLACK_KEY_IMAGE = '../pictures/black_key.gif'
BLACK_KEY_PRESSED_IMAGE = '../pictures/black_key_pressed.gif'
```

The symbol `../` used previously is a way to specify a file path relative to the current working directory. A single `../` means—go back one directory, a set of two `../../` means go back two directories, and so on. This system is generally honored by most modern operating systems. However, some very old operating systems might not support it. So a better but a more verbose way is to use the `os` module of Python to traverse directories.

Next, we will define a method named `create_key` that creates a piano key for us at a given `x` location:

```
def create_key(self, img, key_name, x_coordinate):
    key_image = PhotoImage(file=img)
    label = Label(self.keyboard_frame, image=key_image, border=0)
    label.image = key_image
    label.place(x=x_coordinate, y=0)
    label.name = key_name
    label.bind('<Button-1>', self.on_key_pressed)
```

```
label.bind('<ButtonRelease-1>', self.on_key_released)
self.keys.append(label)
return label
```

Here's a brief code description:

- Note that since we want to place keys at a specific x coordinate we use the `place` geometry manager. We briefly touched upon the place geometry manager in `Chapter 1`, *Meet Tkinter*. Now is a good place to see this rarely used geometry in action.
- This method also takes an image location as its input and creates a `PhotoImage` class, which is then attached to the label widget using the `image=key_image` option in the previous example.
- A third parameter, `key_name`, is attached to the created label widget by using the command `widget.name = key_name`. This is needed to later identify which particular key was pressed. For example, to create the first key *C1*, we attach the name *C1* to the label widget and then later this string value can be accessed by calling `widget.name`
- We bind the label to two events, `'<Button-1>'` and `'<ButtonRelease-1>'`, to handle mouse press events.
- Finally, we add a reference to the newly created widget into an attribute newly defined here as `self.keys`. We keep this reference as we will need to change the image of these widgets to highlight the keys.

Now that we have attached events to two callbacks, let's define them next:

```
def on_key_pressed(self, event):
  print(event.widget.name + ' pressed')
  self.change_image_to_pressed(event)

def on_key_released(self, event):
  print(event.widget.name + ' released' )
  self.change_image_to_unpressed(event)
```

For now, the previous methods print the name of the key pressed and then call another two methods that change the image of the pressed label to a different colored image on button press and release:

```
def change_image_to_pressed(self, event):
  if len(event.widget.name) == 2:
    img = WHITE_KEY_PRESSED_IMAGE
  elif len(event.widget.name) == 3:
    img = BLACK_KEY_PRESSED_IMAGE
```

```
key_img = PhotoImage(file=img)
event.widget.configure(image=key_img)
event.widget.image = key_img

def change_image_to_unpressed(self, event):
    if len(event.widget.name) == 2:
        img = WHITE_KEY_IMAGE
    elif len(event.widget.name) == 3:
        img = BLACK_KEY_IMAGE
    key_img = PhotoImage(file=img)
    event.widget.configure(image=key_img)
    event.widget.image = key_img
```

The white key widget will have a name of length 2 (for example, C1, D2, G1), while a black key will have an image length of 3 (for example, C#1, D#1). We utilize this fact to decide if to use a black key image or a white key image. The rest of the preceding code should be self-explanatory.

Putting the keyboard together

Now it's finally time to combine all the preceding methods to build our complete keyboard of two octaves.

We begin by defining the exact x_coordinates for all the keys from *C1* to *B2* in the file constants.py as follows:

```
WHITE_KEY_X_COORDINATES = [0,40, 80,120, 160, 200, 240,280, 320, 360, 400,
440, 480,520]
BLACK_KEY_X_COORDINATES = [30,70,150,190, 230, 310, 350, 430,470, 510]
```

The preceding *x* coordinate numbers have been obtained simply by trial and error as to emulate their location on a keyboard.

Then we modify the previously defined build_keyboard_frame method as follows:

```
def build_keyboard_frame(self):
    self.keyboard_frame = Frame(self.root, width=WINDOW_WIDTH,
                height=KEYBOARD_HEIGHT,   background='LavenderBlush2')
    self.keyboard_frame.grid_propagate(False)
    self.keyboard_frame.grid(row=4, column=0, sticky="nsew")
    for index, key in enumerate(WHITE_KEY_NAMES):
        x = WHITE_KEY_X_COORDINATES[index]
        self.create_key(WHITE_KEY_IMAGE, key, x )
    for index, key in enumerate(BLACK_KEY_NAMES):
        x = BLACK_KEY_X_COORDINATES[index]
```

```
self.create_key(BLACK_KEY_IMAGE, key, x)
```

The first three lines of the previous method remain as defined in the previous iteration. We then go through all white and black keys creating labels for them at given *x* coordinates.

That concludes the iteration. If you now run `7.02 view.py`, you should see a two-octave keyboard. When you press any key, the key's image should change to blue and it should print the name of the key pressed or released in the Terminal:

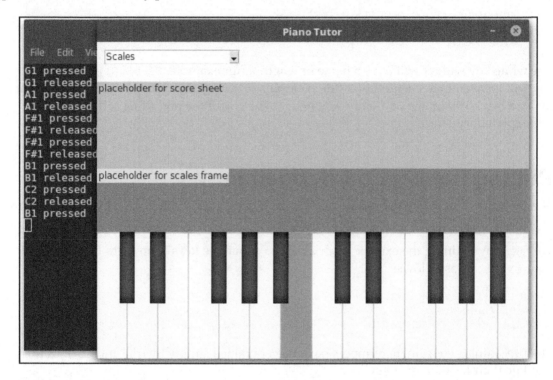

Playing audio

To begin with, we have added 24 sound samples in `.wav` format in a folder named `sounds` in this chapter's code folder. These audio files correspond to the 24 notes on our keyboard. The audio files are named according to the note name it represents.

In order to keep the audio processing separate from the GUI code, we create a new file called audio.py (7.03). The code is defined as follows:

```
import simpleaudio as sa
from _thread import start_new_thread
import time

def play_note(note_name):
  wave_obj = sa.WaveObject.from_wave_file('sounds/' + note_name + '.wav')
  wave_obj.play()

def play_scale(scale):
  for note in scale:
    play_note(note)
    time.sleep(0.5)

def play_scale_in_new_thread(scale):
    start_new_thread(play_scale, (scale,))

def play_chord(scale):
    for note in scale:
        play_note(note)

def play_chord_in_new_thread(chord):
    start_new_thread(play_chord, (chord,))
```

The code description is as follows:

- The play_note method follows the API provided by simpleaudio to play an audio file
- The play_scale method takes in a list of notes and plays them sequentially, giving a time gap between each played note
- The play_chord method takes a list of notes and plays them all together
- The last two methods call these methods in new threads as we don't want to block the main GUI thread when playing these notes

Next, let's import this file (7.03 view.py):

```
from audio import play_note
```

Next, modify the on_key_pressed method to play the given note:

```
def on_key_pressed(self, event):
  play_note(event.widget.name)
  self.change_image_to_pressed(event)
```

This concludes the iteration. If you now run the code and press any key on the keyboard, it should play the note for that key.

Next, we start with building the actual tutor. The next three sections will develop the scales, chords, and chord progression sections. We will start by building the scales tutor.

Building the scales tutor

All the rules for defining which notes to play for a given scale are added in a JSON file named `scales.json` within a folder named `json`. Let's take a look at the first few lines in the `scales.json` file:

```
{
  "Major": [ 0, 2, 4, 5, 7, 9, 11 ],
  "Minor": [ 0, 2, 3, 5, 7, 8, 10 ],
  "Harmonic minor": [ 0, 2, 3, 5, 7, 8, 11 ],
  "Melodic minor": [ 0, 2, 3, 5, 7, 9, 11 ],
  "Major blues": [ 0, 2, 3, 4, 7, 9 ],
  "Minor blues": [ 0, 3, 5, 6, 7, 10 ],
  ...
}
```

Recall that a scale is a set of notes played sequentially. The first note of the scale is called its **root** or **key**. So if you play a scale starting at say the note *B*, you are playing the scale in the key of *B*.

Let's take the fourth item in the key-value pairs. The key is named `"Melodic minor"` and its associated value is `[ 0, 2, 3, 5, 7, 9, 11 ]`. This means that, to play a melodic minor scale in the key of *B*, you will take *B* as the first item—that is represented by 0 in the values list. The next key is two semitones above *B*, the third key is three semitones above *B*, and the next is 5, followed by 7, 9, and 11 semitones above *B*.

So to summarize—in order to play Melodic minor in the key of *B* you will play the following keys:

```
B, B+2, B+3, B+5, B+7, B+9 and B+11 keys
```

Where the preceding numbers represent semitones.

So our task is—given a scale and the key for the scale, our program should highlight the keys and play it out:

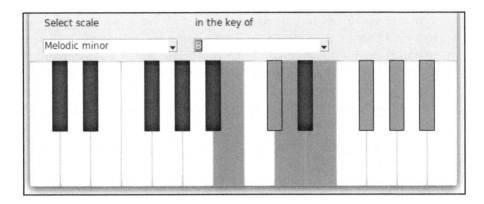

The first thing is to build two combobox for the scale and keys as shown previously. This should be easy for you as we have built combobox several times in the previous chapters.

The second step involves reading the JSON file into our program.

Quoting from json.org (http://json.org/):

> JSON (JavaScript Object Notation) is a lightweight data-interchange format. It is easy for humans to read and write. It is easy for machines to parse and generate. These are universal data structures. Virtually all modern programming languages support them in one form or another. It makes sense that a data format that is interchangeable with programming languages is also be based on these structures. Read more about JSON at https://www.json.org.

Python implements a standard module for reading and writing JSON data too. The module is rightfully called json.

We first import the built-in json module in our namespace:

```
import json
```

We next add a new method, self.load_json_files(), and call it from the class __init__ method:

```
def load_json_files(self):
    with open(SCALES_JSON_FILE, 'r') as f:
        self.scales = json.load(f, object_pairs_hook=OrderedDict)
```

The SCALES_JSON_FILE path is defined in the file constants.py. This loads up the scales data as a dictionary in the self.scales attribute:

You can read JSON files by using the `json.load` command. You can write to a JSON file by using the `json.dump` command. However, `json.load` methods do not preserve key order from a parsed JSON document. That is to say, `json.load` jumbles up the order of the keys. We do not want to jumble up the order of the keys and want them to appear in the order they are mentioned in the file. We therefore use the `OrderedDict` class from the `collections` module to preserve the key order. This is achieved by passing the second argument as `object_pairs_hook=OrderedDict`. An `OrderedDict` is a Python dictionary object that remembers the order that keys were first inserted.

Now that we have the scales data available as the `self.scales` dictionary, our next task is to figure out the keys to highlight. We start by creating a new attribute in the class __init__ method:

```
self.keys_to_highlight = []
```

Next, we define methods to highlight a key and another method to highlight a list of keys:

```
def highlight_key(self, key_name):
  if len(key_name) == 2:
    img = WHITE_KEY_PRESSED_IMAGE
  elif len(key_name) == 3:
    img = BLACK_KEY_PRESSED_IMAGE
  key_img = PhotoImage(file=img)
  for widget in self.keys:
   if widget.name == key_name:
     widget.configure(image=key_img)
     widget.image = key_img

def highlight_list_of_keys(self, key_names):
   for key in key_names:
     self.highlight_key(key)
```

The preceding code is similar to the previous code we wrote to highlight a key when it is pressed. Next, we also need methods to remove existing highlights:

```
def remove_key_highlight(self, key_name):
  if len(key_name) == 2:
    img = WHITE_KEY_IMAGE
  elif len(key_name) == 3:
    img = BLACK_KEY_IMAGE
  key_img = PhotoImage(file=img)
  for widget in self.keys:
   if widget.name == key_name:
```

```
    widget.configure(image=key_img)
    widget.image = key_img

def remove_all_key_highlights(self):
  for key in self.keys_to_highlight:
    self.remove_key_highlight(key)
  self.keys_to_highlight = []
```

The logic here is exactly similar to the one we applied for highlighting keys.

Now that we have methods to highlight and remove highlights from keys, let's define the callbacks attached to the two combobox for scale and key selection:

```
def on_scale_changed(self, event):
  self.remove_all_key_highlights()
  self.find_scale(event)

def on_scale_key_changed(self, event):
  self.remove_all_key_highlights()
  self.find_scale(event)
```

Lastly, here is the logic to select which keys to highlight. Furthermore, once we have the list of keys to be highlighted, we pass it to the previously defined play_scale_in_new_thread method that plays the actual sound for the scale:

```
def find_scale(self, event=None):
  self.selected_scale = self.scale_selector.get()
  self.scale_selected_key = self.scale_key_selector.get()
  index_of_selected_key = KEYS.index(self.scale_selected_key)
  self.keys_to_highlight = [ ALL_KEYS[i+index_of_selected_key] \
    for i in self.scales[self.selected_scale]]
  self.highlight_list_of_keys(self.keys_to_highlight)
  play_scale_in_new_thread(self.keys_to_highlight)
```

Do notice the highlighted part of the code.

So given the index of the selected key, we simply add all items in the list of selected scale to obtain the list of keys to be highlighted.

We also want to call this method as soon as the program runs. So we add a call to self.find_scale() right in our __init__ method. That ensures that we are greeted by playing of C Major scale (the default selection in combobox) as soon as the program runs.

This concludes the iteration. Now if you go and run 7.04 view.py and select the appropriate scale and key name, the keyboard will highlight the keys and also play it out for you.

Building the chord finder section

Now that we have had a glimpse of working with *JSON* files, this should be easy. Let's take a look at the first few lines of the `chords.json` file from the `json` directory:

```
{
  "Major" : [0, 4, 7],
  "Minor" : [0, 3, 7],
  "Sus4" : [0, 5, 7],
  "5" : [0, 4, 6],
  "Diminished" : [0, 3, 6],
  ...
}
```

This is very similar to the scales structure. Let's say we want to figure out what the *C#* major chord would look like. So we start with the *C#* key, which is 0. Then we look at the list of major chords, which read: `[0, 4, 7]`. So starting at *C#* the next key to highlight is 4 semitones above and the next is 7 semitones above *C#*. So the final chord structure for the *C#* major chord would be:

```
C#,     (C# + 4 semitones) ,     (C# + 7 semitones)
```

The GUI is also very similar to the scales section:

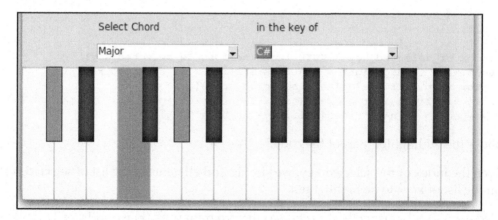

We begin by adding a constant for the path to the `chords.json` file in `7.05 constants.py`:

```
CHORDS_JSON_FILE = '../json/chords.json'
```

Next, we read the contents of this file in a new class attribute, `self.chords`:

```
with open(CHORDS_JSON_FILE, 'r') as f:
    self.chords = json.load(f, object_pairs_hook=OrderedDict)
```

We then modify the chords frame GUI to add two `combobox` (see the complete GUI in `7.05 view.py build_chords_frame`):

```
self.chords_selector = ttk.Combobox(self.chords_frame, values=[k for k
    in self.chords.keys()])
self.chords_selector.current(0)
self.chords_selector.bind("<<ComboboxSelected>>", self.on_chord_changed)
self.chords_selector.grid(row=1, column=1, sticky='e', padx=10,
    pady=10)
self.chords_key_selector = ttk.Combobox(self.chords_frame, values=[k
    for k in KEYS])
self.chords_key_selector.current(0)
self.chords_key_selector.bind("<<ComboboxSelected>>",
self.on_chords_key_changed)
```

Next, we added the two event callbacks defined previously:

```
def on_chord_changed(self, event):
    self.remove_all_key_highlights()
    self.find_chord(event)

def on_chords_key_changed(self, event):
    self.remove_all_key_highlights()
    self.find_chord(event)
```

The `find_chord` method queries the `self.chords` dict for the keys to be highlighted, adds the key offsets from the root note, and calls it to be highlighted and played:

```
def find_chord(self, event=None):
    self.selected_chord = self.chords_selector.get()
    self.chords_selected_key = self.chords_key_selector.get()
    index_of_selected_key = KEYS.index(self.chords_selected_key)
    self.keys_to_highlight = [ ALL_KEYS[i+index_of_selected_key] for \
                            i in self.chords[self.selected_chord]]
    self.highlight_list_of_keys(self.keys_to_highlight)
    play_chord_in_new_thread(self.keys_to_highlight)
```

The final code in this iteration modifies the `on_mode_changed` method to highlight the chord as soon as the chord mode is selected:

```
def on_mode_changed(self, event):
    self.remove_all_key_highlights()
```

```
selected_mode = self.mode_selector.get()
if selected_mode == 'Scales':
  self.show_scales_frame()
  self.find_scale()
elif selected_mode == 'Chords':
  self.show_chords_frame()
  self.find_chord()
elif selected_mode == 'Chord Progressions':
  self.show_progressions_frame()
```

That concludes the iteration. If you now run `7.05 view.py`, you will find a functional chords section that lets us find chords of different varieties in different scales.

Building the chord progression tutor

The GUI component of the chord progression section is slightly more evolved than the previous two sections. Here's how a typical chord progression GUI looks like:

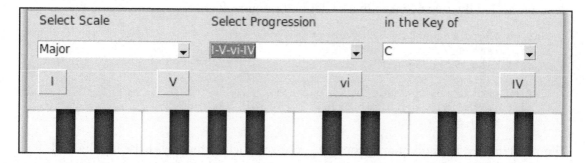

Notice that this section has the combobox as opposed to two for the earlier sections. Depending on what progression is chosen in the middle combobox, we need to draw a number of buttons, each button representing one chord in the complete chord progression.

In the preceding screenshot, note that the progression combobox has a value of **I-V-vi-IV**. This is a total of four roman numbers separated by a dash. This means that this chord progression is made up of four chords. Also notice that a few of the roman numbers (**I, V, IV**, and so on) are written in capital letters and others (**vi**) are written in small letters. All capital letters in the series denote major chords, while each small letter represents a minor chord.

Next, let us take a look at the `progressions.json` file from the `json` folder:

```
{
```

```
    "Major": {
    "I-IV-V": [ "0", "5", "7" ],
    "ii-V-I": [ "2", "7", "0" ],
    "I-V-vi-IV": [ "0", "7", "9", "5" ],
    ... more here},
    "Minor": {
    "i-VI-VII": [ "0", "9", "11"],
    "i-iv-VII": [ "0", "5", "11"],
    "i-iv-v": [ "0", "5", "7" ],
    ..more here
    }
    }
```

As a first observation, the chord progressions are broadly of two types—major and minor. Each type has a list of chord progressions, which is identified by a set of roman numerals.

Let's see an example of how this would work.

Say we want to display the major chord progression ii-V-I in the key of C, as shown in the following screenshot:

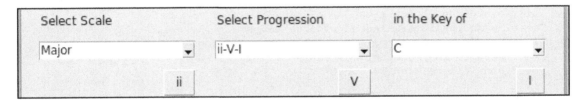

The JSON file lists the progression under the **Major** section as:

```
    "ii-V-I": [ "2", "7", "0" ]
```

Let's first lay down the 12 notes in a table starting at the key of the chord progression (C in our example). We need to pick up the 2nd, 7th, and 0th keys for this progression:

0	1	2	3	4	5	6	7	8	9	10	11
C	C#	D	D#	E	F	F#	G	G#	A	A#	B

The keys are D(2nd), G(7th), and C(0th). With the keys in hand—we next need to identify if each of the keys plays a major or minor chord. This is simple. Those roman numbers written in lower case play a minor chord, while those written in capitals play a major chord.

Given this rule, our final chords in the chord progression in the key of C are:

D Minor - G Major - C Major

Having identified these, our program should dynamically create three buttons. Clicking on these buttons should then play the preceding three chords, respectively.

Let's code this feature. We begin by defining the location of the chords progression file in `7.06 constants.py`:

```
PROGRESSIONS_JSON_FILE = '../json/progressions.json'
```

We then load it from the method `load_json_files()` into an attribute named `self.progressions`:

```
with open(PROGRESSIONS_JSON_FILE, 'r') as f:
    self.progressions = json.load(f, object_pairs_hook=OrderedDict)
```

Next, we modify the progression frame to add three `combobox` elements. See the `build_progressions_frame` code `7.06 view.py`.

The three combobox are attached to the following three callbacks:

```
def on_progression_scale_changed(self, event):
  selected_progression_scale = self.progression_scale_selector.get()
  progressions = [k for k in
    self.progressions[selected_progression_scale].keys()]
  self.progression_selector['values'] = progressions
  self.progression_selector.current(0)
  self.show_progression_buttons()

def on_progression_key_changed(self, event):
  self.show_progression_buttons()

def on_progression_changed(self, event):
  self.show_progression_buttons()
```

The most complex of the three combobox is the progression scale combobox. It lets you choose between *Major* and *Minor* progression scales. Depending on the choice you make there, it populates the second combobox with the progression values from the JSON file. This is what the first four lines of the `on_progression_scale_changed` method do.

Other than that, all three preceding callback methods defined make a call to the `show_progression_buttons` method, which is defined as follows:

```
def show_progression_buttons(self):
  self.destroy_current_progression_buttons()
  selected_progression_scale = self.progression_scale_selector.get()
  selected_progression = self.progression_selector.get().split('-')
  self.progression_buttons = []
```

```
for i in range(len(selected_progression)):
    self.progression_buttons.append(Button(self.progressions_frame,
        text=selected_progression[i],
        command=partial(self.on_progression_button_clicked, i)))
    sticky = 'W' if i == 0 else 'E'
    col = i if i > 1 else 1
    self.progression_buttons[i].grid(column=col, row=2, sticky=sticky,
        padx=10)
```

The preceding code dynamically creates buttons—one for each chord in the chord progression and stores all the buttons in a list named `self.progression_buttons`. We will keep this reference because we will have to destroy the buttons and create fresh ones every time a new chord progression is selected.

 Note the use of the `partial` method from the `functools` module to define the button command callbacks. Since the buttons are being created dynamically, we need to keep track of the button number. We use this handy method `partials` that lets us call a method with only a partial number of arguments. Quoting from Python's documentation -
The `partial()` function is used for partial function application, which *freezes* some portion of a function's arguments and/or keywords resulting in a new object with a simplified signature. You can read more about partials at `https://docs.python.org/3/library/functools.html#functools.partial`.

The preceding code calls a `destroy_button` method whose task is to clear the frame for drawing the next set of buttons, in case a new progression is selected. The code is as follows:

```
def destroy_current_progression_buttons(self):
    for buttons in self.progression_buttons:
        buttons.destroy()
```

Finally, we want to display an individual chord from the chord progression when a button is clicked. This is defined as follows:

```
def on_progression_button_clicked(self, i):
    self.remove_all_key_highlights()
    selected_progression = self.progression_selector.get().split('-')[i]
    if any(x.isupper() for x in selected_progression):
        selected_chord = 'Major'
    else:
        selected_chord = 'Minor'
    key_offset = ROMAN_TO_NUMBER[selected_progression]
    selected_key = self.progression_key_selector.get()
```

```
index_of_selected_key = (KEYS.index(selected_key)+ key_offset)% 12
self.keys_to_highlight = [ ALL_KEYS[j+index_of_selected_key] for j in
                             self.chords[selected_chord]]
self.highlight_list_of_keys(self.keys_to_highlight)
play_chord_in_new_thread(self.keys_to_highlight)
```

Here's a brief description of the preceding code:

- We first split the text, say `ii-V-I`, using the dash (–) delimiter. We then loop through the list and check if it is in uppercase or lowercase. If it is uppercase, the `selected_chord` variable is set to `Major`, if not it is set to `Minor`.
- The index of the keys is calculated by adding the key to the numbers mentioned in the JSON file. We apply modulo operator (%) to the added value to ensure that the value does not exceed the limits of 12 notes.
- Since the numbers are stored as roman numerals (this is the convention used by musicians), we need to convert it to integers. We do that by defining a simple key-value mapping in `7.05/constants.py`:

  ```
  ROMAN_TO_NUMBER = { 'I':0, 'II': 2, 'III':4, 'IV':5, 'V': 7,
  'VI':9, 'VII': 11, 'i':0, 'ii': 2, 'iii':4, 'iv':5, 'v': 7,
  'vi':9, 'vii': 11}
  ```

- Note that we have mapped all numbers starting at 0 and the mapping follows the Major scale pattern (`W  W  H  W  W  S`), where `W` stands for whole tone (two keys jump) and `S` stands for semitone (one key jump).
- Now that we know that if the chord is a major or a minor, the rest of the code is exactly the same as we earlier used to identify the individual chords. We then highlight and play the individual chord.

To end, we modify the `on_mode_changed` to add a call to `show_progression_buttons()` so that every time we switch to the chord progression section, the first chord progression buttons are laid down for us.

This completes the iteration. Our chord progression section is ready. Run code `7.06/view.py`. Inside the chord progression tutor, you can select the chord progression type (major or minor), the progression, and its key from the comboboxes and it will create one button for each of the chords in the chord progression. Press the individual buttons and it will play you the chords in that progression.

Building the score maker

Let us now build the score maker. This will display whatever is played on the piano in music notation. For the sake of program modularity, we will build the program in a separate file named `score_maker.py`.

We start by defining a class `ScoreMaker`. Since we will be showing just two octaves of notes, we will define a constant `NOTES` listing all the notes (`7.06/score_maker.py`):

```
class ScoreMaker:

NOTES = ['C1','D1', 'E1', 'F1', 'G1','A1', 'B1', 'C2','D2', 'E2', 'F2',
'G2','A2', 'B2']
```

The __init__ method of this class takes the container as an argument. This is the container on which this class will draw the score (`7.06/score_maker.py`):

```
def __init__(self, container):
    self.canvas = Canvas(container, width=500, height = 110)
    self.canvas.grid(row=0, column = 1)
    container.update_idletasks()
    self.canvas_width = self.canvas.winfo_width()
    self.treble_clef_image = PhotoImage(file='../pictures/treble-clef.gif')
    self.sharp_image = PhotoImage(file='../pictures/sharp.gif')
```

Note the use of `update_idletasks()` on the `container` frame. Calling this method here is necessary because we created a canvas in the previous line of code, which requires a redrawing of widgets. However, the redraw will only take place after the next run of the event loop. But we want to know the canvas width immediately after it was created. An explicit call to `update_idletasks` immediately carries out all pending events including geometry management. This ensures that we get the correct width of the canvas in the very next step. If you comment out the `update_idletasks` line and try to print the width of the canvas, it will print 1 even though we have explicitly set it to 500.

We also initialize two `.gif` images that we will use to draw the score. The `treble_clef` image will be used to draw the treble clef to the left of the score, while the `sharp_image` will draw a sharp (#) symbol prior to any sharp note (notes on the black keys).

Tkinter uses the concept of event loop to handle all events. Here's an excellent article that explains the concept in depth http://wiki.tcl.tk/ 1527. update_idletask is an example of the method available on all widgets. Visit http://effbot.org/tkinterbook/widget.htm to see a list of methods that are available to be called on all widgets.

Our first task is to draw five equally spaced lines on the canvas. We accordingly define a new method to do that:

```
def _draw_five_lines(self):
    w = self.canvas_width
    self.canvas.create_line(0,40,w,40, fill="#555")
    self.canvas.create_line(0,50,w,50, fill="#555")
    self.canvas.create_line(0,60,w,60, fill="#555")
    self.canvas.create_line(0,70,w,70, fill="#555")
    self.canvas.create_line(0,80,w,80, fill="#555")
```

This creates five parallel lines each 10 pixels apart. The underscore in the method name is an indication that this is to be treated as a private method of the class. While Python does not enforce method privacy, this tells the users not to use this method directly in their program.

Let's then build a method that actually calls the previous method and adds a treble clef to the left, thereby creating an empty staff on which we can draw notes:

```
def _create_treble_staff(self):
    self._draw_five_lines()
    self.canvas.create_image(10, 20, image=self.treble_clef_image, anchor=NW)
```

At the outset, we need to differentiate between drawing a chord and drawing notes of the scale. Since all the notes of a chord are played together, the notes of a chord are drawn at a single *x* location. In contrast, the notes in a scale are drawn at regular *x* offsets, as shown here:

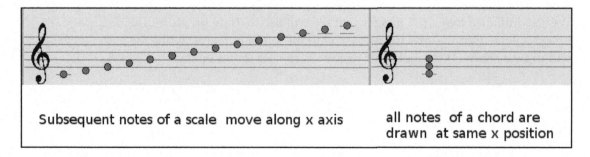

Subsequent notes of a scale move along x axis

all notes of a chord are drawn at same x position

Since we need to offset the *x* value for scales at regular intervals, we use the `count` method from the `itertools` module to provide an ever-increasing value of *x*:

```
import itertools
self.x_counter = itertools.count(start=50, step=30)
```

Now every subsequent call to `x = next(self.x_counter)` increments *x* by 30.

Now here's the code that draws the actual note on the canvas:

```
def _draw_single_note(self, note, is_in_chord=False):
    is_sharp = "#" in note
    note = note.replace("#","")
    radius = 9
    if is_in_chord:
        x = 75
    else:
        x = next(self.x_counter)
    i = self.NOTES.index(note)
    y = 85-(5*i)
    self.canvas.create_oval(x,y,x+radius, y+ radius, fill="#555")
    if is_sharp:
        self.canvas.create_image(x-10,y, image=self.sharp_image, anchor=NW)
    if note=="C1":
        self.canvas.create_line(x-5,90,x+15,  90, fill="#555")
    elif note=="G2":
        self.canvas.create_line(x-5,35,x+15,  35, fill="#555")
    elif note=="A2":
        self.canvas.create_line(x-5,35,x+15,  35, fill="#555")
    elif note=="B2":
        self.canvas.create_line(x-5,35,x+15,  35, fill="#555")
        self.canvas.create_line(x-5,25,x+15,  25, fill="#555")
```

The description of the preceding code is as follows:

- The method accepts a note name, for example, C1 or D2#, and draws an oval at an appropriate place.
- We need to get the *x*, *y* values for drawing an oval.
- We first calculate the *x* value. If the note is part of a chord, we fix the *x* value at 75 px, whereas if the note is part of a scale, the *x* value is incremented by *30* pixels from the previous *x* value by calling `next` on the `itertool counter` method.

Next, we calculate the *y* value. The code to do this is as follows:

```
i = self.NOTES.index(note)
y = 85-(5*i)
```

Basically, the *y* offset is calculated based on the index of the note in the list and each subsequent note is offset by 5 pixels. The number 85 is found by trial and error.

Now that we have the *x* and *y* value, we simply draw the oval of given `radius`:

```
self.canvas.create_oval(x,y,x+radius, y+ radius, fill="#555")
```

If the note is a sharp note, that is, if it contains the character #, it draws the # image 10 pixels left of the oval for the note.

The notes C1, G2, A2, and B2 are drawn outside the five lines. So in addition to oval we need to draw a small line crossing horizontally through them. This is what the last 11 lines of if...else statements achieve.

Finally, we have the `draw_notes` method and `draw_chord` method that given a list of notes draw out the notes and chords, respectively. These are the only two methods that do not have an underscore before their names. This means we expose the interface of our program only using these two methods:

```
def draw_notes(self, notes):
    self._clean_score_sheet()
    self._create_treble_staff()
    for note in notes:
        self._draw_single_note(note)

def draw_chord(self, chord):
    self._clean_score_sheet()
    self._create_treble_staff()
    for note in chord:
        self._draw_single_note(note, is_in_chord=True)
```

Now that we have our `ScoreMaker` ready, we simply import it into 7.07/view.py:

```
from score_maker import ScoreMaker
```

We modify `build_score_sheet_frame` to instantiate the `ScoreMaker`:

```
self.score_maker = ScoreMaker(self.score_sheet_frame)
```

We then modify `find_scale` to add this line (7.07/view.py):

```
self.score_maker.draw_notes(self.keys_to_highlight)
```

We similarly modify `find_chord` and `on_progression_button_clicked` to add this line (`7.07/view.py`):

```
self.score_maker.draw_chord(self.keys_to_highlight)
```

That brings us to the end of this project. If you now run `7.07/view.py`, you should see a functional score maker and a functional **Piano Tutor**.

However, let's end this chapter with a brief discussion on window responsiveness.

A note on window responsiveness

We used `.grid_propagate(False)` in this program to ensure that our frames did not shrink to fit their contents, but rather stayed at a fixed height and width that we had specified while making the frames.

This served us well for this example, but this made our window and its content fixed in size. This is what you would typically call a non-responsive window.

Let us take a look at the program `nonresponsive.py` as an example of a non-responsive window. This program simply draws 10 buttons in a row:

```
from tkinter import Tk, Button
root = Tk()

for x in range(10):
 btn = Button(root, text=x )
 btn.grid(column=x, row=1, sticky='nsew')

root.mainloop()
```

Run this program and resize the window. These buttons are drawn on the root window and are not responsive. The buttons remain fixed in size. They do not adapt in size to change in the window size. If the window size is made smaller, some of the buttons even disappear from view.

In contrast, let us take a look at the program `responsive.py`:

```
from tkinter import Tk, Button, Grid

root = Tk()

for x in range(10):
 Grid.rowconfigure(root, x, weight=1)
```

```
Grid.columnconfigure(root, x, weight=1)
btn = Button(root, text=x )
btn.grid(column=x, row=1, sticky='nsew')

root.mainloop()
```

If you run this program and resize the window, you will see that the buttons respond by resizing themselves to fit the container root window. So what's the difference between the two previous pieces of code? We simply added these two lines to the second program:

```
Grid.rowconfigure(root, x, weight=1)
Grid.columnconfigure(root, x, weight=1)
```

These two lines add **non-zero weights** (weight=1) to the xth button widget in the container (root in the preceding example).

The key here is to understand the importance of weights. If we have two widgets, widget1 and widget2, and we assign them weights of 3 and 1, respectively. Now when you resize its parent, widget1 will take up 3/4th of the space, while widget2 will take up 1/4th of the space.

 Here's the documentation of rowconfigure and columnconfigure: http://infohost.nmt.edu/tcc/help/pubs/tkinter/web/grid-config. html.

Experimenting with the code

The best way to experience this piece of code is to make the following tweaks one by one, run the program, and resize the window to see the effect of each option.

As a first tweak, change the weights to 0:

```
Grid.rowconfigure(root, x, weight=0)
Grid.columnconfigure(root, x, weight=0)
```

This will make the window non-responsive again.

Next, reassign the weights back to 1 and then comment out one of the two lines and see the difference. If you comment out the rowconfigure line the buttons will be responsive in the y direction, but non-responsive in the x direction and vice versa for columnconfigure.

Restore the program to its original state and then assign a different weight in each loop by changing the weight to x:

```
Grid.rowconfigure(root, x, weight=x)
Grid.columnconfigure(root, x, weight=x)
```

So the first button will have a weight of 0, the second button will have a weight of 1, and so on. Now if you run the program and resize the window, the last button with weight=9 will be the most responsive (will take up the largest proportion of the available space), while the first button with a weight of 0 will be completely non-responsive (fixed size), as shown in the following screenshot:

As the last tweak, restore the program to its original state and change the value of the second argument to a fixed number, say 2:

```
Grid.rowconfigure(root, 2, weight=1)
Grid.columnconfigure(root, 2, weight=1)
```

This will assign the weight only to the third button (counting starts with 0), so the third button becomes responsive, while the others stay non-responsive, as shown in the following screenshot:

As a matter of fact, in this last case since we are assigning weight only to a single widget, we could have as well assigned it outside the loop.

Handling widget resize with \<Configure\>

There might be occasions when you \<indexentry content="window responsiveness:widget resize, handling with "\>want to do some specific action when a user resizes a window or a widget. Tkinter provides an event named \<Configure\>, which can be bound to a callback to react to changes in widget size.

Here is a simple example (see `handle_widget_resize.py`):

```
from tkinter import Tk, Label, Pack

root= Tk()
label = Label(root, text = 'I am a Frame', bg='red')
label.pack(fill='both', expand=True)

def on_label_resized(event):
  print('New Width', label.winfo_width())
  print('New Height', label.winfo_height())

label.bind("<Configure>", on_label_resized)
root.mainloop()
```

The description of the code is as follows:

- We have a Label widget in a `root` window. We set the pack options for the label to (`fill='both', expand=True`) as we want it to resize every time the root window resizes.
- We attach a callback to the \<Configure\> event to listen for any changes in the size of the label widget. As soon as the label widget changes, it triggers a call to the method `on_label_resized`.

Now if you resize the window, the label resizes and that triggers `on_label_resized`, which prints the new height and width of the label widget to the console. This can be used for adjusting the placement of items on the screen.

That concludes our brief discussion on window responsiveness.

Summary

We worked with several useful standard modules such as `functools`, `itertools`, and `json`.

We saw how to work with *JSON* files. JSON helps us present complex rules about our domain and are an easier and more portable alternative to storing the same information in say a database.

We looked at the practical usage of `widget.grid_propagate(False)` along with some of its limitations in terms of non-responsiveness.

We saw the usage of `OrderedDict` from the `collections` module and `partials` from the `functools` module.

We looked at various root window methods such as `root.geometry`, `root.winfo_screenwidth`, and `root.resizable`.

We looked at `widget.update_idletasks`, which lets us clear all pending updates without having to wait for the next run of mainloop.

Finally, we looked at the steps involved in making a window responsive in Tkinter.

QA section

Before you proceed to the next chapter, make sure you can answer these questions to your satisfaction:

- What is `partial` from the `functools` module used for?
- When and why do we need to use `widget.update_idletasks` in a Tkinter program?
- If needed, how can we handle resizing of the main window or any other widget in Tkinter?
- What are the data structures available in JSON? (read about it here: `https://www.json.org/`)
- How do you make widgets responsive in Tkinter?

Further reading

Read more about JSON data structures. They are popular and are used everywhere. An alternative structure is XML. Read about XML and JSON and when and why one should be preferred over the other.

The collections module of Python provides some very versatile and useful data structures such as `namedtuple`, `deque`, `Counter`, `dict`, `OrderedDict`, `defaultdict`, `chainMap`, `UserDict`, `UserList`, and `userString`. These can be suitably used in a wide variety of use cases. More information can be found at: `https://docs.python.org/3/library/collections.html`.

We used external audio files and external images in our program. This means that they need to be bundled with the program if it has to be packaged and distributed. An alternative packaging of audio files and images can be done using what is called **base-64 encoding**. The audio files and the images can be base-64 encoded in a text file and then read back and decoded by the program to be used as audio files or image files. Read about base-64 encoding and if you feel motivated enough, try to convert all audio files and images used in this program into base-64 encoding. More information on base-64 encoding can be found here: `https://en.wikipedia.org/wiki/Base64`.

The Python implementation of base-64 encoding can be found here: `https://docs.python.org/3/library/base64.html`.

8
Fun with Canvas

Canvas is undoubtedly one of the most versatile widgets of Tkinter. Given that it provides direct control over the drawing of each individual pixel, combine it with some maths and it can be used to create all sorts of neat visualizations. While the possibilities are endless, we will explore how to implement some of the important mathematical ideas in this chapter.

The key objectives for this chapter are:

- Learning to animate with the Tkinter canvas
- Understanding the usage of polar and Cartesian coordinates on the canvas
- Implementing ordinary differential equations
- Modeling simulations given a list of formulas
- Modeling 3D graphics and studying some common transformation matrices used in 3D animation

Note that many of the code samples in this chapter requires heavy computations. However, code optimization for speed is not our first preference. The primary goal here is comprehension of the underlying concepts.

Building a screen saver

We will start by building a screen saver. The program will consist of several random-colored and random-sized balls bouncing all over the screen at random velocity, as shown in the following screenshot:

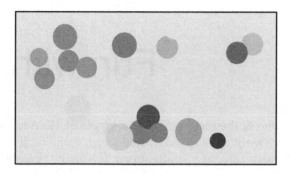

Let's create a class to generate balls with random attributes. Accordingly, we define a new class named RandomBall. Refer the code file 8.01_screensaver:

```
class RandomBall:

def __init__(self, canvas):
 self.canvas = canvas
 self.screen_width = canvas.winfo_screenwidth()
 self.screen_height = canvas.winfo_screenheight()
 self.create_ball()

def create_ball(self):
 self.generate_random_attributes()
 self.create_oval()

def generate_random_attributes(self):
 self.radius = r = randint(40, 70)
 self.x_coordinate = randint(r, self.screen_width - r)
 self.y_coordinate = randint(r, self.screen_height - r)
 self.x_velocity = randint(6, 12)
 self.y_velocity = randint(6, 12)
 self.color = self.generate_random_color()

def generate_random_color(self):
 r = lambda: randint(0, 0xffff)
 return '#{:04x}{:04x}{:04x}'.format(r(), r(), r())

def create_oval(self):
```

```
  x1 = self.x_coordinate - self.radius
  y1 = self.y_coordinate - self.radius
  x2 = self.x_coordinate + self.radius
  y2 = self.y_coordinate + self.radius
  self.ball = self.canvas.create_oval( x1, y1, x2, y2, fill=self.color,
    outline=self.color)

def move_ball(self):
  self.check_screen_bounds()
  self.x_coordinate += self.x_velocity
  self.y_coordinate += self.y_velocity
  self.canvas.move(self.ball, self.x_velocity, self.y_velocity)

def check_screen_bounds(self):
  r = self.radius
  if not r < self.y_coordinate < self.screen_height - r:
    self.y_velocity = -self.y_velocity
  if not r < self.x_coordinate < self.screen_width - r:
    self.x_velocity = -self.x_velocity
```

Here's the description for the preceding code:

- Two key methods here are `create_ball` and `move_ball`. All other methods are helpers to these two methods. The `__init__` method takes a `canvas` as a parameter and then calls the `create_ball` method to draw the ball on the given canvas. To move the ball around, we will explicitly need to call the `move_ball` method.

- The `create_ball` method uses the `canvas.create_oval()` method and `move_ball` uses the `canvas.move(item, dx, dy)` method, where `dx` and `dy` are `x` and `y` offsets for the canvas item.

- Also, note how we create a random color for the ball. Because the hexadecimal color coding system uses up to four hexadecimal digits for each of red, green, and blue, there are up to `0xffff` possibilities for each color. We, therefore, create a lambda function that generates a random number from `0-0xffff`, and use this function to generate three random numbers. We convert this decimal number to its two-digit equivalent hexadecimal notation using the format specifier `#{:04x}{:04x}{:04x}` to get a random color code for the ball.

That is all there is to the `RandomBall` class. We can use this class to create as many ball objects as we want to display in our screensaver.

Next, let's create the `ScreenSaver` class that will show the actual screensaver:

```
class ScreenSaver:

balls = []

def __init__(self, number_of_balls):
 self.root = Tk()
 self.number_of_balls = number_of_balls
 self.root.attributes('-fullscreen', True)
 self.root.attributes('-alpha', 0.1)
 self.root.wm_attributes('-alpha',0.1)
 self.quit_on_interaction()
 self.create_screensaver()
 self.root.mainloop()

def create_screensaver(self):
 self.create_canvas()
 self.add_balls_to_canvas()
 self.animate_balls()

def create_canvas(self):
 self.canvas = Canvas(self.root)
 self.canvas.pack(expand=1, fill=BOTH)

def add_balls_to_canvas(self):
 for i in range(self.number_of_balls):
    self.balls.append(RandomBall(self.canvas))

def quit_on_interaction(self):
  for seq in ('<Any-KeyPress>', '<Any-Button>', '<Motion>'):
    self.root.bind(seq, self.quit_screensaver)

def animate_balls(self):
 for ball in self.balls:
    ball.move_ball()
 self.root.after(30, self.animate_balls)

def quit_screensaver(self, event):
   self.root.destroy()
```

The description of the code is as follows:

- The __init__ method of the ScreenSaver class takes the number of balls (number_of_balls) as its argument
- We use root.attributes (-fullscreen, True) to remove the enclosing frame from the parent window and make it a full-screen window.

- The `quit_on_interaction` method binds the root to call our `quit_screensaver` method in case of any interactions from the user's end.

- We then create a canvas to cover the entire screen with `Canvas(self.root)` with `pack ( expand=1, fill=BOTH )` options to fill the entire screen.

- We create several random ball objects using the `RandomBall` class, passing along the Canvas widget instance as its arguments.

- We finally make a call to the `animate_balls` method, which uses the standard `widget.after()` method to keep running the animation in a loop at a regular interval of 30 milliseconds.

- To run the screen saver, we instantiate an object from our `ScreenSaver` class, passing the number of balls as its argument as follows: `ScreenSaver(number_of_balls=18)`

Our screensaver is now ready! In fact, if you are working on the Windows platform, and when you learn to create an executable program from Python programs (discussed in `Chapter 10`, *Miscellaneous Tips*), you can create an executable file with a `.exe` extension for this screensaver. You can then change its extension from `.exe` to `.scr`, right-click, and select **Install** to add it to your list of screensavers.

Graphing with Tkinter

Tkinter is not a graphing tool. However, should you need to draw graphs with Tkinter, you can use the Canvas widget to draw graphs.

In this iteration, we will draw the following graphs:

- Pie chart (`8.02_pie_chart.py`)
- Bar graph (`8.03_bar_graph.py`)
- Scatter plot (`8.04_scatter_plot.py`)

The three graphs show up as follows:

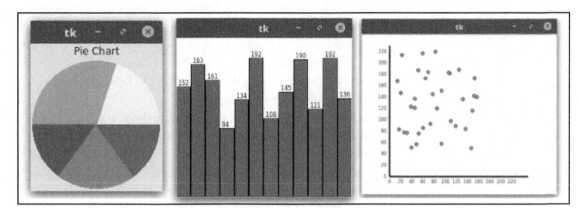

Let's look at the pie chart first. You can easily create a pie chart in Tkinter using the Canvas widget's create_arc method.

The create_arc method has the following signature:

```
item_id = canvas.create_arc(x1, y1, x2, y2, option, ...)
```

Point (x1, y1) is the top-left corner and point (x2, y2) is the bottom-right corner of the rectangle into which the arc fits. If the bounding rectangle is a square, it makes a circle. The method also takes two arguments, named start and extent, which we will use to create the pie chart.

The start option specifies the start angle for the arc, measured in degrees from the +x direction. When omitted, you get the complete ellipse. The extent option specifies the width of the arc in degrees.

The arc begins at the angle given by the start option and draws counterclockwise up to the degrees specified by the extent option.

To create the pie chart, let's define a method that, given a number *n*, divides the circle into, say, 1,000 equal parts and then, given a number less than 1,000, returns the equivalent angle in the arc. Since there are 360 degrees in a circle, the method is defined as follows:

```
total_value_to_represent_by_pie_chart = 1000
def angle(n):
    return 360.0 * n / total_value_to_represent_by_pie_chart
```

Next, we plot the various sections of the pie chart using code like this:

```
canvas.create_arc((2,2,152,152), fill="#FAF402", outline="#FAF402",
start=angle(0), extent = angle(200))
```

You can check out an example of a pie chart in 8.02_pie_chart.py.

Next, the bar graph. This is very simple. We use create_rectangle to draw a bar graph:

```
plot_data= [random.randint(75,200) for r in range(12)]
for x, y in enumerate(plot_data):
  x1 = x + x * bar_width
  y1 = canvas_height - y
  x2 = x + x * bar_width + bar_width
  y2 = canvas_height
  canv.create_rectangle(x1, y1, x2, y2, fill="blue")
  canv.create_text(x1+3, y1, font=("", 6),
    text=str(y),anchor='sw' )
```

One important thing to note here. Since the Canvas widget represents the y coordinate starting from the top-left corner, we need to subtract the y position from the canvas height to get the y coordinate for the graphs.

You can check out the complete code of the bar graph in 8.03_bar_graph.py.

Similarly, we use the create_oval method to draw the scatter plot. Check out the code for the scatter plot in 8.04_scatter_plot.py.

Next, let us see how to embed matplotlib graphs in Tkinter.

Using the Tkinter canvas to draw graphs may work fine for trivial cases. However, Tkinter is not the best choice when it comes to drawing more sophisticated and interactive graphs.

Several Python modules have been developed for making graphs. However, matplotlib stands out as a clear winner for producing professional-quality interactive graphs with Python.

Although a detailed discussion on matplotlib is beyond the scope of this book, we will take a brief look at embedding matplotlib-generated graphs on a Tkinter canvas.

You can install matplotlib and NumPy (a dependency for matplotlib) using the following commands:

```
pip3 install matplotlib
pip3 install numpy
```

The `matplotlib` targets many types of use cases and output formats. Some of the different use cases for `matplotlib` are to:

- Make interactive graphs from the Python shell
- Embed `matplotlib` in GUI modules such as Tkinter, wxPython, or PyGTK
- Generate postscript images from simulations
- Serve on web pages from backend web servers

In order to target all these use cases, `matplotlib` uses the concept of a backend. In order to display a `matplotlib` graph on Tkinter, we use a backend called `TkAgg`.

We import the backend into `matplotlib` as follows:

```
import tkinter as tk
from numpy import arange, sin, pi
from matplotlib.backends.backend_tkagg import
FigureCanvasTkAgg, NavigationToolbar2TkAgg
from matplotlib.figure import Figure
```

We then create the `matplotlib` graph as we would normally do in the `matplotlib` API:

```
f = Figure(figsize=(5,4), dpi=100)
a = f.add_subplot(111)
t = arange(-1.0, 1.0, 0.001)
s = t*sin(1/t)
a.plot(t, s)
```

Finally, we embed the generated graph in the `tkinter` main loop using the `TkAgg` backend as follows:

```
canvas = FigureCanvasTkAgg(f, master=root)
canvas.get_tk_widget().pack(side=tk.TOP, fill=tk.BOTH, expand=1)
```

We can also embed the navigation toolbar of `matplotlib` using the command:

```
toolbar = NavigationToolbar2TkAgg(canvas, root )
toolbar.update()
```

The preceding code (`8.05_matplotlib_embedding_graphs.py`) generates a graph as shown in the following diagram:

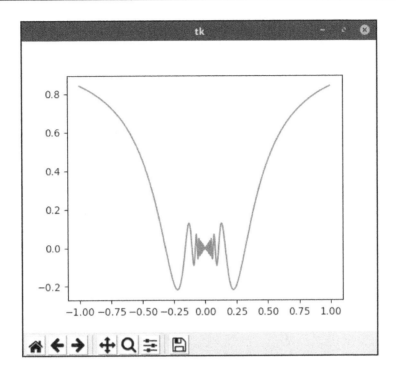

Polar plots with Tkinter

A point in space can be represented using the Cartesian coordinate using two numbers **x** and **y**. The same point can also be represented in the polar coordinate by using the distance from the origin (**r**) and the angle from the *x* axis (theta), as shown in the following diagram:

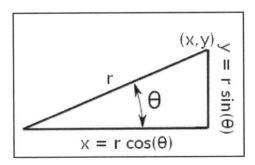

To convert between polar and Cartesian coordinates, we use the following equalities:

$$x = r\ cos(\theta)\ and\ y = rsin(\theta)$$

It is easier to plot equations expressed in terms of **r** and **θ** on a special kind of graph called the **polar plot**, which is divided into small concentric circles and radial lines emanating from the center. The radial lines are normally spaced at intervals of 15∘, while the radius of concentric circles depends on the scale on which the distance is to be measured from the center. Here's an example of a polar plot that we will draw:

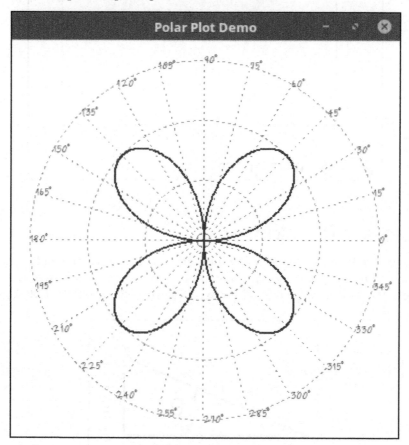

The Tkinter canvas understands Cartesian coordinates. It is, however, easy to convert from polar to Cartesian coordinates. We accordingly define a method named `polar_to_cartesian`; see `8.06_polar_plot.py`:

```
def polar_to_cartesian(r, theta, scaling_factor, x_center, y_center):
    x = r * math.cos(theta) * scaling_factor + x_center
    y = r * math.sin(theta) * scaling_factor + y_center
    return(x, y)
```

Here's a brief description of the preceding code:

- The method converts an input of (r, theta) value to (x, y) coordinates using the equalities *x= r cos(θ) and y = rsin(θ)*.
- The `scaling_factor` in the preceding equation decides how many pixels will equal to one unit in our polar plot and is set to a constant value. Changing it changes the size of the plot.
- We add the `x_center` and `y_center` values to the final results. `x_center` is defined as half the `window_width` while `y_center` is half the window size. We add these as offsets because Canvas considers *(0,0)* as the top left of the canvas, while we want to consider the center of the canvas as *(0,0)*.

We begin by creating a canvas in a Tkinter root window, and add radial lines and concentric circles to the canvas using the following code:

```
# draw radial lines at interval of 15 degrees
for theta in range(0,360,15):
    r = 180
    x, y = x_center + math.cos(math.radians(theta))*r, \
           y_center - math.sin(math.radians(theta)) *r
    c.create_line(x_center, y_center, x, y, fill='green', dash=(2, 4),\
                  activedash=(6, 5, 2, 4) )
    c.create_text(x, y, anchor=W, font="Purisa 8", text=str(theta) + '°')

# draw concentric_circles
for radius in range(1,4):
    x_max = x_center + radius * scaling_factor
    x_min = x_center - radius * scaling_factor
    y_max = y_center + radius * scaling_factor
    y_min = y_center - radius * scaling_factor
    c.create_oval(x_max, y_max, x_min, y_min, width=1, outline='grey', \
                  dash=(2, 4), activedash=(6, 5, 2, 4))
```

Now that our graph paper is ready, it's time to plot the actual polar plot. The following code plots 3000 points of the polar equation `r = 2*math.sin(2*theta)` on the graph:

```
for theta in range(0, 3000):
    r = 2*math.sin(2*theta)
    x, y = polar_to_cartesian(r, theta, scaling_factor, x_center, y_center)
    c.create_oval(x, y, x, y, width=1, outline='navy')
```

This creates the curve of the `form. r = a sin nθ`, where n is even. It is a **2n-leaved rose**. If n is odd, it will form an **n-leaved rose**. There are many other good looking plots that you can plot by changing the `r` equation in the previous method. A few other equations that you can try are as follows:

```
r = 0.0006 * theta    # an archimedean spiral
r = 1 + 2*math.cos(theta) # cardoid pattern
r = 3 * math.cos(theta) # circle
r = 2*math.sin(5*theta) # 5 leaved rose
r = 3 * math.cos(3*theta) # 3 leaved rose
r = 2 * math.sin(theta)**2 # a  lemniscate
r = (4 * math.cos(2*theta))**1/2 # another lemniscate
```

You can also play with the parameters of the individual equation to see the difference they make to the plot.

This concludes the iteration.

Gravity simulation

Let's now simulate gravity. We will simulate the movement of four planets (Mercury, Venus, Earth, and Mars), and our very own Moon, using Newton's law of universal gravitation.

Our simulation assumes the Sun at the center, but it does not draw an oval for the Sun as that would make our planets invisible at that scale. Our simulation programs shows the four planets and moon revolving in circular orbits (`8.07_gravity_simulation.py`):

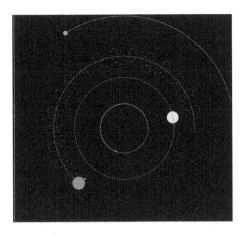

 While the system could be extended to include other planets from the solar system - putting them all on the rectangular window of our screen would not be possible as the differences in planet sizes and distances are so disproportionate that making one planet, such as Jupiter, show up would make sizes and distances of planets such as Earth smaller than a pixel, making them invisible. So our visualization sticks to just the four relatively nearby planets and our Moon. A very insightful interactive visualization of the entire solar system, titled *If the moon were only 1 pixel*, can be found here: http://joshworth.com/dev/pixelspace/pixelspace_solarsystem.html.

Newton's law of gravitation established the fact that gravitation is universal and that all objects attract each other with a force of gravity that is related to the mass of the two bodies and the distance between them, using this formula:

$$F = G\frac{m_1 \cdot m_2}{d^2}$$

Where:

- **F** = Force of attraction between two objects
- **m1** = Mass of object 1
- **m2** = Mass of object 2
- **d** = Distance between the two objects
- **G** = 6.673 x 10^{-11} N m^2/kg^2

Once the preceding equation yields us the gravitational force, we can then find the angular velocity of the object using this formula:

$$AngularVelocity(\alpha) = -\sqrt{\frac{F}{m * d}}$$

The preceding formula holds true for motion in circular paths, which is somewhat an approximation of the actual motion of planets in an elliptical orbit. With angular velocity in hand, we can get the angular position (θ):

$$\theta = \omega. t$$

With the distance from the Sun (center) and θ in hand, we can convert it from a polar coordinate to a Cartesian coordinate as we have done in previous examples. Next, it's just a matter of drawing spheres on the Tkinter canvas at various locations.

With the formulas in hand, we define a `Planet` class (`8.07_gravity_simulation.py`):

```
class Planet:
  sun_mass = 1.989 * math.pow(10, 30)
  G = 6.67 * math.pow(10, -11)

  def __init__(self, name, mass, distance, radius, color, canvas):
    self.name = name
    self.mass = mass
    self.distance = distance
    self.radius = radius
    self.canvas = canvas
    self.color = color
    self.angular_velocity = -math.sqrt(self.gravitational_force() /
                            (self.mass * self.distance))
    self.oval_id = self.draw_initial_planet()
    self.scaled_radius = self.radius_scaler(self.radius)
    self.scaled_distance = self.distance_scaler(self.distance)
```

While most of the preceding code is a simple instantiation of variables, note that it takes in a canvas as an input on which it will draw the planet.

We also need to scale down the planet distances and radii to fit into our window screen, so we have defined two methods in the class to scale distance and radius (`8.07_gravity_simulation.py`):

```
def distance_scaler(self, value):
  #[57.91, 4497.1] scaled to [0, self.canvas.winfo_width()/2]
```

```
    return (self.canvas.winfo_width() / 2 - 1) * (value - 1e10) /
        (2.27e11 - 1e10) + 1

def radius_scaler(self, value):
    #[2439, 6051.8] scaled to [0, self.canvas.winfo_width()/2]
    return (16 * (value - 2439) / (6052 - 2439)) + 2
```

For scaling the distance, we take the maximum distance and scale it to fit in half of the canvas width. For scaling radius, we take the maximum and minimum radii from the first four planets and multiply them with the arbitrary number 16, so that the planets' scales look acceptable on the screen. Most of the preceding code was obtained by experimenting with what looks best on the screen, and the numbers were chosen purely arbitrarily.

The constructor then calls a method, `draw_initial_planet`, which creates an oval of a scaled radius and at a scaled distance on the canvas. It also returns the unique ID of the created oval so that the oval's position can be updated using the id as a handle.

We then define two helper methods using the formulas we discussed earlier:

```
def gravitational_force(self):
    force = self.G * (self.mass * self.sun_mass) / math.pow(self.distance, 2)
    return force

def angular_position(self, t):
    theta = self.angular_velocity * t
    return theta
```

Now we calculate the angular position (`theta`), convert it from polar to Cartesian coordinates, and update the *x*, *y* position for the oval pertaining to the planet. We also leave a 1-pixel trail for the planet's position using `create_rectangle`:

```
def update_location(self, t):
    theta = self.angular_position(t)
    x, y = self.coordinates(theta)
    scaled_radius = self.scaled_radius
    self.canvas.create_rectangle(x, y, x, y, outline="grey")
    self.canvas.coords(self.oval_id, x - scaled_radius, y - scaled_radius,
                    x + scaled_radius, y + scaled_radius)
```

The code to convert from polar to Cartesian coordinates is as follows:

```
def coordinates(self, theta):
    screen_dim = self.canvas.winfo_width()
    y = self.scaled_distance * math.sin(theta) + screen_dim / 2
    x = self.scaled_distance * math.cos(theta) + screen_dim / 2
    return (x, y)
```

Next, we define a `Moon` class, which is similar in all aspects to the `Planet` class, so it inherits from the `Planet` class. However, the most important difference is that instead of taking distance from the Sun and the mass of the Sun as a reference, it takes distance from Earth and the mass of Earth as a reference. As scaling on actual values would have made the Moon's size smaller than 1 pixel, we have also hardcoded the scaled distance and scaled radius values for Moon to make it visible on the screen. Since Moon needs to go round Earth, we also need to pass Earth as an extra argument to the __init__ method of the `Moon` class (`8.07_gravity_simulation.py`).

Finally, we create the four planets and the Moon, passing in their actual values taken from Wikipedia:

```
#name,mass,distance,radius, color, canvas
mercury = Planet("Mercury", 3.302e23, 5.7e10, 2439.7, 'red2', canvas)
venus = Planet("Venus", 4.8685e24, 1.08e11, 6051.8, 'CadetBlue1', canvas)
earth = Planet("Earth", 5.973e24, 1.49e11, 6378, 'RoyalBlue1', canvas)
mars = Planet("Mars", 6.4185e23, 2.27e11, 3396, 'tomato2', canvas)
planets = [mercury, venus, earth, mars]
moon = Moon("Moon", 7.347e22, 3.844e5, 173, 'white', canvas, earth)
```

Then we create a Tkinter canvas and define an `update_bodies_positions` method that runs every 100 ms, as follows:

```
time = 0
time_step = 100000

def update_bodies_position():
 global time, time_step
 for planet in planets:
   planet.update_location(time)
 moon.update_location(time)
 time = time + time_step
 root.after(100, update_bodies_position)
```

That concludes the gravity simulation project. If you now go and run `8.07_gravity_simulation.py`, you can see the planets and our Moon responding to gravitational force.

Drawing fractals

A fractal is a never-ending pattern that repeats itself at all scales. Fractals are found everywhere in nature. We find them in our blood vessels, branches of trees, and in the structure of our galaxies, and the beauty of them lies in the fact that they are made out of simple formulas.

We will demonstrate the simplicity of these seemingly complex-looking phenomena by drawing a fractal named a Mandelbrot set. We assume a basic knowledge of set theory and complex numbers in this section. Our code produces a Mandelbrot set that looks like the following diagram:

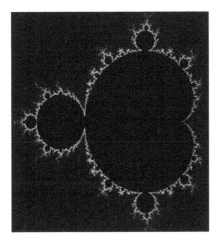

The Mandelbrot set is defined as a set of complex numbers, c:

$$M = \{c \in \mathbb{C} \mid \lim_{n \to \infty} Z_n \neq \infty\}$$

So that the complex number c obeys the following recurrence relation:

$$z_{n+1} = z_n^2 + c$$

Think of recurrence relations as functions where the last output is fed as input into the same function in the next iteration.

So the Mandelbrot set is a set that only includes those complex numbers for which the previous equation does not, after any number of iterations, blow up the value of z_n to infinity.

For a clearer understanding, if we take the number 1 as c and apply it to the preceding equation (note that 1 is also a complex number with no imaginary component—so real numbers are a subset of complex numbers and hence they too lie on the complex plane):

Value of z after n iterations(z_n)	Value of $z_{n+1} = z^2_n + c$ for c = 1
z_0	$0^2 + 1 = 1$
z_1	$1^2 + 1 = 2$
z_2	$2^2 + 1 = 5$
z_3	$5^2 + 1 = 26$

It is clear that the previous series will blow up to infinity as the number of iterations tends to infinity. Since this complex number 1 blows up the equation, it is not a part of the Mandelbrot set.

Contrast this with another number, $c = -1$ the values for which are plotted in the next table:

Value of z after n iterations(z_n)	Value of $z_{n+1} = z^2_n + c$ for c = -1
z_0	$0^2 + -1 = -1$
z_1	$-1^2 + -1 = 0$
z_2	$0^2 + -1 = -1$
z_3	$-1^2 + -1 = 0$

Note that you may continue the preceding series up to infinity but the value will keep alternating between -1 and 0, thus never exploding. This makes the complex number -1 eligible for inclusion in the Mandelbrot set.

Now, let us try to model the preceding equation.

One immediate problem to overcome is that we cannot model infinity in the previous equation. Fortunately, it can be seen from the equation that if the absolute value of z ever exceeds 2, the equation will eventually blow up.

So a definitive way to check whether the equation blows up is to check whether the magnitude of Z > 2. The magnitude of a complex number $a + ib$ is defined as follows:

$$\sqrt{a^2 + b^2}$$

So in order to check whether a complex number $a+ib$ blows up the preceding equation, we need to check the following:

$$\sqrt{a^2 + b^2} > 2$$

Or:

$$a^2 + b^2 > 4$$

The next question to consider is how many times should we iterate Zn to see if its magnitude exceeds 2 or not?

The answer to this depends on the kind of image resolution you seek to obtain in the final image. In general, the higher the maximum number of iterations, the greater the image resolution, subject to the limitation of individual pixel size, beyond which you can never go in terms of details. In practice, an iteration of a few hundred times is sufficient. We use a maximum iteration of 200 as that is enough to determine whether or not the equation blows up for a small-scale image that we will draw. Accordingly, we define a variable in 8.08_Mandelbrot.py as follows:

```
max_number_of_iterations = 200
```

Next, we define a method that takes in the real and imaginary components of a complex number, and tells whether the equation blows up for the complex number input.

For example, the method should return 2 for an input of 1, as the path to blow up is sensed right in the second iteration for the input value 1. However, if we give it an input of −1, the equation never blows up so it runs for the maximum number of iterations and returns the maximum_iteration_count, which we have defined as 200 and is akin to saying that the said number belongs to the Mandelbrot set (8.08_Mandelbrot.py):

```
print(mandelbrot_set_check(1, 0)) # returns 2
print(mandelbrot_set_check(-1, 0)) # returns 200
```

Accordingly, we define the `mandelbrot_set_check` method as follows
(`8.08_Mandelbrot.py`):

```
def mandelbrot_set_check(real, imaginary):
    iteration_count = 0
    z_real = 0.0
    z_imaginary = 0.0
    while iteration_count < max_number_of_iterations and \
            z_real * z_real + z_imaginary * z_imaginary < 4.0:
        temp = z_real * z_real - z_imaginary * z_imaginary + real
        z_imaginary = 2.0 * z_real * z_imaginary + imaginary
        z_real = temp
        iteration_count += 1
    return iteration_count
```

The code simply implements the recurrence relation for the Mandelbrot set.

While it's sufficient to know whether a complex number lies in the Mandelbrot set, we also keep a track of the iteration count, also called the escape time, which is the number of iterations it took a complex number to blow up, if it does blow up. If the iteration count returns as `maximum_number_of_iterations`, it means the complex number does not blow up the equation and the escape time is infinite, that is, the number is a part of the Mandelbrot set. We keep track of the iteration count as we will use this data to paint areas with different escape times in different colors.

Now that we have a way to tell whether or not a complex number belongs to the Mandelbrot set, we need a set of complex numbers to run through this method. In order to do that, we first define a maximum and a minimum complex number, between which we will check for inclusion in the Mandelbrot set. Note that in the following example, we have set the range of complex numbers between *-1.5-1i and 0.7+1i*.

You can try different ranges of these complex numbers, as long as the area falls inside a circle of radius 2, and it will print different regions of the Mandelbrot set:

```
min_real, max_real, min_imaginary, max_imaginary = -1.5, 0.7, -1.0, 1.0
```

Let's next proceed by defining the `image_width` and `image_height` variables as follows:

```
image_width = 512
image_height = 512
```

To draw the Mandelbrot set in an image, we need to map each pixel coordinate of the image to our complex numbers. Having defined the maximum and minimum range for the real and imaginary parts of our complex numbers, it's simply a matter of interpolating the complex numbers to map them to the pixel coordinates.

The following two methods do that for us (8.08_Mandelbrot.py):

```
def map_pixels_to_real(x):
    real_range = max_real - min_real
    return x * (real_range / image_width) + min_real

def map_pixels_to_imaginary(y):
    imaginary_range = max_imaginary - min_imaginary
    return y * (imaginary_range / image_height) + min_imaginary
```

Now we are ready to draw the actual image. We create a Tkinter root window, draw a canvas atop it, and then run the following loops:

```
for y in range(image_height):
 for x in range(image_width):
    real = map_pixels_to_real(x)
    imaginary = map_pixels_to_imaginary(y)
    num_iterations = mandelbrot_set_check(real, imaginary)
    rgb = get_color(num_iterations)
    canvas.create_rectangle([x, y, x, y], fill=rgb, width=0)
```

The preceding code takes each pixel in the image, maps its x, y coordinates to a real and imaginary number respectively, and then send this number out to the mandelbrot_set_check method, which in turn returns the number of iterations it took for the number to blow up. If the number did not blow up, it returns the value of maximum_number_of_iterations. With this number in hand, we call another method that gives an RGB color code, which is just based on some arbitrary numbers. It just adds the cosmetic value, and you can play with different arbitrarily designed color mapping schemes to generate Mandelbrot images of different colors. Finally, we use this color to fill the $(x, y)^{th}$ pixel on the canvas.

This concludes the iteration. Our code can now generate the Mandelbrot set. However, note that this code takes some time to generate the Mandelbrot set.

Voronoi diagrams

We will now draw a Voronoi diagram. Voronoi diagrams are a simple yet very powerful tool used in modeling lots of physical systems. Wikipedia (https://en.wikipedia.org/wiki/Voronoi_diagram#Applications) lists more than 20 disciplines of science and technology where Voronoi diagrams are used to model and solve real-world problems.

There are many little variations to the rules for drawing Voronoi diagrams, but the most common type of Voronoi diagram is made by choosing a finite number of points on a 2D plane. We call these points the seeds or the attractors. The tiny blue dots shown in the following image are attractor points. We then map or attach all the points on the plane to their nearest attractor point. All points closer to a particular attractor point is drawn in one color, which partitions the plane into what are called **Voronoi cells**, as shown in the following diagram:

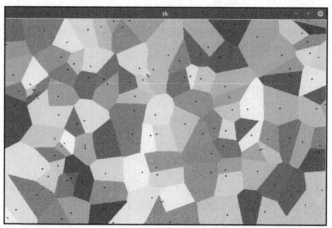

Voronoi diagrams can be drawn in spaces of arbitrary dimensions, but we stick to studying them in a two-dimensional plane.

There are many efficient but complicated algorithms for drawing Voronoi diagrams. However, we will use the simplest algorithm to understand. However, being simple comes at a cost. The algorithm requires more time to compute when compared to other faster but more complex algorithms.

We will begin by creating a fixed number of random attractor points on a canvas of given width and height. Accordingly, we define three variables in the program (`8.09_vornoi_diagram.py`):

```
width = 800
height = 500
number_of_attractor_points = 125
```

Next, we create a canvas on a Tkinter root window with the preceding width and height and pass the canvas to a method named `generate_vornoi_diagram`, which does all the processing and drawing for us. Its code is as follows:

```
def create_voronoi_diagram(canvas, w, h, number_of_attractor_points):
    attractor_points = []
```

```
colors = []
for i in range(number_of_attractor_points):
  attractor_points.append((random.randrange(w), random.randrange(h)))
  colors.append('#%02x%02x%02x' % (random.randrange(256),
                                   random.randrange(256),
                                   random.randrange(256)))
for y in range(h):
  for x in range(w):
    minimum_distance = math.hypot(w , h )
    index_of_nearest_attractor = -1
    for i in range(number_of_attractor_points):
      distance = math.hypot(attractor_points[i][0] - x,
        attractor_points[i][1] - y)
      if distance < minimum_distance:
        minimum_distance = distance
        index_of_nearest_attractor = i
    canvas.create_rectangle([x, y, x, y],
      fill=colors[index_of_neasrest_attractor], width=0)
for point in attractor_points:
  x, y = point
  dot = [x - 1, y - 1, x + 1, y + 1]
  canvas.create_rectangle(dot, fill='blue', width=1)
```

Here's a brief description of the preceding code:

- We begin by creating two lists. The first `for` loop is used to populate the `attractor_points` list with tuples (*x*, *y*) for each of the attractor points. We also create another list, `colors`, which holds the random color hexadecimal string for the cell of each attractor point.
- The second triple nested `for` loops goes through each pixel on the canvas and finds the index of the nearest attractor. Once that has been established, it colors the individual pixel using the color assigned to that attractor point.
- The last `for` loop then draws an overlapping blue colored square for each of the attractor points. This loop is deliberately run last to ensure that the attractor point draws over the colored cell region.

Since the preceding code has to go through three nested loops for checking each *x,y* location on the plane against each attractor point, it has a computational complexity of $O(n^3)$ as per Big-O notation. This means that the algorithm is not at all scalable to drawing images of larger sizes and explains why this code takes some time to generate the Voronoi diagram, even for this modest-sized image. More efficient algorithms are available and if you do not want to reinvent the wheel, you can even use the `Voronoi` class from the `scipy.spatial` module to implement this much faster. That is left as an exercise for you to explore.

This concludes the section. If you now run the `8.09_vornoi_diagram.py` program, it should generate a Voronoi diagram.

Spring pendulum simulation

A lot of real-world phenomena can be called **dynamical systems**. The state of such systems varies with time. Modeling such systems requires the use of **differential equations**. We will take here an example of modeling a pendulum attached to a spring, as shown in the following image. The pendulum swings to and fro. Furthermore, since the bob is attached to a spring, the bob also oscillates up and down:

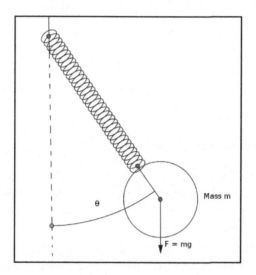

We study the evolution of two variables over time:

- Length l of the spring
- Angle (θ) between the spring and the center line, as shown in the preceding diagram.

Since there are two variables changing over time, the state of our system at any time can be represented by using four state variables:

- Spring length (l)
- Change in spring length (dl/dt), which is velocity

- Angle (θ)
- Change in angle (dθ/dt), which is the angular velocity

They are modeled by the following four differential equations:

$$v = \frac{dL}{dt}$$

$$\frac{d^2 L}{dt^2} = (L_0 + L)\frac{d}{dt}\theta - \frac{k}{m}L + g\cos(\theta)$$

$$\Omega = \frac{d\theta}{dt}$$

$$\frac{d^2\theta}{dt^2} = -\frac{1}{L + L_0}\left[g\sin(\theta) + 2\frac{dL}{dt}\frac{d\theta}{dt}\right]$$

The first equation measures linear velocity, which is the rate of change of L over time. The second equation is a second derivative and gives us the acceleration. The third equation measures change in theta over time and hence represents the angular velocity. The last equation is the second derivative of theta over time and hence it represents the angular acceleration.

Let us begin by defining the following constants:

```
UNSTRETCHED_SPRING_LENGTH = 30
SPRING_CONSTANT = 0.1
MASS = 0.3
GRAVITY = 9.8
NUMBER_OF_STEPS_IN_SIMULATION = 500
```

Accordingly, let us begin by defining the initial value for all these four state variables:

```
state_vector = [ 1, 1, 0.3, 1 ]
# 4 values represent 'l', 'dl/dt', 'θ', 'dθ/dt' respectively
```

Then, we define the `differentials_functions` method which returns an array of the four differential functions defined previously:

```
def differential_functions(state_vector, time):
  func1 = state_vector[1]
  func2 = (UNSTRETCHED_SPRING_LENGHT + state_vector[0]) *
    state_vector[3]**2 -
```

```
        (SPRING_CONSTANT / MASS * state_vector[0]) + GRAVITY *
            np.cos(state_vector[2])
    func3 = state_vector[3]
    func4 = -(GRAVITY * np.sin(state_vector[2]) + 2.0 * state_vector[1] *
        state_vector[3]) / (UNSTRETCHED_SPRING_LENGHT + state_vector[0])
    return np.array([func1, func2, func3, func4])
```

Next, we will use `scipy.integrate.odeint` to solve the differential equations. This method can be used to solve a system of ordinary differential equations of the following form:

$$\frac{dy}{dx} = func(y, x_0)$$

Here's the signature of `scipy.integrate.odeint`:

```
scipy.integrate.odeint(func, y0, t, optional arguments)
```

Where:

- `func`: Callable(y, t0, ...), which computes the derivative of y at t0
- `y0`: Array of initial condition (can be a vector)
- `t`: Array of time points for which to solve for y

The initial value point should be the first element of this sequence.

This method takes as input the derivative function (`func`), an array of initial state values (`y0`), and an array of times (`t`). It returns an array of state values corresponding to those times.

Since we are differentiating against time, we need a variable to track time (`8.10_spring_pendulum.py`):

```
time = np.linspace(0, 37, NUMBER_OF_STEPS_IN_SIMULATION)
```

The number 37 here is the step size for sampling time. Changing this value will change the speed of simulation.

Now we finally solve the sets of differential equations using `scipy.integrate.odeint` as follows (`8.10_spring_pendulum.py`):

```
ode_solution = odeint(differential_functions, state_vector, time)
```

Since we have set the number of simulation steps to 500 and there are four state variables, the `odeint` method returns a numpy array of the shape (*500, 4*), where each row represents the value of the four state variables at a given point of time.

Now recall that our state vector is a list of four values, `['l',  'dl/dt',  'θ',  'dθ/dt']`. So the 0th column returns the value `'l'` and the 2nd column represents the value `'θ'`. This is the polar format representation. Our canvas understands the Cartesian coordinate system. So we obtain the Cartesian coordinates (*x, y*) for the values of each value of (*l, θ*) as follows (`8.10_spring_pendulum.py`):

```
x_coordinates = (UNSTRETCHED_SPRING_LENGHT + ode_solution[:, 0])
                * np.sin(ode_solution[:, 2])
y_coordinates = (UNSTRETCHED_SPRING_LENGHT + ode_solution[:, 0])
                * np.cos(ode_solution[:, 2])
```

With that data in hand, it's now just a matter of plotting it on the canvas. So we create a Canvas widget in a `mainloop` and call an `update_graph` method that runs every 15 milliseconds, deleting everything on the canvas and redrawing the line and an oval (pendulum bob). We also add an increment variable, `plot_step`, which is reset to zero every time the simulation ends. This keeps the pendulum swinging forever (`8.10_spring_pendulum.py`):

```
plot_step = 0

def update_graph():
 global plot_step
 if plot_step == NUMBER_OF_STEPS_IN_SIMULATION: # simulation ended
   plot_step = 0 # repeat the simulation
 x, y = int(x_coordinates[plot_step]) + w / 2,
   int(y_coordinates[plot_step] + h / 2)
 canvas.delete('all')
 canvas.create_line(w / 2, 0, x, y, dash=(2, 1), width=1, fill="gold4")
 canvas.create_oval(x - 10, y - 10, x + 10, y + 10, outline="gold4",
   fill="lavender")
 plot_step = plot_step + 1
 root.after(15, update_graph)
```

This will create a spring pendulum, as shown in the following screenshot:

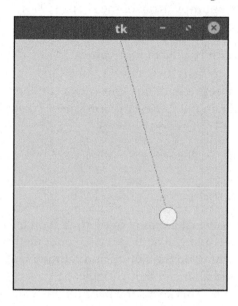

That concludes the iteration. You can explore this simulation by changing the values of the constants (mass, spring constant, and gravity). Also, change the initial state vector elements, such as the angle and velocity, and the program should respond as it would in a real-world situation.

We saw how to obtain ODE, which is a derivative with respect to only one variable. An extension of this concept is **partial differential equations (PDEs)**, which are derivatives with respect to several variables. More complex phenomena, such as electromagnetism, fluid mechanics, heat transfer, electromagnetic theory and various biological models, are all modeled by partial differential equations.

> The FEniCS computing platform (`https://fenicsproject.org/`) is a popular open-source software tool for solving PDEs with a Python binding.

Chaos game – building triangles out of randomness

The Chaos game refers to the emergence of fractal patterns with random numbers when the selection of random numbers are subject to some constraints. Let's look at the rules of one of the simplest chaos games:

1. We start by creating three points on a plane to form a triangle.
2. To begin the game, we draw a random point inside the triangle.
3. We then roll a dice. Given the outcome, we move halfway between the last point and any one of the vertices of the triangle. For example, if the outcome is 1 or 2, we move halfway between the last point and vertex A. If the outcome is 3 or 4, we move halfway from the current point towards vertex B, or if the outcome is 5 or 6, we draw the next point halfway between the current point and vertex C, as shown in the following image. This is repeated over and over again:

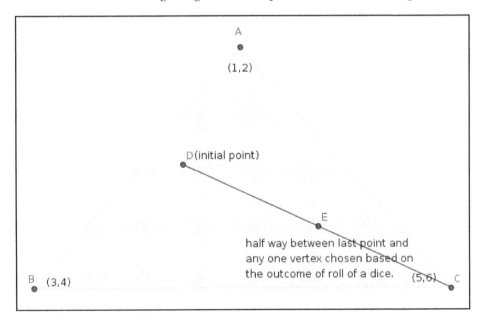

Here is the surprise part of it. While all the points except for the three vertexes were selected at random, the end result is not a haphazard set of points but rather a fractal—a set of repeating patterns of triangles called the Sierpinski triangle, shown in the following screenshot. This, according to some mathematicians, is a glimpse into the orderliness of the universe hidden inside what appears to be otherwise chaotic:

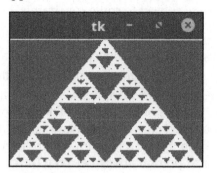

 Note that repeating this same rule inside a set of four points does not create a fractal. However, placing some specific kinds of restrictions on the choice of vertices produces a variety of interesting fractal shapes. You can read more about different varieties of fractals generated out of chaos games at https://en.wikipedia.org/wiki/Chaos_game.

Let us now code this program. We first define the three vertices of the triangle, as shown in the preceding screenshot:

```
v1 = (float(WIDTH/2), 0.0)
v2 = (0.00, float(HEIGHT))
v3 = (float(WIDTH), float(HEIGHT))
```

Here, WIDTH and HEIGHT are the window dimensions.

Our next task is to choose a random point inside our triangle as the starting point. This can be done using what are called **barycentric coordinates**.

Let *V1, V2, V3* be the three vertices of a triangle. A point *P* inside the triangle can be expressed as $P = aV_1 + bV_2 + cV_3$, where *a+b+c=1* and *a,b,c* are each ≥ 0. If we know and *b*, we can calculate *c* as *1-a-b*.

So we generate two random numbers, a and b, each in the range *[0,1]* so that their sum ≤ 1. If the sum of two random points exceeds 1, we replace a with 1-a and b with 1-b, so that their sum falls back below 1. Then, $aV_1 + bV_2 + cV_3$ is uniformly distributed inside the triangle.

Now that we have the barycentric coordinates a, b, and c, we can compute point P inside the triangle as aV1 + bV2 + cV3. Here is the idea expressed in code (8.11_chaos_game.py):

```
def random_point_inside_triangle(v1, v2, v3):
    a = random.random()
    b = random.random()
    if a + b > 1:
        a = 1-a
        b = 1-b
    c = 1 - a -b
    x = (a*v1[0])+(b*v2[0])+(c*v3[0]);
    y = (a*v1[1])+(b*v2[1])+(c*v3[1]);
    return (x,y)
```

We next define a method to calculate the halfway distance between two points:

```
def midway_point(p1, p2):
    x = p1[0] + (p2[0] - p1[0]) //2
    y = p1[1] + (p2[1] - p1[1]) //2
    return (x,y)
```

This is a simple linear interpolation between two points based on the Pythagorean theorem. Note that in Python, the / operator does floating point division while // does integer division (dropping the remainder).

Next, we put the laws of the game in a method called get_next_point:

```
def get_next_point():
    global last_point
    roll = random.choice(range(6))+1
    mid_point = None
    if roll == 1 or roll == 2:
        mid_point = midway_point(last_point, v1)
    elif roll == 3 or roll == 4:
        mid_point = midway_point(last_point, v2)
    elif roll == 5 or roll == 6:
        mid_point = midway_point(last_point, v3)
    last_point = mid_point
    return mid_point
```

Finally, we create a Tkinter canvas and define a method, `update`, to draw the individual pixels every 1 millisecond as follows:

```
def update():
  x,y = get_next_point()
  canvas.create_rectangle(x, y, x, y, outline="#FFFF33")
  root.after(1, update)
```

Calling this `update` method creates the fractal pattern in our chaos game.

Phyllotaxy

Phyllotaxy is derived from the Greek words phýllon (meaning leaf) and táxis (meaning arrangement). Accordingly, phyllotaxy is the study of the spiral arrangements found in leaves and flowers.

In this section, we will code the following floral pattern:

The mathematical details for this program have been taken from *Chapter 4* of the book *Algorithmic Botany of Plants*—a PDF of which can be obtained from here: `http://algorithmicbotany.org/papers/abop/abop-ch4.pdf`.

Here are the two formulas from the chapter that we will be using:

$$r = c \times \sqrt{n} \quad \text{and} \quad \phi = n \times 137.5°$$

(r, ϕ) represents the polar coordinate of each point on the canvas. As you shall see, our phyllotaxy will be made up of dots arranged in a spiral pattern. So the variable *n* in the preceding example represents the count or the index of the *n*th dot starting at zero at the center of the spiral. The variable c is used as a scale factor that in turn decides how near or far the dots will appear in the final image. The angle 137.5 is related to the golden ratio and the Fibonacci angle and looks the most natural. You can read more about it in the linked PDF.

To begin with, we define all the values that we discussed so far:

```
width, height = 500, 500
number_of_dots = 2000
angle = 137.5
scaling_factor = 4
dot_size = 4
n = np.arange(number_of_dots)
r = np.zeros(number_of_dots)
phi = np.zeros(number_of_dots)
x= np.zeros(number_of_dots)
y= np.zeros(number_of_dots)
dots = []
colors = []
```

Next, we create a Tkinter canvas and add colors to the colors list. We also create the dots using create_oval and save the reference to all ovals in the dots list:

```
for i in n:
    r = (scaling_factor * np.sqrt(i) * 6 ) %256
    color = '#%02x%02x%02x' % (int(r) , 0, 0)
    colors.append(color)
    dots.append(canvas.create_oval(x[i]-dot_size, y[i]-dot_size,
                    x[i]+dot_size, y[i]+dot_size, fill=color ))
```

The color defined in the preceding code is based on the value of r and is purely arbitrary. We could have used any other variable or rule for defining the color.

Lastly, we define the update function, which calculates the value of the r and ∅ values every 15 milliseconds and updates the coordinates of all the ovals on the canvas:

```
def update():
    global angle
    angle +=0.000001
    phi = angle * n
    r = scaling_factor * np.sqrt(n)
    x = r * np.cos(phi) + width/2
```

```
y = r * np.sin(phi) + height/2
for i in n:
canvas.coords(dots[i],x[i]-dot_size, y[i]-dot_size,x[i]+dot_size,
    y[i]+dot_size )
root.after(15, update )
```

You should now see the phyllotaxy pattern. Try changing all the parameters to see how the image changes.

3D graphics with Tkinter

Tkinter's Canvas widget provides for drawing with exact coordinate specifications. Therefore, it can be used to create all sorts of 3D graphics. Furthermore, we have already seen the animation abilities of Tkinter. We can apply these abilities to also animate in 3D.

Let's create a simple application where we create a cube in the center. We add event listeners to rotate the cube on mouse events. We also make a small animation in which the cube keeps rotating by itself when no mouse intervention occurs. In its final form, the application would look as follows (8.13_3D_graphics.py):

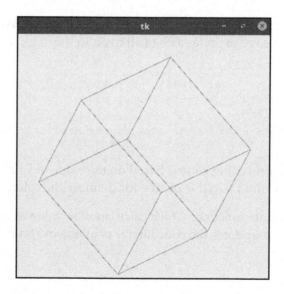

Transposing or unzipping can be done in Python by using the special * operator, any point in a 3D space can be represented by *x, y,* and *z* coordinates. This is usually represented by a vector of the form:

$$Point = [x, y, z]$$

This is an example of a row vector as all three points are written in a single row.

This is convenient for humans to read. However, as per convention and for some mathematical advantage that we will see later, positions are taken as a column vector. So it is written in a column as follows:

$$Point = \begin{bmatrix} x \\ y \\ z \end{bmatrix}$$

Since a shape is a collection of points, it is, therefore, a collection of column vectors. A collection of column vectors is a matrix, where each individual column of the matrix represents a single point in 3D space:

$$Shape/Object = \begin{bmatrix} x_1 & x_2 & x_3 & .. & x_5 \\ y_1 & y_2 & y_3 & .. & y_5 \\ z_1 & z_2 & x_3 & .. & z_5 \end{bmatrix}$$

Let's take the example of a cube. A cube has eight defining vertices. A representative cube could have the following eight points with its center located at [0,0,0]:

```
Vertex 1 : [-100,-100,-100],
Vertex 2 : [-100, 100,-100],
Vertex 3: [-100,-100,100],
Vertex 4: [-100,100,100],
Vertex 5: [100,-100,-100],
Vertex 6: [100,100,-100],
Vertex 7: [100,-100,100],
Vertex 8: [100,100,100]
```

However, here the vertices are represented as row vectors. To represent the vectors as column vectors, we need to transpose the preceding matrix. Since transposition will be a common operation, let's start by building a class called MatrixHelpers and defining a method named transpose_matrix(8.13_3D_graphics.py):

```
class MatrixHelpers():

    def transpose_matrix(self,matrix):
        return list(zip(*matrix))
```

Transposing or unzipping can be done in Python by using the special * operator, which makes zip its own inverse.

Another issue with the preceding coordinates is that it centers at *(0,0,0)*. This means that if we try to plot the preceding points on a canvas, it will show up only partly, centered at the top-left corner of the canvas, something like this:

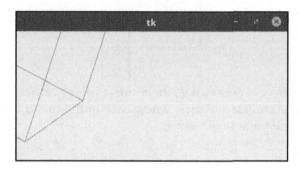

We need to move all the points to the center of the screen. We can achieve this by adding *x* and *y* offset values to the original matrix.

We accordingly define a new method named `translate_matrix` as follows:

```
def translate_vector(self, x,y,dx,dy):
    return x+dx, y+dy
```

Now let's draw the actual cube. We define a new class named `Cube` that inherits from the `MatrixHelper` class because we want to use the `transpose_matrix` and `translate_vector` methods defined in the `MatrixHelper` class (see code `8.13_3D_graphics.py`):

```
class Cube(MatrixHelpers):
    def __init__(self, root):
        self.root = root
        self.init_data()
        self.create_canvas()
        self.draw_cube()
```

The `__init__` method simply calls four new methods. The `init_data` method sets the coordinate values for all the eight vertices of the cube (`8.13_3D_graphics.py`):

```
def init_data(self):
    self.cube = self.transpose_matrix([
            [-100,-100,-100],
```

```
        [-100, 100,-100],
        [-100,-100,100],
        [-100,100,100],
        [100,-100,-100],
        [100,100,-100],
        [100,-100,100],
        [100,100,100]
    ])
```

The `create_canvas` method creates a 400 x 400 sized canvas on top of the root window and assigns a background and fill color to the canvas:

```
def create_canvas(self):
    self.canvas = Canvas(self.root, width=400, height=400,
background=self.bg_color)
    self.canvas.pack(fill=BOTH,expand=YES)
```

Lastly, we define the `draw_cube` method, which uses `canvas.create_line` to draw lines between selected points. We do not want lines between all the points, but rather lines between some selected vertices to create a cube. We accordingly define the method as follows (`8.13_3D_graphics.py`):

```
def draw_cube(self):
  cube_points_to_draw_line = [[0, 1, 2, 4],
            [3, 1, 2, 7],
            [5, 1, 4, 7],
            [6, 2, 4, 7]]
  w = self.canvas.winfo_width()/2
  h = self.canvas.winfo_height()/2
  self.canvas.delete(ALL)
  for i in cube_points_to_draw_line:
   for j in i:
     self.canvas.create_line(self.translate_vector(self.cube[0][i[0]],
       self.cube[1][i[0]], w, h),
     self.translate_vector(self.cube[0][j], self.cube[1][j], w, h), fill
       = self.fg_color)
```

This code draws a cube on the canvas. However, since the cube draws upfront, all we see is a square from the front. In order to see the cube, we need to rotate the cube to a different angle. That brings us to the topic of 3D transformations.

A wide variety of 3D transformations, such as scaling, rotation, shearing, reflection, and orthogonal projections, can be accomplished by multiplying the shape matrix with another matrix known as a transformation matrix.

For example, the transformation matrix for scaling a shape is:

$$Scale\ Transformation\ Matrix\ S = \begin{bmatrix} S_x & 0 & 0 & 0 \\ 0 & S_y & 0 & 0 \\ 0 & 0 & S_z & 0 \\ 0 & 0 & 0 & 1 \end{bmatrix}$$

Where S_x, S_y, and S_z are scaling factors in x, y, and z directions. Multiply any shape matrix with this matrix and you get the matrices for the scaled shape.

Let's, therefore, add a new method named `matrix_multiply` to our `MatrixHelper` class (`8.13_3D_graphics.py`):

```
def matrix_multiply(self, matrix_a, matrix_b):
    zip_b = list(zip(*matrix_b))
    return [[sum(ele_a*ele_b for ele_a, ele_b in zip(row_a, col_b))
            for col_b in zip_b] for row_a in matrix_a]
```

Next, let's add the ability to rotate the cube. We will be using the rotation transformation matrix. Furthermore, since rotation can happen along any of the x, y, or z axes, there are actually three different transformation matrices. The three rotation matrices are as follows:

$$R_x = \begin{bmatrix} 1 & 0 & 0 \\ 0 & cos(a) & -sin(a) \\ 0 & sin(a) & cos(a) \end{bmatrix} R_y = \begin{bmatrix} cos(a) & 0 & sin(a) \\ 0 & 1 & 0 \\ -sin(a) & 0 & cos(a) \end{bmatrix} R_z = \begin{bmatrix} cos(a) & -sin(a) & 0 \\ sin(a) & cos(a) & 0 \\ 0 & 0 & 1 \end{bmatrix}$$

Multiply the shape coordinates by the first matrix for a given value of a and you get the shape rotated by an angle a about the x axis in a counterclockwise direction. Similarly, the other two matrices rotate along the y axis and z axis respectively.

To rotate in a clockwise direction, we simply need to flip the sign of all sin values in the preceding matrix.

Note, however, that the order of rotation matters. So if you first rotate along the x axis and then rotate along the y axis, it is not the same as first rotating along y and then along the x axis.

 More details on rotation matrices can be found at `https://en.wikipedia.org/wiki/Rotation_matrix`.

So now that we know the three rotation matrices, let's define the following three methods in our MatrixHelper class (8.13_3D_graphics.py):

```
def rotate_along_x(self, x, shape):
    return self.matrix_multiply([[1, 0, 0],
                                 [0, cos(x), -sin(x)],
                                 [0, sin(x), cos(x)]], shape)

def rotate_along_y(self, y, shape):
    return self.matrix_multiply([[cos(y), 0, sin(y)],
                                 [0, 1, 0],
                                 [-sin(y), 0, cos(y)]], shape)

def rotate_along_z(self, z, shape):
    return self.matrix_multiply([[cos(z), sin(z), 0],
                                 [-sin(z), cos(z), 0],
                                 [0, 0, 1]], shape)
```

Next, we define a method named continually_rotate and call this method from the __init__ method of our Cube class:

```
def continually_rotate(self):
    self.cube = self.rotate_along_x(0.01, self.cube)
    self.cube = self.rotate_along_y(0.01, self.cube)
    self.cube = self.rotate_along_z(0.01, self.cube)
    self.draw_cube()
    self.root.after(15, self.continually_rotate)
```

The method uses root.after to call itself back every 15 milliseconds. At each loop, the coordinates of the cube are rotated by 0.01 degrees along all three axes. This is followed by a call to draw the cube with a fresh set of coordinates. Now, if you run this code, the cube rotates continuously.

Next, let's bind the rotation of the cube to a mouse button click and mouse motion. This will let the user rotate the cube by clicking and dragging the mouse over the cube.

Accordingly, we define the following method and call it from the __init__ method of the Cube class:

```
def bind_mouse_buttons(self):
    self.canvas.bind("<Button-1>", self.on_mouse_clicked)
    self.canvas.bind("<B1-Motion>", self.on_mouse_motion)
```

The methods linked from the preceding event binding are defined as follows:

```
def on_mouse_clicked(self, event):
```

```
    self.last_x = event.x
    self.last_y = event.y

def on_mouse_motion(self, event):
    dx = self.last_y - event.y
    self.cube = self.rotate_along_x(self.epsilon(-dx), self.cube)
    dy = self.last_x - event.x
    self.cube = self.rotate_along_y(self.epsilon(dy), self.cube)
    self.draw_cube()
    self.on_mouse_clicked(event)
```

Note that the preceding method maps mouse displacements along the *y* axis to rotations along the *x* axis and vice versa.

Also, note that the last line of the code calls `on_mouse_clicked()` to update the value of `last_x` and `last_y`. If you skip that line, the rotation becomes exceedingly fast as you increase the displacement from the last clicked position.

The method also refers to another method, named epsilon, which translates the distance into an equivalent angle for rotation. The epsilon method is defined as follows:

```
self.epsilon = lambda d: d * 0.01
```

The epsilon here is obtained by multiplying the displacement, d, with an arbitrary value of 0.01. You can increase or decrease the sensitivity of rotation to mouse displacement by changing this value.

Now the cube becomes responsive to mouse click and drag over the canvas. This concludes the last project of this chapter.

Here, we have just scratched the surface of 3D graphics. A much more detailed discussion on 3D programming with Tkinter can be found at `https://sites.google.com/site/3dprogramminginpython/`.

There have also been attempts to further abstract and build 3D programming frameworks for Tkinter. You can find an example of a 3D framework for Tkinter at `https://github.com/calroc/Tkinter3D`.

That concludes the chapter, and also our experiments with the Canvas widget. In the next chapter, we will look at some of the most commonly recurring themes of writing GUI applications, such as using a queue data structure, database programming, network programming, interprocess communication, use of the `asyncio` module, and a few other important concepts in programming.

Summary

Let's summarize the concepts we discussed in this chapter.

We built a screen saver and in the process saw how to implement animations on the Tkinter canvas. Next, we saw how to create Cartesian and polar plots on the canvas. We also saw how to embed `matplotlib` plots on a Tkinter window.

We then implemented a basic gravity simulation that showed how we could take a physical model and implement it using a Tkinter canvas. We got a glimpse into the implementation of Voronoi diagrams, which are being used to model and solve so many practical real-world problems.

We also build some nice visualizations such as the Mandelbrot set and Phyllotaxies.

Finally, we learned how to use a Tkinter canvas to draw and animate 3D graphics using transformation matrices.

QA section

Here are a few questions to reflect upon:

- How do you convert between polar and Cartesian coordinates? When should we prefer one coordinate system over the other?
- How do you animate on a Tkinter canvas? What determines the speed of the animation?
- How do we model real-world phenomena on a Tkinter canvas using differential equations?
- What are some real-world applications of fractals?
- Fractals are still under active research. Can you find out more about some cutting-edge technology that relies on the use of fractals?
- What are some of the real-world applications of Voronoi diagrams?
- How can we extend our 3D cube program to show meshes of other objects—say the model of a car, or a human body, or a real-world object?

Further reading

A close cousin of the Mandelbrot set is the Julia set. Read about the Julia set and then modify `8.07_Mandelbrot.py` to produce a Julia set. Fractals are a very interesting topic to study and a lot of the maths behind them is still unexplored. Besides the fact that they are beautiful to look at, they are also used in a lot of practical applications. See `https://en.wikipedia.org/wiki/Fractal#Applications_in_technology`.

If fractals pique your interest, you can also take a look at other variants of the Mandelbrot set such as the Magnet 1 fractal and Buddhabrot.

If you are interested in learning more about chaotic behavior, try to plot Hénon's Function on a Tkinter canvas.

We modeled a spring pendulum and it worked in a deterministic manner. However, adding two pendulums together to form a double pendulum creates a dynamic system that is chaotic. Even though such systems follow the ordinary differential equation, the net outcome may vary immensely, even for a very small change in the initial condition. It may be worth trying to model a double pendulum by modifying our spring pendulum.

We used the built-in odeint method from `scipy`. However, we could have written our own variation using either the Euler's method or Runge-Kutta method. You can read more about these numerical methods for approximating ordinary differential equations over here: `https://en.wikipedia.org/wiki/Numerical_methods_for_ordinary_differential_equations`.

If neat or intriguing visualizations looks like a fun thing to do, here are a few more interesting canvas projects that you can undertake: Barnsley fern, the cellular automata, the Lorenz attractor, and simulating tearable cloth with verlet integration.

Ray tracing is another powerful but very simple to implement 3D rendering technique that can be easily implemented in about 100 lines of code.

9
Multiple Fun Projects

By now, we have explored most of the important features of Tkinter. Let's use this chapter to explore aspects of programming that, though not core to Tkinter, are often encountered while writing GUI applications.

In this chapter, we will develop several small applications from different domains. The applications we will build here include:

- A snake game application
- A weather reporter application
- A port scanner application
- A chat application
- A phone book application
- An ultrasound distance scanner application

Some of the key objectives of the chapter are:

- To learn to use `Queue` module to avoid race conditions and other synchronization issues involved in writing multithreaded programs
- To understand the basics of data mining over the network
- To understand socket programming and to learn the basics of server-client architecture
- To learn database programming
- To learn to use `asyncio` with Tkinter
- To learn how to interface and interact with external hardware components using serial communication

Technical requirements

Most of the projects in this chapter rely on the standard libraries and do not require anything extra. The exception is the ultrasonic range finder project, which requires an Arduino board and an ultrasonic range finder sensor. The hardware is relatively cheap (under 10 dollars). You may also decide not to buy the hardware and still read the project to understand how serial communication takes place between two pieces of equipment.

In addition, you will also need to download and install the Arduino **integrated development environment** (**IDE**), the details of which will be discussed in the project itself.

Building a Snake game

Let's now build a simple Snake game. As usual, we will be making use of the `Canvas` widget to provide the platform for our Snake program. We will use `canvas.create_line` to draw our snake and `canvas.create_rectangle` to draw the snake food.

The primary objective of this project is to learn how to use `Queue` module as a **synchronization technique** in a multithreaded application.

Writing a multithreaded application poses the challenge of synchronization between different threads. When multiple threads try to access shared data simultaneously, the data is likely to get corrupted or modified in ways that were not intended in the program. This is called a **race condition**.

Understanding a race condition

The `9.01_race_condition.py` code demonstrates a race condition. The program is as follows:

```
import threading

class RaceConditionDemo:
  def __init__(self):
    self.shared_var = 0
    self.total_count = 100000
    self.demo_of_race_condition()

  def increment(self):
```

```
      for i in range(self.total_count):
        self.shared_var += 1

  def decrement(self):
    for i in range(self.total_count):
      self.shared_var -= 1

  def demo_of_race_condition(self):
    t1 = threading.Thread(target=self.increment)
    t2 = threading.Thread(target=self.decrement)
    t1.start()
    t2.start()
    t1.join()
    t2.join()
    print("value of shared_var after all increments & decrements :",
self.shared_var)

if __name__ == "__main__":
  for i in range(100):
    RaceConditionDemo()
```

The preceding code consists of two methods named `increment` and `decrement` that both operate on a single shared variable named `shared_var`. These two methods are called from separate threads.

One would expect that an equal number of increments and decrements on a shared variable would produce no change in its value at the end. However, when you run this program, say 100 times as before, it produces a different value for the shared variable in each consecutive run. This is a classic example for how a race condition can make the output of a program nondeterministic.

Race conditions occur because we cannot predict the thread execution order at all. The operating system does it very randomly and so the execution order of threads varies each time the program is run.

Using synchronization primitives

To handle this complexity, the `threading` module provides some synchronization primitives, such as locks, joins, semaphores, events, and condition variables.

`9.02_lock_demo.py` slightly modifies the preceding code by introducing a `lock` using this line:

```
self.lock = threading.Lock()
```

Next, every time `shared_variable` is to be modified, it is done after acquiring a `lock`. The `lock` is released when the variable has been modified, as shown in the following code:

```
self.lock.acquire()
self.shared_var += 1
self.lock.release()
```

This enables us to avoid a race condition. Since this code operates with a `lock`, it produces no change in the shared variable after an equal number of increments and decrements.

It seemed easy to use the `lock` mechanism to avoid a race condition. However, as the complexity of a program grows, there are many places where a variable may be modified. Tracking large code bases for places where a variable may be changed is often a difficult task.

Using queues

In most cases, it is safer and simpler to use **queues**. Simply put, a queue is a compound memory structure that is thread-safe. Queues effectively channel access to a resource to multiple threads in a sequential order, and are a recommended design pattern that uses threads for most of the scenarios that require concurrency.

The `Queue` module provides a way to implement different kinds of queuing, such as FIFO (default implementation), LIFO queues, and priority queues, and this module comes with a built-in implementation of all the locking semantics required for running multithreaded programs.

Here's a quick roundup of the basic usage of the `Queue` module:

```
my_queue = Queue() #create empty queue
my_queue.put(data)# put items into queue
task = my_queue.get () #get the next item in the queue
my_queue.task_done() # called when a queued task has completed
my_queue.join() # awaits for all tasks in queue to get completed
```

Let's see a simple demonstration of using a queue to implement a multithreaded application (see `9.03_threading_with_queue.py`):

```python
import queue
import threading

class Consumer(threading.Thread):

    def __init__(self, queue):
        threading.Thread.__init__(self)
        self.queue = queue

    def run(self):
        while True:
            task = self.queue.get()
            self.do_task(task)

    def do_task(self, task):
        print ('doing task{}'.format(task))
        self.queue.task_done()


def producer(tasks):
    my_queque = queue.Queue()
    # populate queue with tasks
    for task in tasks:
        my_queque.put(task)
    # create 6 threads and pass the queue as its argument
    for i in range(6):
        my_thread = Consumer(my_queque)
        my_thread.daemon = True
        my_thread.start()
    # wait for the queue to finish
    my_queque.join()
    print ('all tasks completed')

if __name__ == "__main__":
    tasks = 'A B C D E F'.split()
    producer(tasks)
```

The description of the code is as follows:

- We first create a `Consumer` class, which inherits from the `threading` module of Python. The `__init__` method takes in a queue as its argument.

- We then override the `run` method of the `threading` module to get each item from the queue using `queue.get()`, which is then passed on to the `task_handler` method, which actually executes the task specified in the current queue item. In our example, it does nothing useful except print the name of the task.
- After the work is done on a particular thread by our `task_handler` method, it sends a signal to the queue telling it that the task has been completed using the `queue.task_done()` method.
- Outside our `Consumer` class, we create an empty queue in our `producer()` module function. This queue is populated with a list of tasks using `queue.put(task)`.
- We then create six different threads and pass this populated queue as its argument. Now that the tasks are handled by the queue, all threads automatically ensure that the tasks are completed in the sequence in which they are encountered by the threads, without causing any deadlocks or two different threads trying to work on the same queued task.
- At the time of creating each thread, we also create a pool of daemon threads using `my_thread.daemon = True`. Doing this passes control to our main program once all threads have completed execution. If you comment out the line, the program would still run, but would fail to exit after all threads have completed executing the tasks in the queue. Without the daemon threads, you'd have to keep track of all the threads and tell them to exit before your program could completely quit.
- Finally, the `queue.join()` method ensures that the program flow waits there until all queued tasks are actually done and the queue is empty.

Building the Snake game

With that background information about using a queue to handle multithreaded applications, let's build our Snake game.

Upon completion, the game will look as follows:

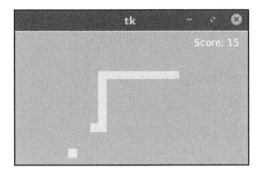

The View class

Let's start coding our game by first creating a basic `View` class. This class will be responsible for creating the GUI, checking for *game over* logic, and most importantly acting as the consumer, taking items from the queue and processing them to update the view (see `9.04_game_of_snake.py`):

```
class View(Tk):
    def __init__(self, queue):
        Tk.__init__(self)
        self.queue = queue
        self.create_gui()

    def create_gui(self):
        self.canvas = Canvas(self, width=495, height=305, bg='#FF75A0')
        self.canvas.pack()
        self.snake = self.canvas.create_line((0, 0), (0,0),fill='#FFCC4C',
            width=10)
        self.food = self.canvas.create_rectangle(0, 0, 0, 0,
            fill='#FFCC4C', outline='#FFCC4C')
        self.points_earned = self.canvas.create_text(455, 15, fill='white',
            text='Score:0')
```

The preceding code should be mostly familiar to you by now as we have written similar code in the past. Note, however, that rather than passing the root instance as an argument to its __init__ method, our `View` class now inherits from the `Tk` class. The line `Tk.__init__(self)` ensures that the root window is available to all methods of this class. This way we can avoid writing a root attribute on every line by referencing root simply as `self`.

This class will also have code to process items put in the queue. We will code the rest of this class after we have coded the classes that put items in the queue.

The Food class

Next, we will create the Food class (see 9.04_game_of_snake.py):

```python
class Food:

def __init__(self, queue):
 self.queue = queue
 self.generate_food()

def generate_food(self):
 x = random.randrange(5, 480, 10)
 y = random.randrange(5, 295, 10)
 self.position = (x, y)
 rectangle_position = (x - 5, y - 5, x + 5, y + 5)
 self.queue.put({'food': rectangle_position})
```

The description of the code is as follows:

- Because we want to process all data centrally from within a queue, we pass the queue as an argument to the __init__ method of the Food class.
- The __init__ method calls another method called generate_food, which is responsible for generating the snake food at random positions on the canvas.
- The generate_food method generates a random (x, y) position on the canvas. However, because the place where the coordinates coincide is just a small point on the canvas, it would be barely visible. We, therefore, generate an expanded coordinate (rectangle_position) ranging from five values less than the (x, y) coordinate up to five values higher than the same coordinate. Using this range, we can create a small rectangle on the canvas that would be easily visible and would represent our food.
- However, we do not create the rectangle here. Instead, we pass the coordinates for the food (rectangle) into our queue using queue.put.

The Snake class

Let's now create the `Snake` class. We have already passed a task to generate our food to the central queue. However, no additional thread was involved in the task. We could also generate our `Snake` class without using threads. However, because we are talking about ways to implement multithreaded applications, let's implement our `Snake` class to work from a separate thread (see `9.04_game_of_snake.py`):

```python
class Snake(threading.Thread):
  is_game_over = False

  def __init__(self, queue):
    threading.Thread.__init__(self)
    self.queue = queue
    self.daemon = True
    self.points_earned = 0
    self.snake_points = [(495, 55), (485, 55), (475, 55), (465, 55),
      (455, 55)]
    self.food = Food(queue)
    self.direction = 'Left'
    self.start()

  def run(self):
    while not self.is_game_over:
      self.queue.put({'move': self.snake_points})
    time.sleep(0.1)
    self.move()

  def on_keypress(self, e):
    self.direction = e.keysym

  def move(self):
   new_snake_point = self.calculate_new_coordinates()
   if self.food.position == new_snake_point:
     self.points_earned += 1
     self.queue.put({'points_earned': self.points_earned})
     self.food.generate_food()
   else:
     self.snake_points.pop(0)
   self.check_game_over(new_snake_point)
   self.snake_points.append(new_snake_point)

  def calculate_new_coordinates(self):
    last_x, last_y = self.snake_points[-1]
    if self.direction == 'Up':
      new_snake_point = (last_x, last_y - 10)
    elif self.direction == 'Down':
```

```
        new_snake_point = (last_x, last_y + 10)
    elif self.direction == 'Left':
        new_snake_point = (last_x - 10, last_y)
    elif self.direction == 'Right':
        new_snake_point = (last_x + 10, last_y)
    return new_snake_point

def check_game_over(self, snake_point):
    x, y = snake_point
    if not -5 < x < 505 or not -5 < y < 315 or snake_point in
self.snake_points:
        self.is_game_over = True
        self.queue.put({'game_over': True})
```

The description of the code is as follows:

- We create a class named Snake to run from a separate thread. This class takes the queue as its input arguments.
- We initialize the points earned by the player from zero and set the initial location of the snake using the attribute self.snake_points. Note that initially, the snake is 40 pixels long.
- Finally, we start the thread and create an infinite loop to call the move() method at small intervals. During every run of the loop, the method populates the queue with a dictionary having the key as move and the value equal to the updated position of the snake, through the self.snake_points attribute.
- First, the move method obtains the latest coordinates for the snake depending on the keyboard event. It uses a separate method called calculate_new_coordinates to get the latest coordinates.
- It then checks whether the location of the new coordinates coincides with the location of the food. If they match, it increases the score of the player by one and calls the Food class' generate_food method to generate a new food at a new location.
- If the current point does not coincide with the food coordinates, it deletes the first item from the snake coordinates using self.snake_points.pop(0).
- Then, it calls another method named check_game_over to check whether the snake collides with the wall or itself. If the snake does collide, it appends a new dictionary item in the queue with the value 'game_over':True.

- Finally, if the game is not over, it appends the new position of the snake to the list `self.snake_points`. This is automatically added to the queue, because we have defined `self.queue.put({'move': self.snake_points } )` in the `Snake` class's `run()` method to update every `0.1` seconds as long as the game is not over.

Queue handler

Now that the queue is getting populated with various actionables, let's create the `queue_handler` method to process the items in the queue and update the `View` accordingly.

We define the `queue_handler()` method in our `View` class as follows:

```
def queue_handler(self):
 try:
   while True:
     task = self.queue.get_nowait()
     if 'game_over' in task:
       self.game_over()
     elif 'move' in task:
       points = [x for point in task['move'] for x in point]
       self.canvas.coords(self.snake, *points)
     elif 'food' in task:
       self.canvas.coords(self.food, *task['food'])
     elif 'points_earned' in task:
       self.canvas.itemconfigure(self.points_earned, text='Score:
                       {}'.format (task['points_earned']))
     self.queue.task_done()
 except queue.Empty:
   self.after(100, self.queue_handler)
```

The description for the code is as follows:

- The `queue_handler` method gets into an infinite loop looking for tasks in the queue using `task = self.queue.get_nowait()`. If the queue becomes empty, the loop is restarted using `canvas.after`.
- When we use `queue_get_nowait()`, the call does not block the calling thread until an item is available. It removes and returns an item from the queue, if available. If the queue is empty, it raises `Queue.Empty`.
- Once a task is fetched from the queue, the method checks its key.

- If the key is `game_over`, it calls another method named `game_over()` which we define next.
- If the key of the task is `move`, it uses `canvas.coords` to move the line to its new position.
- If the key is `points_earned`, it updates the score on the canvas.

When the execution of a task completes, it signals the thread with the `task_done()` method. Finally, we create the main loop as follows:

```python
def main():
    q = queue.Queue()
    gui = View(q)
    snake = Snake(q)
    for key in ("Left", "Right", "Up", "Down"):
        gui.bind("<Key-{}>".format(key), snake.on_keypress)
        gui.mainloop()

if __name__ == '__main__':
    main()
```

Our game is now functional. Go and try controlling the snake while keeping its stomach filled.

Creating a Weather Reporter application

Let's now build a simple Weather Reporter application. The weather data for any given location will be fetched from the network, suitably formatted, and presented to the user.

We will use a higher level module named `urllib` to fetch weather data from the web. The `urllib` module is part of Python's standard library and it provides an easy to use API for working with URLs. It has four submodules:

- `urllib.request`: For opening and reading URLs
- `urllib.error`: For handling exceptions raised by `urllib.request`
- `urllib.parse`: For parsing URLs
- `urllib.robotparser`: For parsing `robots.txt` files

With `urllib.request`, fetching the contents of a web page turns into three lines of code (see `9.05_urllib_demo.py`):

```python
import urllib.request
```

```
with urllib.request.urlopen('http://www.packtpub.com/') as f:
    print(f.read())
```

This prints the entire HTML source code or whatever is the response from the web page `http://www.packtpub.com`. This is, in essence, the core of mining the web for information.

Now that we know how to get data from a URL, let's apply it to building our Weather Reporter application. This application should take the location as an input from the user and fetch relevant weather-related data, as shown in the following screenshot:

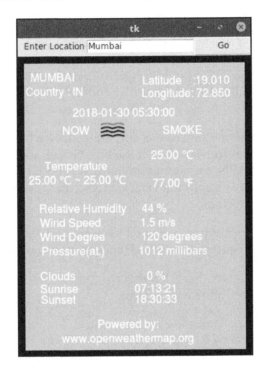

We create a class, `WeatherReporter`, and call it from outside the class within the `mainloop` (see the code of `9.06_weather_reporter.py`):

```
def main():
    root=Tk()
    WeatherReporter(root)
    root.mainloop()

if __name__ == '__main__':
    main()
```

We do not discuss the code for creating this GUI here, as we have done similar coding many times in all the the previous chapters. The weather data is displayed on a canvas (see `9.06_weather_reporter.py`):

When you specify a location and click on the **Go** button, it calls a command callback named `on_show_weather_button_clicked`.

We then fetch the weather data from a website.

There are two ways to fetch data from a website. The first method involves getting an HTML response from a website, and then parsing the received HTML response for data that is relevant to us. This type of data extraction is called **site scraping**.

Scrapy and **Beautiful Soup** are two popular site-scraping frameworks for extracting data from websites. You can find the official documentation of the two libraries at `http://scrapy.org/` and `http://www.crummy.com/software/BeautifulSoup/`.

Site scraping is a rather crude method that is employed only when a given website does not provide a structured way to retrieve data. On the other hand, some websites are willing to share data through a set of APIs, provided you query it for data using the specified URL structure. This is clearly more elegant than site scraping, because data is interchanged in a reliable and *mutually agreed* format.

For our Weather Reporter application, we want to query some weather channels for a given location, and in turn retrieve and display the data on our canvas.

Fortunately, there are several weather APIs that we can use. In our example, we will use the weather data provided by the following website:
`http://openweathermap.org/`

In order to use the API, you need to sign up for a free API key here:
`http://home.openweathermap.org/users/sign_up`

The `OpenWeatherMap` service provides free weather data and forecast APIs. This site collates weather data from more than 40,000 weather stations across the globe, and the data can be assessed by city name and geographic coordinates, or their internal city ID.

The website provides weather data in two data formats:

- **JSON (JavaScript Object Notation)**
- **XML (Extensible Markup Language)**

XML and JSON are two popular interchangeable data serialization formats widely used for interchanging data between different applications, which may be running on different platforms and using different programming languages, thus providing the benefit of interoperability.

JSON is simpler than XML, because its grammar is simpler and it maps more directly onto the data structures used in modern programming languages. JSON is better suited for exchanging data, but XML is good for exchanging documents.

The API documentation tells us of a query such as:

```
api.openweathermap.org/data/2.5/weather?q=London,uk&APPID={APIKEY}
```

The preceding code returns weather data for London in JSON format as follows:

```
{"coord":{"lon":-0.12574,"lat":51.50853},"sys":{"country":"GB","sunrise":13
77147503,"sunset":1377198481},"weather":[{"id":500,"main":"Rain",
"description": "light rain","icon":"10d"}],"base":"gdps
stations","main":{"temp":294.2, "pressure":1020,"humidity":88,
"temp_min":292.04,"temp_max":296.48},"wind":{"speed":1,"deg":0},"rain":{"1h
":0.25},"clouds":{"
all":40},"dt":1377178327,"id":2643743,"name":"London","cod":200}
```

The syntax of JSON is simple. Any piece of JSON data is a name/value pair and each piece of data is separated from the others by commas. JSON uses curly braces {} to hold objects and square brackets [ ] to hold arrays. Accordingly, we define a method to get the weather data in JSON format in our application (see 9.06_weather_reporter.py):

```
def get_data_from_url(self):
  try:
    params = urllib.parse.urlencode( {'q': self.location.get(), 'APPID':
self.APIKEY},
      encoding="utf-8")
    api_url =
('http://api.openweathermap.org/data/2.5/weather?{}'.format(params))
    with urllib.request.urlopen(api_url) as f:
      json_data = f.read()
      return json_data
  except IOError as e:
    messagebox.showerror('Unable to connect', 'Unable to connect %s' % e)
    sys.exit(1)
```

The description for the code is as follows:

- This method uses `urllib` to retrieve responses from the website. It returns the response in JSON format.
- Now, we'll start processing the JSON data. The weather data returned using the API is encoded in JSON format. We need to convert this data into the Python data type. Python provides a built-in `json` module that simplifies the process of encoding/decoding JSON data. We therefore import the `json` module into our current namespace.

Then, we'll use this module to convert the retrieved JSON data into the Python dictionary format (see `9.06_weather_reporter.py`):

```python
def json_to_dict(self, json_data):
  decoder = json.JSONDecoder()
  decoded_json_data = decoder.decode(json_data.decode("utf-8"))
  flattened_dict = {}
  for key, value in decoded_json_data.items():
    if key == 'weather':
      for ke, va in value[0].items():
        flattened_dict[str(ke)] =  str(va).upper()
      continue
    try:
      for k, v in value.items():
      flattened_dict[str(k)] = str(v).upper()
    except:
      flattened_dict[str(key)] = str(value).upper()
  return flattened_dict
```

Now that we have a dictionary of all weather-related information provided by the API, we simply display the retrieved weather data using `canvas.create_text` and `canvas.create_image`. The code for displaying the weather data is self-explanatory (see `9.06_weather_reporter.py`).

Our Weather Reporter application is now functional.

When you access a server from your Python program, it is very important to send requests after small time gaps. A typical Python program is capable of running several million instructions per second. However, the server that sends you the data at the other end is not equipped to work at that speed. If you knowingly or unknowingly send a large number of requests to a server within a short time span, you may prevent it from servicing its routine requests from normal web users. This constitutes what is called a **denial of service (DOS)** attack on the server. You may be banned or, in a worst case scenario, be sued for disrupting a server, if your program does not make a limited number of well-behaved requests.

To summarize the code for the Weather Reporter, we use the `urllib` module to query the weather API provided by our data provider. The data is fetched in JSON format. The JSON data is then decoded into a Python-readable format (dictionary).

The converted data is then displayed on the canvas using the `create_text` and `create_image` methods.

A simple socket demo

The goal of this project is to introduce you to the basics of network programming and how to use it in your GUI application.

Python has great support for network programming. At the lowest level, Python provides a `socket` module that lets you connect and interact with the network using a simple-to-use, object-oriented interface.

For those new to socket programming, **sockets** are the fundamental concept behind any kind of network communication done by your computer. For instance, when you type `www.packtpub.com` in your browser, the operating system on your computer opens a socket and connects to the remote server to fetch the web page for you. The same happens with any application that needs to connect to the network.

More specifically, sockets refer to a communications endpoint that is characterized by a five-element tuple that contains the following information:

```
(protocol, local address, local port, remote address, remote port)
```

This tuple must be unique for communication on a channel between a local machine and a remote machine.

Sockets may be connection-oriented or connectionless. Connection-oriented sockets allow for the flow of data to and fro as required. Connectionless sockets (or datagram sockets) allow only one message at a time to be transmitted, without an open connection.

Sockets can be classified into different types or families. The two most common socket families are AF_INET (for internet connections) and AF_UNIX for interprocess communications on a Unix machine. We will use AF_INET in our chat program.

This is the lowest level at which a programmer can access the network. Underneath the socket layer lie raw UDP and TCP connections, which are handled by your computer's operating system with no direct access points for programmers.

Let's take a brief look at some of the APIs available in the socket module:

API	Description
socket.socket (addressfamily=AF_INET, type=SOCK_STREAM, proto=0, fileno=None)	Creates a socket. The addressfamily represents the format for providing the address, normally the IP address; type is usually SOCK_STREAM for TCP or SOCK_DGRAM for the UDP connection protocol. The protocol number is usually zero and may be omitted. Returns a socket object.
socket.bind(address)	Associates a local address with a socket. The socket must not already be bound. (The format of the address depends on the address family defined when creating the socket.)
socket.listen(backlog)	Announces a willingness to accept connections. The backlog argument specifies the maximum number of queued connections and should be at least zero; the maximum value is system-dependent.
socket.accept()	Passively establishes an incoming connection. Before accepting, the socket must be bound to an address and listening for connections. Returns a (conn, address) pair, where conn is a new socket object usable to send and receive data on the connection, and address is the address bound to the socket on the other end of the connection.
socket.connect()	Actively attempts to establish a connection to a remote socket at the address.

`socket.send(bytes)/socket.sendall(bytes)`	Sends some data over the connection. Unlike `send()`, `sendall()`, this continues to send data from bytes until either all data has been sent or an error occurs. Returns `None` on success.
`socket.recv(bufsize)`	Receives some data over the connection. Returns a bytes object representing the data received. The maximum amount of data to be received at once is specified by `bufsize`.
`socket.close()`	Releases the connection. The underlying system resource (for example, a file descriptor) is also closed.

If you look at the `9.07_socket_demo.py` Python file in the code bundle of this project, you'll find that it sends a very obscure-looking `GET` request to fetch the contents from the URL in the following line of code:

```
message = "GET / HTTP/1.1 \r\nHost:" + host + "\r\n\r\nAccept:
text/html\r\n\r\n"
```

The data received from the server is also sent in packets, and it is our task to collect all the data and assemble it at our end.

Building a port scanner

Now that we know the basics of socket programming, let's build a port scanner.

Ports are to computers what entrances are to houses. A computer has 65,535 ports through which it can communicate with the outside world. Most of the ports are closed by default. However, typically computers need to keep certain ports open for other computers on the network to connect and communicate.

A port scanner then is software that scans all the ports of a computer to find out which ports of the computer are open and listening for incoming communications. Port scanning is used by network administrators to strengthen their security regimes, but it is also used by hackers to look for entry points to break into a computer.

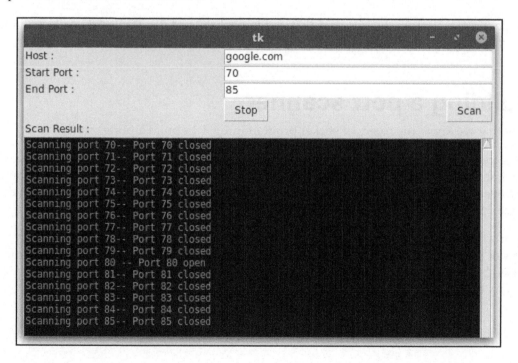

Before you get into scanning random website servers with this tool, it is important to know that port scanning without proper authorization is illegal in a few jurisdictions. Many ISPs ban port scanning. Furthermore, many websites have explicit policies banning any attempts at port scanning. There have been cases of convictions for unauthorized scans. You may even want to consult a lawyer if you are scanning third-party websites with this tool. Even if a website is silent about port scanning, it's always better to get authorization from a website before you scan its ports. Repeated scan attempts on a single target may also cause your IP address to be blocked by the administrators.

We recommend that you use this tool to analyze security vulnerabilities only on computers that you are authorized to scan, or on websites that have a liberal policy allowing for limited and non-disruptive scans.

With that disclaimer out of the way, let's get into building the port scanner. On completion, our port scanner will look as follows:

We do not discuss the code that creates the preceding GUI, as this should be easy for you. See `9.08_port_scanner.py` for the complete code. We instead discuss the code related to port scanning.

There are several techniques used for port scanning. TCP SYN scanning is the most commonly used technique. It exploits the three-way handshake protocol employed by TCP, which involves sending and receiving SYN, SYN-ACK, and ACK messages. Here, SYN stands for synchronize and ACK stands for acknowledge. Visit `https://en.wikipedia.org/wiki/Transmission_Control_Protocol` for more details on this three-way handshake protocol.

A TCP SYN scan involves sending a SYN packet as if you will make a real connection and then waiting for the response. A SYN/ACK response from the target means that the port is open. A RST (reset) response suggests that the port is closed. If no response is received, the port is considered to be filtered.

Another common technique, and the one we will use for port scanning, is called the TCP connect scanner. This involves requesting a connection to the target operating system using the connect system call. This is exactly how web browsers and other high-level clients make a connection.

The connect command establishes an actual connection to the target, as opposed to the half-open scan that TCP SYN scan does. Since a complete connection is established, a connect scan is slower and requires more transmission than an SYN scan to find out whether a port is open. Furthermore, the target machine is more likely to log the connection and it is therefore not as stealthy as an SYN scan.

Accordingly, the code that checks whether a port is open is defined as follows (see `9.08_port_scanner.py`):

```
def is_port_open(self,url, port):
  try:
    s = socket.socket(socket.AF_INET, socket.SOCK_STREAM)
    s.settimeout(1)
    s.connect((socket.gethostbyname(url), port))
    s.close()
    return True
  except:
    return False
```

Note that the preceding code simply uses `socket.connect` to make a connection to probe the port

We call the preceding method from another method, `start_scan`, which simply loops over each of the ports in the range provided by the user:

```
def start_scan(self, url, start_port, end_port):
  for port in range (start_port, end_port+1):
    if not self.stop:
      self.output_to_console("Scanning port{}".format(port))
      if self.is_port_open(url, port):
        self.output_to_console(" -- Port {} open \n".format(port))
      else:
        self.output_to_console("-- Port {} closed \n".format(port))
```

Finally, we do not want a call to this method to block our Tkinter main loop. Therefore, we call the preceding method in a new thread as follows:

```
def scan_in_a_new_thread(self):
  url = self.host_entry.get()
  start_port = int(self.start_port_entry.get())
  end_port = int(self.end_port_entry.get())
  thread = Thread(target=self.start_scan, args=(url, start_port,
    end_port ))
  thread.start()
```

The preceding method gets the values entered by the user and passes them as arguments to the `start_scan` method in a new thread.

The rest of the code simply creates and updates the GUI with the result and should be self-explanatory. This concludes the port scanner project.

Building a chat application

Next, let's build a multi-client chat room. The goal of this program is to explore socket programming in further detail. This section also implements and discusses the client-server architecture that is so common in all network programs.

Our chat program will consist of a chat server, which listens for and receives all incoming messages on a given port.

It also maintains a list of chat clients that connect to the server. It then broadcasts any incoming messages to all connected clients:

Let's start with the code for the chat server.

A server runs on a remote host and has a socket bound to a specific port number. The server just waits, listening to the socket for a client to make a connection request.

Here's the code for a chat server (see `9.09_chat_server.py`):

```python
class ChatServer:
  clients_list = []
  last_received_message = ""

  def __init__(self):
    self.create_listening_server()

  def create_listening_server(self):
    self.server_socket = socket.socket(socket.AF_INET, socket.SOCK_STREAM)
    local_ip = '127.0.0.1'
    local_port = 10319
    self.server_socket.setsockopt(socket.SOL_SOCKET,
      socket.SO_REUSEADDR, 1)
    self.server_socket.bind((local_ip, local_port))
    print("Listening for incoming messages..")
    self.server_socket.listen(5)
    self.receive_messages_in_a_new_thread()

  def receive_messages_in_a_new_thread(self):
    while 1:
      client = so, (ip, port) = self.server_socket.accept()
      self.add_to_clients_list(client)
      print ('Connected to ', ip , ':' , str(port))
      t = threading.Thread(target=self.receive_messages, args=(so,))
```

```
        t.start()

    def receive_messages(self, so):
      while True:
        incoming_buffer = so.recv(256)
        if not incoming_buffer: break
        self.last_received_message = incoming_buffer.decode('utf-8')
        self.broadcast_to_all_clients(so)
        so.close()

    def broadcast_to_all_clients(self, senders_socket):
        for client in self.clients_list:
            socket, (ip, port) = client
            if socket is not senders_socket:
                socket.sendall(self.last_received_message.encode('utf-8'))

    def add_to_clients_list(self, client):
        if client not in self.clients_list:
            self.clients_list.append(client)

if __name__ == "__main__":
ChatServer()
```

The description of the preceding code is as follows:

- We create a TCP socket with an address family of IPv4 using the line `self.server_socket = socket(AF_INET, SOCK_STREAM)`. The IPv4 socket uses a 32-bit number to represent the address size. It is the most popular addressing scheme and accounts for most current internet traffic. IPv6 is a newer numbering system with a 128-bit address size, thereby providing a much larger pool of addresses. IPv6 has seen some adoption but it has not yet become the mainstream standard.

- The `SOCK_STREAM` parameter means that we will be using a TCP connection for the communication. Another less popular option is to use `SOCK_DGRAM`, which refers to the UDP mode of transmission.

- TCP is a more reliable protocol for communication than UDP as it offers a guarantee against packet loss. It also takes care of the proper ordering of bytes at the receiving end. If we use a UDP protocol, we will have to take care of handling packet loss, duplication, and the ordering of packets at the receiving end.

- We used `socket.bind(('127.0.01', 10319))` in the preceding code to bind the socket. We could have alternatively used `socket.bind ((socket.gethostname( ), 10319)` so that the socket would have been visible to the outside world. Alternatively, we could have specified an empty string such as `socket.bind((' ', 10319))` to make the socket reachable by any address the machine could have.

- The `socket.setsockopt(SOL_SOCKET, SO_REUSEADDR, 1)` line of code allows other sockets to `bind()` to this local port, unless there is an active socket already bound to the port. This lets us get around the `Address already in use` error message when a server is restarted after a crash.

- The line `self.server_socket.accept()` returns a value of the form `(socket, (ip, port))` as soon as a remote client connects to the server. Each client is then uniquely identified by the following data: `(socket, (ip, port))`.

- The line `Thread(target=self.receive_messages, args=(so,))` receives each new message on a new thread.

- Finally, the line `socket.sendall(self.last_received_message.encode('utf-8'))` sends the message to individual clients.

- The `receive_messages` method receives messages using the `socket.recv` method. The `socket.recv` method receives messages in buffers. It is your responsibility to call the method again and again until the entire message has been dealt with. When the `socket.recv` method returns 0 bytes, it means that the sender has closed the connection. We then break out of the infinite loop and get the complete message from the buffer.

Also note that message transmission over the network occurs in bytes.

Any message that we send must be converted to byte form using `outgoing_message.encode('utf-8')`. Similarly, any message that we receive from the network must be converted from bytes to a string or any other format.

To convert bytes to a string, we use `incoming_bytes.decode('utf-8')`.

Our chat server is now ready. Next, let's build the chat client.

Our chat client should connect to the remote server and send a message to the server. It should also be listening for any incoming messages from the central chat server. We do not reproduce the entire code for our chat client. Specifically, we omit the code that produces the GUI for our chat client as we have coded similar widgets in the past.

The partial code in our chat client that sends and receives messages to and from the chat server is as follows (see `9.10_chat_client.py`):

```
class ChatClient:
  client_socket = None
  last_received_message = None

  def __init__(self, root):
    self.root = root
    self.initialize_socket()
    self.initialize_gui()
    self.listen_for_incoming_messages_in_a_thread()

  def initialize_socket(self):
    self.client_socket = socket(AF_INET, SOCK_STREAM)
    remote_ip = '127.0.0.1'
    remote_port = 10319
    self.client_socket.connect((remote_ip, remote_port))

  def listen_for_incoming_messages_in_a_thread(self):
    t = Thread(target=self.recieve_message_from_server,
    args=(self.client_socket,))
    t.start()

  def recieve_message_from_server(self, so):
    while True:
      buf = so.recv(256)
      if not buf:
        break
      self.chat_transcript_area.insert('end',buf.decode('utf-8') + '\n')
      self.chat_transcript_area.yview(END)
    so.close()

  def send_chat(self):
    senders_name = self.name_widget.get().strip() + ":"
    data = self.enter_text_widget.get(1.0, 'end').strip()
    message = (senders_name + data).encode('utf-8')
    self.chat_transcript_area.insert('end', message.decode('utf-8') + '\n')
    self.chat_transcript_area.yview(END)
    self.client_socket.send(message)
    self.enter_text_widget.delete(1.0, 'end')
    return 'break'
```

This code is very similar to the code of our chat server. Here's a short description of the code:

- We first create a socket using `socket(AF_INET, SOCK_STREAM)`
- We then connect the socket to the remote IP and the remote port of our chat server using `socket.connect()`
- We receive messages from the server using `socket.recv()`
- We send messages to the server using `socket.send()`

Note that when a client attempts to connect to the server using the `socket.connect` method, the operating system will assign a unique but random port to identify the client when a message is returned by the server.

The port numbers from 0 to 1023 are referred to as the well-known ports, reserved ports, or system ports. They are used by the operating system to provide widely used network services. For example, port 21 is reserved for FTP services, port 80 is reserved for HTTP services, port 22 is reserved for SSH and SFTP, and port 443 is reserved for a secure HTTP service (HTTPS) over TLS/SSL.

The random port that the operating system assigns to our client is selected from a pool of ports that are above the system-reserved ports. The list of all reserved ports can be found at `https://en.wikipedia.org/wiki/List_of_TCP_and_UDP_port_numbers`.

The full code of the chat client can be found in `9.10_chat_client.py`. The chat is now functional, but note that we have not coded the logic for removing users from the `clients_list` in `ChatServer`. This means that even if you close a chat window, the chat server will still try to send a chat message to the closed client as we have not removed the client from the server. We will not implement it here, but should you wish to implement this, you can easily override the window's `close` method and send a message to `ChatServer` to delete the client from the client list.

That concludes the chat application project.

Creating a phone book application

Let's now build a simple phone book application that allows the user to store names and phone numbers.

The main learning objective for this project relates to being able to use a relational database with Tkinter to store and manipulate records. We have already seen some basic examples of object persistence with serialization. Relational databases extend this persistence using rules of relational algebra to store data in tables.

Python provides database interfaces for a wide range of database engines. Some of the commonly used database engines include MySQL, SQLite, PostgreSQL, Oracle, Ingres, SAP DB, Informix, Sybase, Firebird, IBM DB2, Microsoft SQL Server, and Microsoft Access.

We will use SQLite to store data for our phone book application.

SQLite is a serverless, zero-configuration, self-contained SQL database engine suitable for developing embedded applications. The source code for SQLite is in the public domain, which makes it freely available for use in all sorts of commercial and non-commercial projects.

Unlike many other SQL databases, SQLite does not require running a separate server process. Instead, SQLite stores all the data directly onto flat files that get stored on a computer disk. These files are easily portable across different platforms, making it a very popular choice for smaller and simpler database implementation requirements.

Python comes with a built-in standard library for SQLite3 support. However, we need to download the SQLite3 command-line tool that lets us create, modify, and access the database using a command line. The command-line shell for Windows, Linux, and macOS can be downloaded from `http://sqlite.org/download.html`.

Following the instructions on the website, install the SQLite command shell into any location of your choice.

Let's now implement our phone book application. The application will look as follows:

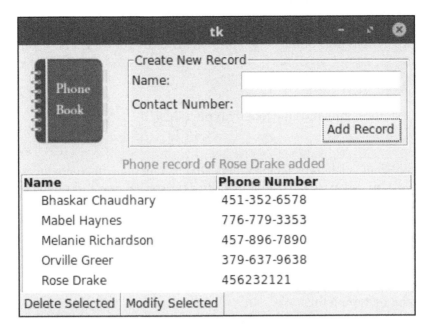

The application will demonstrate some of the common operations involved in database programming. The user should be able to create new records, read existing records, update existing records, and delete records from the database using this application. Together, these activities constitute what are known as **CRUD (Create, Read, Update, and Delete)** operations on a database.

In order to create the database, we open the command-line tool of our operating system. Within the command line, we first navigate to the directory where we need to create the new database file. In order to create the database, we simply use this command:

```
sqlite3 phonebook.db
```

This creates a database file named phonebook.db in the folder from which we execute the command. It also displays a message similar to the following:

```
SQLite version 3.7.17 2018-01-31 00:56:22
Enter ".help" for instructions
Enter SQL statements terminated with a ";"
sqlite>
```

We have now created a database named `phonebook.db`. However, the database file is currently empty. It does not contain any tables or any data. So, we get no results if we run this command:

```
sqlite> .tables
```

For now, let's exit the command-line tool by typing this:

```
sqlite> .exit
```

We want to store contacts in our database, and that is why we will create the `contacts` table. Our database table should store a person's name and phone number. In addition, it is good practice to keep a unique identification number for each person or each entry in the table. This is because multiple people might have the same name or same contact number.

To create a table within our `phonebook.db` database, we again open the command-line tool and navigate to the directory where we had created the database. We again get into the SQLite3 terminal by typing this:

```
sqlite3 phonebook.db
```

This time, a new database is not created. Rather, the command now opens the existing `phonebook.db` database because it is already present on the disk.

Next, we create a table named contacts, and add three columns to the table from the command line:

```
sqlite> CREATE TABLE contacts
(
contactid INTEGER PRIMARY KEY AUTOINCREMENT,
name STRING NOT NULL,
contactnumber INTEGER NOT NULL
);
```

You can verify the contacts table was created by typing the following command:

```
sqlite>.table
```

This prints the name of all the tables present in the currently open database. You will get the following output:

```
sqlite>.table
contacts
```

Let's first create a basic GUI that will let us add, view, delete, and modify the records. We create a class named phoneBook and create all GUI widgets within it.

We do not discuss the entire code that creates the GUI as we have coded similar structures in the past. However, we use a new ttk widget named Treeview. The code for creating Treeview is as follows (9.11_phonebook.py):

```
def create_tree_view(self):
  self.tree = ttk.Treeview(height=5, columns=2)
  self.tree.grid(row=4, column=0, columnspan=2)
  self.tree.heading('#0', text='Name', anchor=W)
  self.tree.heading(2, text='Phone Number', anchor=W)
```

To add items to Treeview, we use the following code:

```
self.tree.insert('', 0, text=row[1], values=row[2])
```

To get all items in Treeview, we use the code:

```
items = self.tree.get_children()
```

To delete items from Treeview, we use the code:

```
self.tree.delete(item)
```

Next, let's prepare the code to query our database:

```
db_filename = 'phonebook.db'

def execute_db_query(self, query, parameters=()):
  with sqlite3.connect(self.db_filename) as conn:
    cursor = conn.cursor()
    query_result = cursor.execute(query, parameters)
    conn.commit()
  return query_result
```

The code description is as follows:

- The method establishes a connection to the phonebook.db database we created earlier.
- The next line, cursor = conn.cursor(), creates a cursor object. The cursor is a control structure that is required as per SQL standards, and it enables us to traverse the records in a database.

- The next line, `cursor.execute(query)`, executes the query against the database.
- The line `conn.commit()` actually commits/saves these changes to the database.

We can now use the preceding method to execute CRUD queries on the database.

Creating a new record

A new record needs to be created every time a user enters a new name and a phone number in the entry widgets provided, and then clicks on the **Add Record** button.

The database query for adding a new record is as follows:

```
query = 'INSERT INTO contacts VALUES(NULL,?, ?)'
parameters = (self.namefield.get(), self.numfield.get())
self.execute_db_query(query, parameters)
```

Reading from the database

The database query for reading all records from the database is as follows:

```
query = 'SELECT * FROM contacts ORDER BY name desc'
phone_book_entries = self.execute_db_query(query)
```

The preceding variable, `phone_book_entries`, contains a list of all the records from the database.

Updating records

To update the phone number of an existing contact, we use the following code:

```
query = 'UPDATE contacts SET contactnumber=? WHERE contactnumber=? AND
name=?'
parameters = (newphone, old_phone_number, name)
self.execute_db_query(query, parameters)
```

Deleting records

To delete the phone number of an existing contact, we use the following code:

```
query = 'DELETE FROM contacts WHERE name = ?'
self.execute_db_query(query, (name,))
```

The rest of the code is the supporting GUI. See `9.11_phonebook.py` for the complete code. We have now completed coding a basic phone book application.

We have seen how to create a database, add tables to the database, and query the database to add, modify, delete, and view items in the database. Our phone book application has demonstrated how to execute basic CRUD operations on a database.

Furthermore, due to the similarity of basic database operations, you can now consider working with other database systems, such as MySQL, PostgreSQL, Oracle, Ingres, SAP DB, Informix, Sybase, Firebird, IBM DB2, Microsoft SQL Server, and Microsoft Access.

Using asyncio with Tkinter

Starting with Python 3.4, a new module named `asyncio` was introduced as a Python standard module.

The term **Asyncio** is made by adding two words: async + I/O. Async is about concurrency, which means doing more than one thing at a time. I/O, on the other hand, refers to handling I/O bound tasks. A **bound task** means the thing that keeps your program busy. If, for instance, you are doing computation-intensive math processing, the processor is taking most of the time—and it is, therefore, a **CPU bound task**. On the contrary, if you are waiting for a result from the network, result from the database, or an input from the user, the task is **I/O bound**.

So in a nutshell, the `asyncio` module provides concurrency, particularly for I/O bound tasks. Concurrency ensures that you do not have to wait for I/O bound results.

Let's say you have to fetch content from multiple URLs, then process the fetched content to extract the title and display it in a Tkinter window. Now you obviously cannot fetch the content in the same thread that runs the Tkinter main loop, as that would make the root window unresponsive while the content is fetched.

So one of the options is to spawn a new thread for each URL. While this can be an option, it is not a very scalable one as spawning thousands or more threads at a time can lead to a lot of code complexity. We already saw a demo of a race condition in the beginning of the current chapter (9.01_race_condition.py), where running multiple threads can make it difficult to control the shared state. Furthermore, as context switching is an expensive and time-consuming affair, the program can become laggy after spawning just a few threads.

Here's where asyncio comes to our rescue. In contrast to multithreading, which relies on threading, asyncio uses a concept of event loops.

To demonstrate, here is a Tkinter program that on the click of a button simulates fetching 10 URLs:

```python
from tkinter import Tk, Button
import asyncio
import threading
import random

def asyncio_thread(event_loop):
  print('The tasks of fetching multiple URLs begins')
  event_loop.run_until_complete(simulate_fetch_all_urls())

def execute_tasks_in_a_new_thread(event_loop):
  """ Button-Event-Handler starting the asyncio part. """
  threading.Thread(target=asyncio_thread, args=(event_loop, )).start()

async def simulate_fetch_one_url(url):
  """ We simulate fetching of URL by sleeping for a random time """
  seconds = random.randint(1, 8)
  await asyncio.sleep(seconds)
  return 'url: {}\t fetched in {} seconds'.format(url, seconds)

async def simulate_fetch_all_urls():
  """ Creating and starting 10 i/o bound tasks. """
  all_tasks = [simulate_fetch_one_url(url) for url in range(10)]
  completed, pending = await asyncio.wait(all_tasks)
  results = [task.result() for task in completed]
  print('\n'.join(results))

def check_if_button_freezed():
  print('This button is responsive even when a list of i/o tasks are in progress')

def main(event_loop):
  root = Tk()
  Button( master=root, text='Fetch All URLs',
```

```
                command=lambda: execute_tasks_in_a_new_thread(event_loop)).pack()
    Button(master=root, text='This will not Freeze',
                        command=check_if_button_freezed).pack()
    root.mainloop()

if __name__ == '__main__':
    event_loop = asyncio.get_event_loop()
    main(event_loop)
```

Here's a brief description of the code (9.12_async_demo.py):

- The first step in using the `asyncio` module is to construct an event loop using the code `event_loop = asyncio.get_event_loop()`. Internally, this `event_loop` will schedule all tasks assigned to it using coroutines and futures to do the I/O bound tasks in an asynchronous manner.
- We pass this `event_loop` as an argument to the Tkinter root window, so that it can use this event loop for scheduling async tasks.
- The method that is in charge of doing the I/O bound task is then defined by appending the keyword `async` in front of the method definition. Essentially, any method that is to be executed from the event loop must be appended with the keyword `async`.
- The method simulates a time-taking I/O blocking task using `await asyncio.sleep(sec)`. In a real case, you will perhaps use this to fetch the contents of a URL or perform a similar I/O blocking task.
- We start executing the async tasks in a new thread. This single thread executes the list of tasks using the `event_loop.run_until_complete(simulate_fetch_all_urls())` command. Note that this is different from creating one thread each for each of the tasks. In this case, we are only creating a single thread to isolate it from the Tkinter main loop.
- The line `all_tasks = [simulate_fetch_one_url(url) for url in range(10)]` combines all the async tasks into a list. This list of all I/O bound tasks is then passed on to `completed, pending = await asyncio.wait(all_tasks)`, which waits for all tasks to be completed in a non-blocking manner. Once all the tasks are completed, the results are populated in the `completed` variable.
- We get the results of individual tasks using `results = [task.result() for task in completed]`.
- We finally print out all the results to the console.

The benefit of using `asyncio` is that we do not have to spawn one thread for each task and as a result, the code does not have to context switch for each individual task. Thus, using `asyncio` we can scale up to fetch thousands of URLs without slowing down our program and without worrying about managing results from each thread individually.

This concludes our brief discussion on using the `asyncio` module with Tkinter.

Interfacing with hardware/serial communication

The **internet of things (IoT)** is now becoming a reality. We are seeing a glimpse of IoT in smart medical devices, driverless cars, smart factories, and smart homes. A large number of such IoT applications are built around the idea of capturing data with sensors and actuators.

The rise of IoT can largely be attributed to the rise in popularity of microcontrollers, which make it very easy to test and build product prototypes for such embedded systems. A microcontroller is a self-contained device with a built-in processor and a programmable memory. Most typical microcontrollers provide general purpose input/output pins which can be used either to receive data from sensors or to send data based on some program that is uploaded to the microcontoller.

In this project, we will use one of the most popular microcontrollers—the Arduino Uno—to demonstrate how to build an application that can read data from an external device. We will build an Ultrasonic Range Finder. If you find this project interesting, you can buy the hardware and build it as well—the total cost of this project is less than five dollars. However, if you do not intend to implement it, you can merely read through this section. Our primary objective here is to show how to get data from external hardware into Tkinter using what is known as serial communication.

Hardware

To begin with, we need an Arduino Uno board (or any other Arduino board). We also need an ultrasonic range finder sensor. A quick web search shows hundreds of rangefinder sensors for less than a quarter of a dollar. We use a sensor named HC-SR04-Ultrasonic Range Finder, but just about any other sensor would do. The sensor we have chosen provides a range-finding capability for distances in a 2 cm - 300 cm range, with an accuracy of up to 3 mm.

These sensors use sonar to determine the distance to an object, just as dolphins and bats do. Here's how the sensor calculates the distance. The module has two units. The transmitter transmits ultrasound, while a receiver reads any ultrasound that reflects back. Since the speed of ultrasound is fixed and known, by calculating the time between transmission and reflection, we can calculate the distance of the object that reflected the ultrasound.

Here's how the hardware is set up:

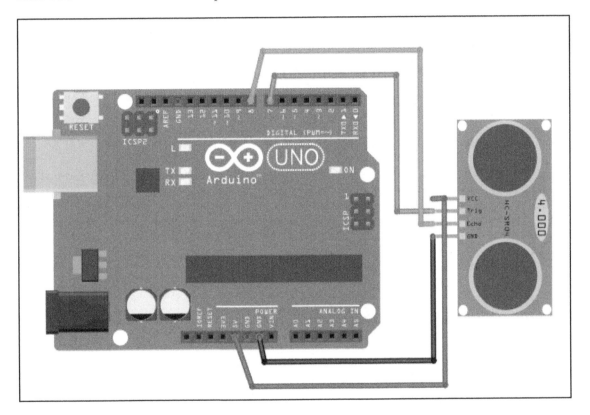

To the left is the Arduino Uno board. The ultrasound sensor is towards the right. As you can see the sensor has four pins marked VCC, Trig, Echo, and GND. The specifications of the sensor states that it needs 5 volts to run. Accordingly, we connect the VCC pin to a pin that reads 5V on the Arduino pin. Similarly, the ground pin (GND) from the sensor is connected to a GND pin on the Arduino board. Now the sensor is powered up. We connect the Trig pin to pin number 8 and the Echo pin to pin number 7 on the Arduino board. Every time we provide a high pulse on Pin 8, the sensor will trigger an ultrasound and then the Echo pin will return the time it took for the ultrasound to reflect back, which we will read into the Arduino on Pin 7.

Writing the Arduino sketch

In the Arduino world, programs that you upload to the microcontroller are called sketches. You can write these sketches in a free **integrated development environment (IDE)** which can be downloaded from here:
https://www.arduino.cc/en/Main/Software

Once you finalize a program, you upload it to your Arduino board using the upload button on the IDE and voila: your board starts doing what you asked it to do.

Every Arduino sketch will have two methods where you get to define the logic of your program:

- setup(): For one-time initialization
- loop(): For things that the board keeps doing forever until it runs out of power

Here's the code that we upload to the Arduino (see 9.13.arduino_sketch.ino):

```
const int triggerPin = 8;
const int echoBackPin = 7;

void setup() {
 Serial.begin(9600);
 pinMode(triggerPin, OUTPUT);
 pinMode(echoBackPin, INPUT);
}

void loop() {
  long duration, distanceIncm;
  // trigger ultrasound ping
  digitalWrite(triggerPin, LOW);
  delayMicroseconds(2);
  digitalWrite(triggerPin, HIGH);
```

```
    delayMicroseconds(5);
    digitalWrite(triggerPin, LOW);
    // receive input from the sensor
    duration = pulseIn(echoBackPin, HIGH);

    //calculate distance
    distanceIncm = duration / 29 / 2;

    // send data over serial port
    Serial.print(distanceIncm);
    Serial.println();
    delay(100);
}
```

The code description is as follows:

- The first two lines indicates that we will use pin numbers 7 and 8 on the Arduino board and we assign them the variable names `triggerPin` and `echoBackPin`.

- The `setup` function initializes the serial port and fixes its baud rate at 9600. Baud rate is defined as the number of signal changes that occur in a second. We will use the same rate when reading data in Tkinter with Python.

- The code `pinMode(triggerPin, OUTPUT)` means that we will now use Pin 8 to send an output pulse to the sensor.

- Similarly, the code `pinMode(echoBackPin, INPUT);` declares that we will use Pin 7 to receive input from the sensor.

- Within the loop, we start by setting pin `triggerPin` to low pulse. We then trigger the sensor to emit ultrasound by triggering a high voltage pulse of 2 microseconds. This triggers the sensor to emit an ultrasound for 5 microseconds. We then mark the pin `LOW` to stop triggering the ultrasound pulse.

- We then time the signal received on `echoBackPin` using `duration = pulseIn(ioPin, HIGH)`. This gives us the time (in microseconds) it took for the ultrasound to reflect back.

- Given that the speed of sound is 340 m/s or 29 microseconds per centimeter, we find the distance using the formula `distance = speed * time`. But since this is the time it took for a reflected sound to travel out and back, the actual distance is half this value. Perhaps the math should be done by Python instead? Doing division here using a `long` method will result in a whole number and so will not be precise. Note that we could have also offloaded this calculation from Arduino to our Python code, as most Arduino processors do not directly support floats in hardware, and doing so in software on such a limited processor could bog it down.

- The line `delay(100)` ensures that the previous code runs every `100` milliseconds, sending pulses of ultrasound and measuring the distance to whatever the sensor is pointed at.

The moment this code is uploaded to the Arduino board, it starts sending 5-microsecond pulses of ultrasound after a delay of 100 milliseconds. It also sends a message to the serial port of your computer in every one of these loops.

Now it's time to read this using Python and then display it in a Tkinter widget.

Reading serial data

We will use the `pyserial` module to read data from the serial port. However, this is not a standard Python module and needs to be installed. We can install it using the following pip command:

```
pip install pyserial
```

Once we are able to get data from the Arduino board, we can further process it or plot it in the way we want. However, the goal here is to simply display whatever data is sent by the Arduino board over the serial port, as shown in the following Tkinter window (`9.14_read_from_serial_port.py`):

In order to read the serial port, we first need to identify the port on which this message is being sent. There are two ways you can do this.

Firstly, you can find the name of the port from your Arduino IDE under the **Tools** menu, as shown here:

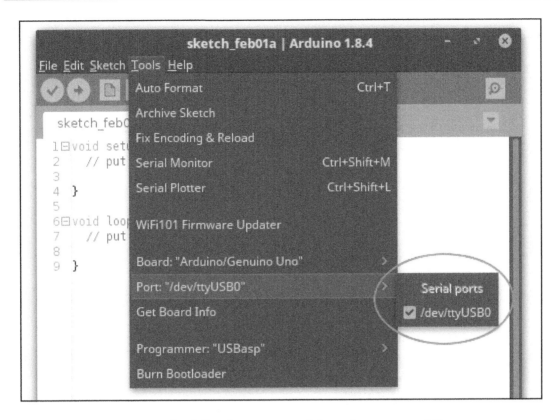

Alternatively, you can run the following command from the command line:

```
python -m serial.tools.list_ports
```

This will print a list of all active serial ports. Once you have the port name at hand, data reading is done using the following code:

```python
from tkinter import Tk, Label
import serial

ser = serial.Serial()
ser.port = "/dev/ttyUSB0"
ser.baudrate = 9600
try:
 ser.open()
except serial.SerialException:
 print("Could not open serial port: " + ser.port)

root = Tk()
root.geometry('{}x{}'.format(200, 100))
```

```
label = Label(root, font=("Helvetica", 26))
label.pack(fill='both')

def read_serial_data():
 if ser.isOpen():
   try:
     response = ser.readline()
     label.config(text='Distance : \n' + response.decode("utf-8").rstrip()
+ ' cm')
   except serial.SerialException:
     print("no message received")

root.after(100, read_serial_data)
read_serial_data()
root.mainloop()
```

The description of the code is as follows:

- We first get an instance of the `Serial` class by calling `ser = serial.Serial()`. We then specify the port name and the baud rate. This is the same baud rate that we used earlier in our Arduino code.
- We then open the serial port by calling `ser.open()` and read the data using `ser.readline()`.
- The rest of the code is Tkinter-specific and creates the GUI and displays the results in a `Label` widget.

This concludes the section and the chapter.

In the next chapter, we will conclude the book with discussions on miscellaneous issues that you may encounter when writing GUI programs.

Summary

Let's summarize the concepts we discussed in this chapter.

We learned about the perils of spawning threads and the resulting race condition.

We learned how to use the queue data structure to program a multithreaded application, without having to worry about synchronization between multiple threads trying to access the same memory, and without using complicated synchronization primitives.

The Weather Reporter application introduced us to the basics of network programming and how to tap into the internet to get data. We discussed two popular structures used for data exchange, namely XML and JSON.

The port scanner and the chat program discussed the basics of socket programming for interprocess and remote communication. We used the TCP/IP protocol to send and receive messages in our chat program. We also saw a basic example of client-server architecture.

We saw how all forms of communication over a network occur in bytes and how we can convert data to bytes and back from bytes to data in the required format.

The phone book application showed us how to work with databases. We saw how to perform basic CRUD operations on a database.

Next, we saw how to use the `asyncio` module to fetch I/O bound tasks in a non-blocking and scalable manner, without having to worry about managing the states of a large number of threads at once.

Finally, we saw how to interface with external hardware to collect data from sensors using serial communication.

QA section

Here are a few questions to reflect upon:

- What is a race condition? How can you avoid a race condition?
- What are the benefits of using the queue data structure?
- What are the most popular open source databases available in the market?
- What are the most common modes of interprocess communication?
- When would you use the `asyncio` module?
- What are some of the advantages and disadvantages of using serial communication? What are some of its alternatives?
- What are the JSON and XML file formats used for? What are their advantages and disadvantages when compared to using a database?

Further reading

We used Python code to perform basic CRUD operations on our database. It would be worthwhile to note that as applications get larger and more complex, the programmer should consider making use of an **ORM (object-relational mapping)** library instead of direct CRUD operations. Read more about ORM and its benefits at `http://blogs.learnnowonline.com/2012/08/28/4-benefits-of-object-relational-mapping-orm/`.

We used a thread lock as a synchronization primitive in `9.02_lock_demo.py`. There are several other synchronization primitives that could have been used instead. Learn about other synchronization primitives at `https://www.usenix.org/legacy/publications/library/proceedings/bsdcon02/full_papers/baldwin/baldwin_html/node5.html`.

Python Enhancement Proposals (PEPs) are official design documents or technical specifications in the Python community that describe a new feature that has been introduced in Python. For instance, PEP 3156 is the specification dealing with and explaining the rationale behind the introduction of the `asyncio` module. You can read this PEP document here:
`https://www.python.org/dev/peps/pep-3156/`

The event loop in `asyncio` internally uses coroutines and futures to implement asynchronous behavior. Learning how to use coroutines and futures can be a valuable tool for writing more efficient and scalable programs.

Sockets are commonly used for interprocess communication. However, there are many other methods for interprocess communication. A brief read of `http://nptel.ac.in/courses/106108101/pdf/Lecture_Notes/Mod%207_LN.pdf` is well worth the effort.

10
Miscellaneous Tips

We have reached the final chapter of this book. Let's end our discussion on Tkinter by looking at some concepts that, though very common in many **graphical user interface (GUI)** programs, did not appear in the previous chapters.

We will cover the following in this chapter:

- Tracing Tkinter variables and attaching callbacks that are triggered when the value of a variable changes
- Understanding the default keyboard widget traversal rules to provide a consistent user experience
- Validating user inputs using built-in Tkinter mechanisms
- Formatting a widget's content as the user interacts with the widget
- Understanding how Tkinter handles fonts and the best practices involved in using custom fonts in Tkinter
- Redirecting the command-line output to Tkinter
- Taking a look at the source code of Tkinter to understand class hierarchy
- Highlighting some current best practices involved in program design and implementation
- Getting an insight into code cleanup and program optimization
- Distributing Tkinter applications as standalone programs to end users
- Understanding the limitations of Tkinter
- Exploring alternatives to Tkinter and understanding when it is better to use them instead of Tkinter and the tradeoffs involved
- Backporting Tkinter programs are written in Python 3.x versions to older Python 2.x versions

Let's begin!

Tracing Tkinter variables

When you specify a Tkinter variable, such as `textvariable`, for a widget (`textvariable = myvar`), the widget automatically gets updated whenever the value of the variable changes. However, there might be times when, in addition to updating the widget, you need to do some extra processing at the time of reading or writing (or modifying) the variable.

Tkinter provides a method to attach a callback method that will be triggered every time the value of a variable is accessed. Thus, the callback acts as a variable observer.

The callback creation method is named `trace_variable(self, mode, callback)` or simply `trace(self, mode, callback)`.

The mode argument can take a value of `r`, `w`, or `u`, which stand for *read*, *write*, or *undefined*. Depending upon the mode specifications, the callback method is triggered when the variable is read or written.

By default, the callback method gets three arguments. The arguments, in order of their position, are as follows:

- The name of the Tkinter variable
- The index of the variable in case the Tkinter variable is an array, otherwise, it's an empty string
- The access modes (`r`, `w`, or `u`)

Note that the triggered callback function may also modify the value of the variable. However, this modification does not trigger additional callbacks.

Let's look at an example of variable tracing in Tkinter. Take a look at how a change in a traced Tkinter variable triggers a callback (see code `10.01_trace_variable.py`):

```
from tkinter import Tk, Label, Entry, StringVar
root = Tk()
my_variable = StringVar()

def trace_when_my_variable_written(var, indx, mode):
    print ("Traced variable {}".format(my_variable.get()))

my_variable.trace_variable("w", trace_when_my_variable_written)

Label(root, textvariable = my_variable).pack(padx=5, pady=5)
Entry(root, textvariable = my_variable).pack(padx=5, pady=5)
```

```
root.mainloop()
```

The following line of code attaches a callback to `trace` the variable:

```
my_variable.trace_variable("w", trace_when_my_variable_written)
```

Now, every time you write in the entry widget, it modifies the value of `my_variable`. Because we have set a `trace` on `my_variable`, it triggers the callback method that, in our example, simply prints the new value into the console, as shown in the following screenshot:

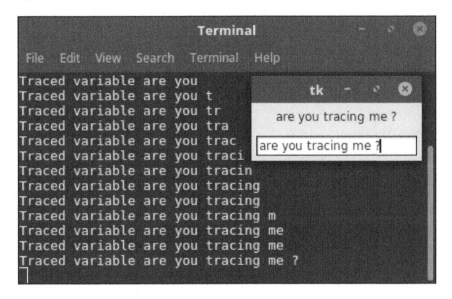

The `trace` on a variable is active until it is explicitly deleted. You can delete a `trace` using the following command:

```
trace_vdelete(self, mode, callback_to_be_deleted)
```

The `trace` method returns the ID and name of the callback method. This can be used to get the name of the callback method that needs to be deleted.

Widget traversal

If a GUI has more than one widget, a given widget can come under focus when you explicitly click on the widget. Alternatively, the focus can be shifted to other widgets in the order that the widgets were created in the program by pressing the *Tab* key on the keyboard.

Therefore, it is vital to create widgets in the order that we want the user to traverse through them. Otherwise, the user will have a tough time navigating between the widgets using the keyboard.

Different widgets are designed to behave differently to different keyboard strokes. Therefore, let's spend some time trying to understand the rules of traversing through widgets using the keyboard.

Have a look at the 10.02_widget_traversal.py file to understand the keyboard traversal behavior for different widgets. The code displays a window like the one shown in the following screenshot:

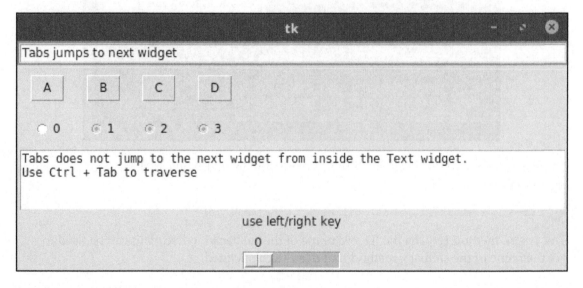

The code will not be given here as it is very simple (see the 10.02_widget_traversal.py code). It simply adds an entry widget, a few buttons, a few radio buttons, a text widget, a label widget, and a scale widget.

The code demonstrates the default keyboard traversal behaviors for these widgets in Tkinter.

The following are a few important points that you should note:

- The *Tab* key can be used to traverse forward, and *Shift + Tab* can be used to traverse backward.
- A user can traverse through the widgets in the order that they were created. A parent widget is visited first (unless it is excluded using `takefocus = 0`), followed by all of its children widgets.
- You can use `widget.focus_force()` to force the input focus on a widget.
- You cannot traverse a text widget by using the *Tab* key because the text widget can contain tab characters as its content. Instead, the text widget can be traversed by using *Ctrl + Tab*.
- Buttons on the widget can be pressed using the spacebar. Similarly, check buttons and radio buttons can also be traversed using the spacebar.
- You can go up and down the items in a Listbox widget by using the up and down arrows.
- The Scale widget responds to the left and right arrow keys and the up and down arrow keys. Similarly, the Scrollbar widget responds to the left/right or up/down arrow keys, depending on their orientation.
- By default, most of the widgets (except Frame, Label, and Menus) get an outline when they have the focus set on them. This outline is normally displayed as a thin black border around the widget. You can even set the Frame and Label widgets to show this outline by setting the `highlightthickness` option to a nonzero integer value for these widgets.
- We can change the color of the outline by using `highlightcolor= 'red'` in the code.
- Frame, Label, and Menu are not included in the tab's navigation path. However, they can be included in the navigation path by using the `takefocus = 1` option. You can explicitly exclude a widget from the tab's navigation path by using the `takefocus = 0` option.

Validating user input

Let's discuss input data validation in Tkinter.

Most of the applications that we have developed in our book are point-and-click-based (the drum machine, the chess game, and the drawing application), where a validation of user input is not required. However, data validation is a must in programs such as the phone book application, where a user enters some data and we store it in a database.

Ignoring user input validation can be dangerous in such applications because input data can be misused for SQL injection. In general, an application in which a user can enter textual data is a good candidate for the validation of user input. In fact, not trusting user inputs is almost considered a maxim.

Wrong user inputs may be intentional or accidental. In either case, if you fail to validate or sanitize data, unexpected errors may occur in your program. In a worst-case scenario, user input can be used to inject harmful code that may be capable of crashing a program or wiping out an entire database.

Widgets, such as Listbox, Combobox, and Radiobuttons, allow limited input options and hence, they normally cannot be misused to input wrong data. On the other hand, widgets such as the Entry widget, the Spinbox widget, and the Text widget allow a large possibility of user inputs, and hence, they need to be validated for correctness.

To enable validation on a widget, you need to specify an additional option of the `validate = 'validationmode'` form to the widget.

For example, if you want to enable validation on an Entry widget, you begin by specifying the validate option, as follows:

```
Entry( root, validate="all", validatecommand=vcmd)
```

Validation can occur in one of the following validation modes:

Validation Mode	Explanation
none	This is the default mode. No validation occurs if `validate` is set to `none`.
focus	When validate is set to focus, the `validate` command is called twice—once when the widget receives focus, and once when the focus is lost.
focusin	The `validate` command is called when the widget receives focus.

focusout	The `validate` command is called when the widget loses focus.
key	The `validate` command is called when the entry is edited.
all	The `validate` command is called in all the aforementioned cases.

The `10.03_validation_mode_demo.py` code file demonstrates all of these validation modes by attaching them to a single `validation` method. In the code, note the different ways in which different Entry widgets respond to different events. Some Entry widgets call the `validation` method on the focus events, others call the `validation` method at the time of entering keystrokes into a widget, and still others use a combination of the focus and key events.

Although we did set the validation mode to trigger the `validate` method, we need some data to validate against the rules. This is passed to the `validate` method using percent substitution. For instance, we passed the mode as an argument to the `validate` method by performing a percent substitution on the `validate` command, as demonstrated in the following command:

```
vcmd = (self.root.register(self.validate_data), '%V')
```

This was followed by passing the value of v as an argument to the `validate` method:

```
def validate_data(self, v)
```

In addition to %V, Tkinter recognizes the following percent substitutions:

Percent substitutions	Explanation
%d	The type of action that is performed on a widget (1 for insert, 0 for delete, and –1 for a focus, forced, or `textvariable` validation).
%i	The index of the char string that is inserted or deleted, if any. Otherwise, it will be –1.
%P	The value of the entry in case the edit is allowed. If you are configuring the Entry widget to have a new `textvariable`, this will be the value of that `textvariable`.
%s	The current value of the entry prior to editing.
%S	The text string being inserted or deleted if any. Otherwise, {}.
%v	The type of validation that has been currently set.

%V	The type of validation that triggers the callback method (key, focusin, focusout, and forced).
%W	The name of the Entry widget.

These substitution values provide us with the necessary data to validate the input.

Let's pass all of these values and just print them through a dummy validate method just to see what kind of data that we can expect to get on carrying out the validations (see the 10.04_percent_substitutions_demo.py code):

```
class PercentSubstitutionsDemo():
  def __init__(self):
    self.root = tk.Tk()
    tk.Label(text='Type Something Below').pack()
    vcmd = (self.root.register(self.validate), '%d', '%i', '%P', '%s',
                                               '%S', '%v', '%V', '%W')
    tk.Entry(self.root, validate="all", validatecommand=vcmd).pack()
    self.root.mainloop()

  def validate(self, d, i, P, s, S, v, V, W):
    print("Following Data is received for running our validation checks:")
    print("d:{}".format(d))
    print("i:{}".format(i))
    print("P:{}".format(P))
    print("s:{}".format(s))
    print("S:{}".format(S))
    print("v:{}".format(v))
    print("V:{}".format(V))
    print("W:{}".format(W))
    # returning true for now
    # in actual validation you return true if data is valid
    # else return false
    return True
```

Note the line where we register a validate method by passing all the possible percent substitutions to the callback.

Take particular note of the data returned by %P and %s because they pertain to the actual data entered by the user in the Entry widget. In most cases, you will be checking either of these two data sources against the validation rules.

Now that we have a background of rules for data validation, let's have a look at two practical examples that demonstrate input validation.

Key validation mode demo

Let's assume that we have a form that asks for a username. We want users to input only alphabetical or space characters in the name. Thus, a number of special characters should not be allowed, as shown in the following screenshot of the widget:

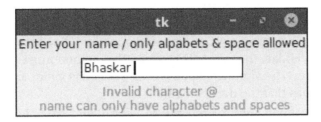

This is clearly a case for the `key` validation mode because we want to check whether an entry is valid after every keypress. The percent substitution that we need to check is `%S` because it yields the text string being inserted or deleted in the Entry widget. Therefore, the code that validates the Entry widget is as follows (see the `10.05_key_validation.py` code):

```python
import tkinter as tk

class KeyValidationDemo():
  def __init__(self):
    root = tk.Tk()
    tk.Label(root, text='Enter your name / only alpabets & space
      allowed').pack()
    vcmd = (root.register(self.validate_data), '%S')
    invcmd = (root.register(self.invalid_name), '%S')
    tk.Entry(root, validate="key",validatecommand=vcmd,
              invalidcommand=invcmd).pack(pady=5, padx=5)
    self.error_message = tk.Label(root, text='', fg='red')
    self.error_message.pack()
    root.mainloop()

  def validate_data(self, S):
    self.error_message.config(text='')
    return (S.isalpha() or S == ' ')

  def invalid_name(self, S):
    self.error_message.config(text='Invalid character %s \n
                  name can only have alphabets and spaces' % S)
    app = KeyValidationDemo()
```

The description of the preceding code is as follows:

- We first register two options, namely `validatecommand ( vcmd )` and `invalidcommand ( invcmd )`.
- In the example, `validatecommand` is registered to call the `validate_data` method, and the `invalidcommand` option is registered to call another method named `invalid_name`.
- The `validatecommand` option specifies a method that needs to be evaluated, which will validate the input. The validation method must return a Boolean value, where `True` signifies that the data entered is valid, and a `False` return value signifies that the data is invalid.
- In case the validate method returns `False` (invalid data), no data is added to the Entry widget and the script registered for `invalidcommand` is evaluated. In our case, a False validation will call the `invalid_name` method. The `invalidcommand` method is generally responsible for displaying error messages or setting back the focus to the Entry widget.

Focus-out validation mode demo

The previous example demonstrated validation in the `key` mode. This means that the validation method was called after every keypress to check whether an entry was valid.

However, there are situations where you might want to check the entire string entered into the widget rather than checking individual keystroke entries.

For example, when an Entry widget accepts a valid email address, we would ideally like to check the validity after the user has entered the entire email address and not after every keystroke entry. This will qualify for a validation in the `focusout` mode.

Check out `10.06_focus_out_validation.py` for a demonstration of email validation in the `focusout` mode, which gives us the following GUI:

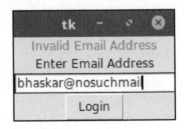

The code for the aforementioned demo is as follows:

```python
import tkinter as tk
import re

class FocusOutValidationDemo():
    def __init__(self):
        self.master = tk.Tk()
        self.error_message = tk.Label(text='', fg='red')
        self.error_message.pack()
        tk.Label(text='Enter Email Address').pack()
        vcmd = (self.master.register(self.validate_email), '%P')
        invcmd = (self.master.register(self.invalid_email), '%P')
        self.email_entry = tk.Entry(self.master, validate="focusout",
                    validatecommand=vcmd, invalidcommand=invcmd)
        self.email_entry.pack()
        tk.Button(self.master, text="Login").pack()
        tk.mainloop()

    def validate_email(self, P):
        self.error_message.config(text='')
        x = re.match(r"[^@]+@[^@]+\.[^@]+", P)
        return (x != None)

    def invalid_email(self, P):
        self.error_message.config(text='Invalid Email Address')
        self.email_entry.focus_set()

app = FocusOutValidationDemo()
```

This code has a lot of similarities to the previous validation example. However, note the following differences:

- The validate mode is set to `focusout` in contrast to the `key` mode in the previous example. This means that the validation will be done only when the Entry widget loses focus. The validation occurs when you hit the *Tab* key. Thus, the input box does not lose its focus in case the input is invalid.

- This program uses data provided by the `%P` percentage substitution, while the previous example used `%S`. This is understandable because `%P` provides the value entered in the Entry widget, but `%S` provides the value of the last keystroke.

- This program uses regular expressions to check whether the entered value corresponds to a valid email format. Validation usually relies on regular expressions. A whole lot of explanation is required to cover this topic, but that is beyond the scope of this book. For more information on regular expression modules, visit `http://docs.python.org/3.6/library/re.html`.

This concludes our discussion on input validation in Tkinter. Hopefully, you should now be able to implement input validation to suit your custom needs.

Formatting widget data

Input data such as date, time, phone number, credit card number, website URL, and IP number, have an associated display format. For instance, the date can be better represented in a MM/DD/YYYY format.

Fortunately, it is easy to format data in the required format as the user enters it in the widget, as shown in the following screenshot:

The 10.07_formatting_entry_widget_to_display_date.py code automatically formats user input to insert forward slashes at the required places to display the date entered by a user in the MM/DD/YYYY format:

```python
from tkinter import Tk, Entry, Label, StringVar, INSERT

class FormatEntryWidgetDemo:
  def __init__(self, root):
    Label(root, text='Date(MM/DD/YYYY)').pack()
    self.entered_date = StringVar()
    self.date_entry = Entry(textvariable=self.entered_date)
    self.date_entry.pack(padx=5, pady=5)
    self.date_entry.focus_set()
    self.slash_positions = [2, 5]
    root.bind('<Key>', self.format_date_entry_widget)

  def format_date_entry_widget(self, event):
    entry_list = [c for c in self.entered_date.get() if c !='/']
    for pos in self.slash_positions:
      if len(entry_list) > pos:
        entry_list.insert(pos, '/')
    self.entered_date.set(''.join(entry_list))
    # Controlling cursor
    cursor_position = self.date_entry.index(INSERT) # current cursor
      position
```

```
    for pos in self.slash_positions:
      if cursor_position == (pos + 1): # if cursor position is on slash
        cursor_position += 1
    if event.keysym not in ['BackSpace', 'Right', 'Left','Up', 'Down']:
      self.date_entry.icursor(cursor_position)

root = Tk()
FormatEntryWidgetDemo(root)
root.mainloop()
```

The description of the preceding code is as follows:

- The Entry widget is bound to the keypress event, where every new keypress calls the related `format_date_entry_widget` callback method.
- First, the `format_date_entry_widget` method breaks down the entered text into an equivalent list named `entry_list` and ignores the slash/symbol that may have been entered by a user.
- It then iterates through the `self.slash_positions` list and inserts the slash symbol at all the required positions in `entry_list`. The net result of this is a list that has slashes inserted at all the right places.
- The next line converts this list into an equivalent string using `join()` and then sets the value of the Entry widget to this string. This ensures that the Entry widget text is formatted into the aforementioned date format.
- The remaining pieces of code simply control the cursor to ensure that the cursor advances by one position whenever it encounters the slash symbol. It also ensures that keypresses, such as *Backspace*, right, left, up, and down are handled properly.

Note that this method does not validate the date value, and users may add an invalid date. The method defined here will simply format it by adding a forward slash at the third and sixth positions. Adding date validation to this example is left as an exercise for you to complete.

This concludes our brief discussion on formatting data within widgets. Hopefully, you should now be able to create formatted widgets for a wide variety of input data that can be better displayed in a given format.

More on fonts

Many Tkinter widgets let you specify custom font specifications either at the time of widget creation or later by using the `configure()` option. For most cases, default fonts provide a standard look and feel. However, if you want to change font specifications, Tkinter lets you do so. There is one caveat, though.

When you specify your own font, you need to make sure that it looks good on all the platforms where your program is intended to be deployed because a font might look good on a particular platform, but it may look awful on another platform. Unless you know what you are doing, it is always advisable to stick to Tkinter's default fonts.

Most platforms have their own set of standard fonts that are used by the platform's native widgets. So, rather than trying to reinvent the wheel on what looks good on a given platform or what would be available for a given platform, Tkinter assigns these standard platform-specific fonts to its widget, thus providing a native look and feel on every platform.

Tkinter assigns nine fonts to nine different names; you can use these fonts in your programs. The font names are as follows:

- `TkDefaultFont`
- `TkTextFont`
- `TkFixedFont`
- `TkMenuFont`
- `TkHeadingFont`
- `TkCaptionFont`
- `TkSmallCaptionFont`
- `TkIconFont`
- `TkTooltipFont`

Accordingly, you can use them in your programs in the following way:

```
Label(text="Sale Up to 50% Off !", font="TkHeadingFont 20")
Label(text="**Conditions Apply", font="TkSmallCaptionFont 8")
```

Using these kinds of fonts markups, you can rest assured that your font will look native across all platforms.

Finer control over font

In addition to the aforementioned method of handling fonts, Tkinter provides a separate `Font` class implementation. The source code for this class is located in the same folder as the source code for Tkinter.

On my Linux machine, the source code is located in `/usr/local/lib/python3.6/tkinter/font.py`. On Windows (with a default Python 3.6 install) the location is `C:\Program Files (x86)\Python36-32\Lib\tkinter\font.py`.

To use this module, you need to import fonts into your namespace, as follows (see the `10.08_font_demo.py` code):

```
from tkinter import Tk, Label, Pack
from tkinter import font
root = Tk()
label = Label(root, text="Humpty Dumpty was pushed")
label.pack()
current_font = font.Font(font=label['font'])
print ('Actual :', str(current_font.actual()))
print ('Family : ', current_font.cget("family"))
print ('Weight : ', current_font.cget("weight"))
print ('Text width of Dumpty : {}'.format(current_font.measure("Dumpty")))
print ('Metrics:', str(current_font.metrics()))
current_font.config(size=14)
label.config(font=current_font)
print ('New Actual :', str(current_font.actual()))
root.mainloop()
```

The console output of this program on my terminal is as follows:

```
Actual: {'slant': 'roman', 'underline': 0, 'family': 'DejaVu Sans',
'weight': 'normal', 'size': -12, 'overstrike': 0}
Family: DejaVu Sans
Weight: normal
Text width of Dumpty: 49
Metrics: {'fixed': 0, 'descent': 3, 'ascent': 12, 'linespace':15}
New actual: {'slant': 'roman', 'underline': 0, 'family': 'DejaVu Sans',
'weight': 'normal', 'size': 14, 'overstrike': 0}
```

As you can see, the `font` module provides much better fine-grained control over various aspects of fonts that are otherwise inaccessible.

Building a font selector

Now that we have seen the basic features that are available in Tkinter's `font` module, let's implement a font selector like the one shown in the following screenshot:

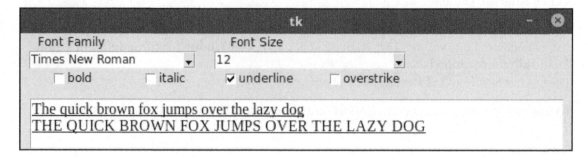

The key to building the font selector shown in the preceding screenshot is to fetch a list of all the fonts installed on a system. A call to the `families()` method from the `font` module fetches a tuple of all the fonts available on a system. Accordingly, when you run the following code, a tuple of all the fonts available on the system gets printed (see the `10.09_all_fonts_on_a_system.py` code):

```
from tkinter import Tk, font
root = Tk()
all_fonts = font.families()
print(all_fonts) # this prints the tuple containing all fonts on a system.
```

Note that since `font` is a submodule of Tkinter, it needs an instance of `Tk()`, which loads the Tcl interpreter, before it can fetch the tuple.

Now that we have a tuple of all the fonts available on a system, we just need to create the GUI shown in the preceding screenshot and attach relevant callbacks to all the widgets.

We will not discuss the code that creates the GUI shown in the preceding screenshot. Check out `10.10_font_selector.py` for the complete code. However, note that the code attaches the following callback to all the widgets:

```
def on_value_change(self, event=None):
    self.current_font.config(family=self.family.get(), size=self.size.get(),
            weight=self.weight.get(), slant=self.slant.get(),
            underline=self.underline.get(),
            overstrike=self.overstrike.get())
    self.text.tag_config('fontspecs', font=self.current_font)
```

Here, `fontspecs` is a custom tag that we attached to the sample text in the text widget, as follows:

```
self.text.insert(INSERT, '{}\n{}'.format(self.sample_text,
                        self.sample_text.upper()), 'fontspecs')
```

This concludes our brief discussion on playing with fonts in Tkinter.

Redirecting the command-line output to Tkinter

You may occasionally need to redirect the output of a command line to a GUI such as Tkinter. The ability to pass outputs from the command line to Tkinter opens a large pool of possibilities for using the inherent powers of the shell on Unix and Linux operating systems and the Windows shell on a Windows machine.

We will demonstrate this by using the `subprocess` Python module, which lets us spawn new processes, connect to the input, output, and error pipes of this new process, and obtain the return codes from the programs.

A detailed discussion on the `subprocess` module can be found at `https://docs.python.org/3/library/subprocess.html`.

We will use the `Popen` class from the `subprocess` module to create a new process.

The `Popen` class provides a cross-platform way to create new processes, and it has the following long signature to handle most of the common and esoteric use cases:

```
subprocess.Popen(args, bufsize=-1, executable=None, stdin=None,
stdout=None, stderr=None, preexec_fn=None, close_fds=True, shell=False,
cwd=None, env=None, universal_newlines=False, startupinfo=None,
creationflags=0, restore_signals=True, start_new_session=False,
pass_fds=())
```

Here's a simple program that shows how we can redirect the output of the `ls` Bash shell command to Tkinter's text widget. As a reminder, the `ls` command in the Bash scripting language returns a list of all files and directories (see the `10.11_reading_from_command_line.py` code):

```
from tkinter import Tk, Text, END
from subprocess import Popen, PIPE
root = Tk()
```

```
text = Text(root)
text.pack()

#replace "ls" with "dir" in the next line on windows platform
with Popen(["ls"], stdout=PIPE, bufsize=1, universal_newlines=True) as p:
    for line in p.stdout:
        text.insert(END, line)

root.mainloop()
```

Windows users should note that you will have to replace ls with dir in the highlighted part of the preceding code to get an equivalent result.

Furthermore, note that you can pass extra arguments to Popen by using the following format:

```
Popen(['your command', arg0, arg1, ...])
```

Even better, you can pass the name of the script file that needs to be executed in the new process. The code used to run a script file is as follows:

```
Popen('path/toexecutable/script',stdout=sub.PIPE,stderr=sub.PIPE)
```

However, the script file that needs to be executed must include a proper shebang declaration to let the program choose a proper executing environment for your script. For instance, if you intend to run a Python script, your script must begin with the shebang of the #!/usr/bin/env python3 form. Similarly, you need to include #!/bin/sh to run a Bourne-compatible shell script. A shebang isn't necessary on Windows. It is also not required for binary executables.

Running the preceding program produces a window, and a listing of all the files from the current directory are added to the text widget, as shown in the following screenshot:

While the preceding program is simple, this technique can have a lot of practical uses. For instance, you may recall that we built a chat server in the previous chapter. Every time a new client connected to the server, it printed the client details to the terminal. We could have easily redirected that output into a new Tkinter app. This would enable us to create a dashboard for the server; from there, we could have monitored all the incoming connections to the server.

This opens the door for us to reuse any command-line script written in any other programming language, such as Perl or Bash, and directly integrate it with a Tkinter program.

This concludes the brief section on the redirection of command-line outputs into Tkinter programs.

The class hierarchy of Tkinter

As programmers, we hardly need to understand the class hierarchy of Tkinter. After all, we have been able to code all the applications so far without bothering with the overall class hierarchy. However, knowing the class hierarchy enables us to `trace` the origin of a method within the source code or source documentation of a method.

In order to understand the class hierarchy of Tkinter, let's take a look at the source code of Tkinter. On the Windows installation, the source code of Tkinter is located at `path\of\Python\Installation\Lib\tkinter\`. On my Linux machine, the source code is located at `/usr/lib/python3.6/tkinter/`.

If you open the __init__.py file from this folder in a code editor and look at its list of class definitions in Tkinter, you will see the following structure:

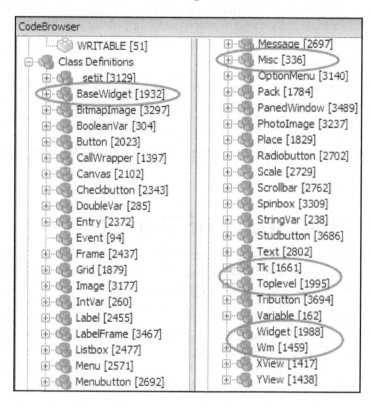

So, what can you see here? We have class definitions for each core Tkinter widget.

In addition to this, we have class definitions for different geometry managers and variable types defined within Tkinter. These class definitions are what you would normally expect to be there.

However, in addition to these, you will see some more class names, such as BaseWidget, Misc, Tk, Toplevel, Widget, and Wm. All of these classes are circled in the preceding screenshot. So, what services do these classes provide, and where do they fit in the larger scheme of things?

Let's use the `inspect` module to look at the class hierarchy of Tkinter. We will first inspect the class hierarchy of the Frame widget as a representation of class hierarchies for all the other widgets. We will also look at the class hierarchy of the `Tk` and `Toplevel` classes to estimate their role in the overall class hierarchy of Tkinter (`10.12_tkinter_class_hierarchy.py`):

```
import tkinter
import inspect

print ('Class Hierarchy for Frame Widget')

for i, classname in enumerate(inspect.getmro(tkinter.Frame)):
  print( '\t{}: {}'.format(i, classname))

print ('Class Hierarchy for Toplevel')
for i, classname in enumerate(inspect.getmro(tkinter.Toplevel)):
  print ('\t{}:{}'.format(i, classname))

print ('Class Hierarchy for Tk')
for i, classname in enumerate(inspect.getmro(tkinter.Tk)):
  print ('\t{}: {}'.format(i, classname))
```

The output of the preceding program is as follows:

```
Class Hierarchy for Frame Widget
        0: <class 'tkinter.Frame'>
        1: <class 'tkinter.Widget'>
        2: <class 'tkinter.BaseWidget'>
        3: <class 'tkinter.Misc'>
        4: <class 'tkinter.Pack'>
        5: <class 'tkinter.Place'>
        6: <class 'tkinter.Grid'>
        7: <class 'object'>
Class Hierarchy for Toplevel
        0:<class 'tkinter.Toplevel'>
        1:<class 'tkinter.BaseWidget'>
        2:<class 'tkinter.Misc'>
        3:<class 'tkinter.Wm'>
        4:<class 'object'>
Class Hierarchy for Tk
        0: <class 'tkinter.Tk'>
        1: <class 'tkinter.Misc'>
        2: <class 'tkinter.Wm'>
        3: <class 'object'>
```

The description of the preceding code is as follows:

- The getmro(classname) function from the inspect module returns a tuple consisting of all the ancestors of classname in the order specified by the **method resolution order** (**MRO**). MRO refers to the order in which base classes are searched when looking for a given method.
- By inspecting the MRO and the source code, you will come to know that the Frame class inherits from the Widget class, which in turn inherits from the BaseWidget class.
- The Widget class is an empty class with the following class definition: class Widget(BaseWidget, Pack, Place, Grid).
- As you can see, this is how methods defined in the geometry manager (the pack, place, and grid mix-ins) are made available to all the widgets.
- The BaseWidget class has the following class definition: class BaseWidget(Misc). This class exposes the destroy method that can be used by programmers.
- All the utility methods defined in the Misc class are made available to the widgets at this hierarchy level.
- The Misc class is a generic mix-in that provides a lot of functionality that we have used in our applications. Some of the methods that we have used in our programs, as defined within the Misc class, are after(), bbox(), bind_all(), bind_tag(), focus_set(), mainloop(), update(), update_idletask(), and winfo_children(). For a complete list of functionalities provided by the Misc class, run the following commands in the Python interactive shell:

```
>>> import tkinter
>>> help(tkinter.Misc)
```

Now, let's take a look at the Tk and Toplevel classes:

- The Tk class returns a new Toplevel widget on the screen. The __init__ method of the Tk class is responsible for the creation of a new Tcl interpreter by calling a method named loadtk(). The class defines a method named report_callback_exception(), which is responsible for the reporting of errors and exceptions on sys.stderr.

- The __init__ method of the `Toplevel` class of Tkinter is responsible for the creation of the main window of an application. The constructor of the class takes various optional arguments such as `bg`, `background`, `bd`, `borderwidth`, `class`, `height`, `highlightbackground`, `highlightcolor`, `highlightthickness`, `menu`, and `relief`.
- To obtain a list of all the methods provided by the `Toplevel` and `Tk` classes, run the following command in the Python interactive shell:
  `help(tkinter.Toplevel); help(tkinter.Tk)`.
- In addition to inheriting from the `Misc` mixin class, the `Toplevel` and `Tk` classes also inherit methods from the `Wm` mixin class.
- The `Wm` (short for the Window manager) `mixin` class provides many methods to let us communicate with the window manager. Some commonly used methods from this class include `wm_iconify`, `wm_deiconify`, `wm_overrideredirect`, `title`, `wm_withdraw`, `wm_transient`, and `wm_resizable`. For a complete list of functions provided by the `Wm` class, run the following command in the Python interactive shell: `help(tkinter.Wm)`.

After translating the class hierarchy, as obtained from the previous program and by inspecting the source code, we get a hierarchy structure of Tkinter, as shown in the following diagram:

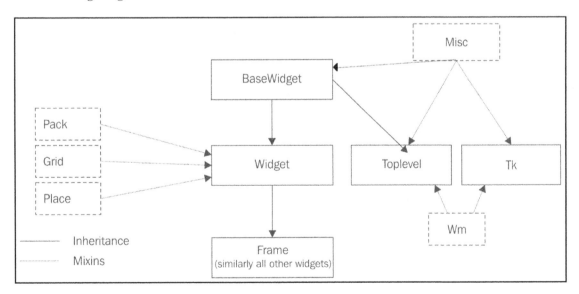

In addition to the normal inheritance relation, which is shown in the preceding diagram with the help of unbroken lines, Tkinter provides a list of mixins (or helper classes).

A `mixin` is a class that is designed not to be used directly, but to be combined with other classes using multiple inheritances.

Tkinter mixins can be broadly classified into the following two categories:

- Geometry mixins: These include the `Grid`, `Pack`, and `Place` classes
- Implementation mixins: These include the following classes:
    - The `Misc` class, which is used by the root window and `widget` classes, provides several Tk and window-related services
    - The `Wm` class, which is used by the root window and the Toplevel widget, provides several window manager services

This concludes our brief under-the-hood tour of Tkinter. Hopefully, this should give you some insight into the inner workings of Tkinter. If you ever have a doubt about the documentation of any given method, you can take a peek directly into the actual implementation of the method.

Tips for program design

Let's take a look at a few generic tips for program design.

The model-first policy versus the code-first policy

A well-designed model is half the work done. That said, the model is sometimes not very evident when you start writing the program. In such cases, you can break the rules and try out the code-first philosophy. The idea is to build your program incrementally from the ground up, refactor your code, and model, as your vision for the program becomes clearer.

Separating the model from the view

The need to separate the model or data structure from the view is the key to building scalable applications. While it is possible to intermix the two components, you will soon find your program getting messy and difficult to maintain.

Selecting the right data structure

Selecting the right data structure can have a profound impact on the performance of a program. If your program requires you to spend considerable time on lookups, use a dictionary, if feasible. When all that you need is to traverse over a collection, prefer lists over dictionaries because dictionaries take up more space. When your data is immutable, prefer tuples over lists because tuples can be traversed faster than lists.

Naming variables and methods

Use meaningful and self-documenting names for your variables and methods. The name should leave no scope for confusion about the intent of the variable or the method. Use plural names for collections and singular names otherwise. Methods that return Boolean values should be appended with words such as *is* or *has*. Stick to the style guidelines, but you should also know when to break them.

The Single Responsibility Principle

The Single Responsibility Principle suggests that a function/class/method should do only one thing and that it should do it all and do it well. This means that we should not try to handle multiple things from within a function.

Loose coupling

Whenever possible, reduce coupling or dependence in your program. The following is a famous quote on this subject:

> *All problems in computer science can be solved by another level of indirection.*
> *– David Wheeler*

Let's suppose that your program has a play button. An immediate impulse may be to link it to the `play` method of your program. However, you can further break it up into two methods. You could probably link the play button to a method named `on_play_button_clicked`, which in turn calls the actual `play` method. The advantage of this is that you may want to handle additional things when the play button is clicked, such as displaying the current track information somewhere in your program.

Thus, you can now use the `on_play_button_clicked` method to decouple the click event from the actual play method and then handle calls to multiple methods.

However, you must resist the temptation of adding too many levels of indirection, as your program may quickly start getting messy and it may get out of control.

Handling errors and exceptions

Python follows the **EAFP** (short for **easier to ask for forgiveness than permission**) style of coding as opposed to the **LBYL** (**look before you leap**) style that is followed by most programming languages.

Therefore, handling exceptions in a way that is similar to the following one is normally cleaner in Python than checking conditions using the if-then block.

So when coding in Python, rather than using the following style in coding:

```
if some_thing_wrong:
    do_something_else()
else:
    do_something_normal()
```

Consider using this instead:

```
try:
    do_some_thing_normal()
except some_thing_wrong:
    do_some_thing_else()
```

Handling cross-platform differences

Even though Tkinter is a cross-platform module, you might come across occasions when code written for one operating system might not work as expected on other operating systems. We already saw one such example in the case of getting command-line results in the previous Redirecting the command-line output to Tkinter. In such cases, you can overcome these cross-platform discrepancies by first identifying the operating system on which the program is being run and then using a conditional statement to run different lines of code for different operating systems.

Here's a brief snippet that demonstrates this concept:

```
from platform import uname
operating_system = uname()[0]
if ( operating_system == "Linux" ):
  canvas.bind('<Button-4>', wheelUp) # X11
  canvas.bind('<Button-5>', wheelDown)
elif ( operating_system == "Darwin" ):
  canvas.bind('<MouseWheel>', wheel) # MacOS
else:
  canvas.bind_all('<MouseWheel>', wheel) # windows
```

The particular problem here is that the mouse wheel event is denoted by the <MouseWheel> event name on Windows and macOS, but as <Button-4> and <Button-5> on Linux distributions. The preceding code uses the platform module of Python to identify the operating system and follows a different line of code for different operating systems.

Tips for program optimization

Next, let's take a look at some generic tips to optimize your programs.

Using filter and map

Python provides two built-in functions, named filter and map, to manipulate collections directly rather than having to iterate over each item in the collection. The filter, map, and reduce functions are faster than loops because a lot of the work is done by the underlying code written in C.

The filter(function, list) function returns a list (iterators in Python 3.x) that contains all the items for which the function returns a true value. The following command is an example:

```
print filter(lambda num: num>6, range(1,10))# prints [7, 8,9]
```

This is faster than running a conditional if-then check against the list.

The `map(function_name, list)` function applies `function_name` to each item in the list and returns the values in a new list (returns iterators instead of lists in Python 3.x). The following command is an example:

```
print map(lambda num: num+5, range(1,5)) #prints [6, 7, 8,9]
```

This is faster than running the list through a loop and adding 5 to each element.

Optimizing variables

The way you select variables in your program can considerably affect the speed of the execution of your program. For instance, if you do not need to change the content or attributes of a widget after its instantiation, do not create a class-wide instance of the widget.

For example, if a Label widget needs to remain static, use `Label(root, text='Name').pack(side=LEFT)` instead of using the following snippet:

```
self.mylabel = Label(root, text='Name')
self.mylabel.pack(side=LEFT)
```

Similarly, do not create local variables if you are not going to use them more than once. For example, use `mylabel.config (text= event.keysym)` instead of first creating a local variable named key and then using it only once:

```
key = event.keysym
mylabel.config (text=key)
```

If the local variable needs to be used more than once, it may make sense to create a local variable.

Profiling your program

Profiling involves generating detailed statistics to show how often and for how long various routines of a program execute. This helps you isolate the offending parts of a program, and those parts probably need redesigning.

Python provides a built-in module named `cProfile`, which enables the generation of detailed statistics pertaining to a program. The module gives details such as the total program running time, the time taken to run each function, and the number of times each function is called. These statistics make it easy to determine the parts of the code that need optimization.

In particular, cProfile provides the following data for a function or script:

- ncalls: This indicates the number of times a function is called
- tottime: This indicates the time spent on a function, which excludes the time spent on calling other functions
- percall: This is tottime divided by ncalls
- cumtime: This indicates the time spent on a function, including calls to other functions
- percall: This is cumtime divided by tottime

To profile a function named spam(), use the following code:

```
import cProfile
cProfile.run('spam()','spam.profile')
```

You can then view the results of profiling by using another module called pstats, as follows:

```
import pstats
stats = pstats.Stats('spam.profile')
stats.strip_dirs().sort_stats('time').print_stats()
```

More importantly, you can profile an entire script. Let's assume that you want to profile a script named myscript.py. You can simply navigate to the directory of the script using a command-line tool and then type and run the following command:

python -m cProfile myscript.py

Here's a partial output from running the preceding command on the 8.08_vornoi_diagram code from Chapter 8, *Fun With Canvas*:

```
57607465 function calls (57607420 primitive calls) in 110.040 seconds
Ordered by: standard name
ncalls tottime percall cumtime percall filename:lineno(function)
 1 50.100 50.100 95.452 95.452
8.09_vornoi_diagram.py:15(create_voronoi_diagram)
 1 0.000 0.000 110.040 110.040 8.09_vornoi_diagram.py:5(<module>)
 400125 2.423 0.000 14.616 0.000 __init__.py:2313(_create)
 400125 0.661 0.000 15.277 0.000 __init__.py:2342(create_rectangle)
 400128 1.849 0.000 2.743 0.000 __init__.py:95(_cnfmerge)
 625 0.001 0.000 0.003 0.000 random.py:170(randrange)
 625 0.002 0.000 0.002 0.000 random.py:220(_randbelow)
 50400000 30.072 0.000 30.072 0.000 {built-in method math.hypot}
 1 14.202 14.202 14.358 14.358 {method 'mainloop' of '_tkinter.tkapp'
objects}
```

I specifically chose to profile this program because it takes a long time to execute. In this case, it took ~110 seconds to run and most of the time was spent running the `create_vornoi_diagram` function (~95 seconds). So now this function is a perfect candidate for optimization.

In addition to the `cProfile` module, there are other modules, such as `PyCallGraph` and `objgraph`, and they provide visual graphs for the profile data.

Other optimization tips

Optimization is a vast topic, and there is a lot that you can do. If you are interested in knowing more about code optimization, you can start with the official Python optimization tips that are available at `http://wiki.python.org/moin/PythonSpeed/PerformanceTips`.

Distributing a Tkinter application

So, you have your new application ready and want to share it with the rest of the world. How do you do that?

You, of course, need Python installed for your programs to run. Windows does not have Python preinstalled. Most modern Linux distributions and macOS have Python preinstalled, but you don't need just any version of Python. You need a version of Python that is compatible with the version on which the program was originally written.

Furthermore, if your program uses third-party modules, you need the appropriate module installed for the required Python version. This surely is too much diversity to handle.

Fortunately, we have tools, such as Freeze tools, that allow us to distribute Python programs as standalone applications.

Given the diversity of platforms that need to be handled, there are a large number of Freeze tool options from which you can choose. Therefore, a detailed discussion on any one of these tools is beyond the scope of this book.

We will list some of the most evolved freezing tools in the following sections. If you find a tool that fits into your distribution requirements, you can look at its documentation for more information.

py2exe

If you only need to distribute your Python application on Windows, py2exe is perhaps the most hardened tool. It converts Python programs into executable Windows programs that can run without requiring a Python installation.

More information, a download link, and tutorials on this are available at `http://www.py2exe.org/`.

py2app

The py2app performs the same tasks in macOS that py2exe does for Windows. If you just need to distribute your Python application on macOS, py2app is a time-tested tool. More information is available at `https://pythonhosted.org/py2app/`.

PyInstaller

PyInstaller has gained popularity as a freezing tool in the last few years because it supports a wide variety of platforms, such as Windows, Linux, macOS X, Solaris, and AIX.

In addition, executables created using PyInstaller claim to take up less space than other freezing tools because it uses transparent compression. Another important feature of PyInstaller is its out-of-the-box compatibility with a large number of third-party packages. The full list of features, downloads, and documentation can be viewed by visiting `http://www.pyinstaller.org/`.

Other freezing tools

The following are a few other freezing tools:

- **Freeze**: This tool is shipped with the standard Python distribution. Freeze can only be used to compile executables on Unix systems. However, the program is overly simplistic, as it fails to handle even the common third-party libraries. More information on this is available at `http://wiki.python.org/moin/Freeze`.
- **cx_Freeze**: This tool is similar to py2exe and py2app, but it claims to be portable across all platforms on which Python works. More information on this is available at `http://cx-freeze.sourceforge.net/index.html`.

If you're distributing a small program, a freezing tool might be just what you need.

However, if you have a large program, say, with lots of external third-party library dependencies, or dependencies that are not supported by any existing freezing tool, your application might be the right candidate for bundling the Python interpreter with your application.

The limitations of Tkinter

We have already explored the power of Tkinter. Perhaps the greatest power of Tkinter lies in its ease of use and lightweight footprint. Tkinter exposes a very powerful API, especially with the Text widget and the Canvas widget.
However, its ease of use and the fact that it is lightweight also result in some limitations.

A limited number of core widgets

Tkinter provides only a small number of basic widgets and lacks a collection of modern widgets. It needs Ttk, Pmw, TIX, and other extensions to provide some really useful widgets. Even with these extensions, Tkinter fails to match the range of widgets provided by other GUI tools, such as the advanced wxPython widget set and PyQt.

For instance, wxPython's HtmlWindow widget lets users display HTML content with ease. There have been attempts to provide similar extensions in Tkinter, but they are far from satisfactory. Similarly, there are other widgets from the Advanced User Interface Library and mixins in wxPython, such as floating/docking frames and perspective loading and saving; Tkinter users can only hope that these widgets will be included in future releases.

Non-Python objects

Tkinter widgets are not first-class Python objects. Thus, we have to use workarounds such as `Intvar`, `StringVar`, and `BooleanVar` to handle variables in Tkinter. This adds a small layer of complexity, as error messages returned by the Tcl interpreter are not very Python-friendly, which makes it harder to debug.

No support for printing

Tkinter is rightly criticized for not providing any support for printing features.

The Canvas widget allows for limited printing support in the PostScript format. The PostScript format is too limited in what it can be used for. Compare this to wxPython, which provides a complete printing solution in the form of a printing framework.

No support for newer image formats

Tkinter does not natively support image formats such as JPEG and PNG. The `PhotoImage` class of Tkinter can read images only in the GIF and PGM/PPM formats. Although there are workarounds, such as using the `ImageTk` and `Image` submodules from the `PIL` module, it would have been better if Tkinter natively supported popular image formats.

Inactive development community

Tkinter is often criticized for having a relatively inactive development community. This is true to a large extent. The documentation for Tkinter has remained a work in progress for many years now.

A large number of Tkinter extensions have appeared over the years, but most of them have not been under active development for a long time.

Tkinter supporters refute this with the argument that Tkinter is a stable and mature technology that does not need frequent revisions, unlike some other GUI modules that are still being developed.

Alternatives to Tkinter

If a program can be written in Tkinter, this is probably the best way to go in terms of simplicity and maintainability. However, in case the aforementioned limitations get in your way, you can explore some other alternatives to Tkinter.

In addition to Tkinter, there are several other popular Python GUI toolkits. The most popular ones include wxPython, PyQt, PySide, and PyGTK. Here's a brief discussion of these toolkits.

wxPython

wxPython is a Python interface for `wxWidgets`, a popular open source GUI library. The code written in wxPython is portable across most major platforms, such as Windows, Linux, and macOS.

The wxPython interface is generally considered to be better than Tkinter at building complex GUIs, primarily because it has a large base of natively supported widgets. However, Tkinter supporters do contest this claim.

The `wxWidgets` interface was originally written in the C++ programming language. Hence, wxPython inherits a large portion of the complexity that is typical of C++ programs. wxPython provides a very large base of classes, and it often takes more code to produce the same interface than it would take in Tkinter. However, in exchange for this complexity, wxPython provides a larger base of built-in widgets than Tkinter offers.

Owing to its inherent complexity, wxPython has seen the emergence of several GUI builder toolkits, such as **wxGlade, wxFormBuilder,** and **wxDesigner.** The wxPython installation comes with demo programs that can help you quickly get started with the toolkit. To download the toolkit, or for more information on wxPython, visit `http://wxpython.org/`.

PyQt

PyQt is a Python interface for a cross-platform GUI toolkit named Qt, a project currently developed and maintained by a British firm named Riverbank Computing.

PyQt, with several hundred classes and thousands of functions, is perhaps the most fully featured GUI library currently available for GUI programming in Python. However, this feature load brings in a lot of complexity and a steep learning curve.

Qt, and hence pyQt, has a very rich set of supported widgets. In addition to this, it includes built-in support for network programming, SQL databases, threads, multimedia frameworks, regular expressions, XML, SVG, and much more. The designer feature of Qtletsus generates GUI code from a **WYSIWYG (what you see is what you get)** interface.

PyQt is available under a variety of licenses, including GNU, **General Public License (GPL)**, and a commercial license. However, its greatest disadvantage is that unlike Qt, it is unavailable under the **Lesser General Public License (LGPL)**.

PySide

If you are looking for an LGPL Version of Qt bindings for Python, you may want to explore PySide. PySide was originally released under the LGPL in August 2009 by Nokia, the former owners of the Qt Toolkit. It is now owned by Digia. More information on PySide can be obtained by visiting `http://qt-project.org/wiki/PySide`.

PyGTK

PyGTK is a collection of Python bindings for the GTK + GUI library. PyGTK applications are cross-platform and can run on Windows, Linux, macOS, and others. PyGTK is free and is licensed under the LGPL. Therefore, you can use, modify, and distribute it with very few restrictions.

More information about PyGTK can be obtained by visiting `http://www.pygtk.org/`.

Other options

Besides these popular toolkits, there are a range of toolkits available for GUI programming in Python.

Java programmers who are comfortable with Java GUI libraries, such as Swing and AWT, can seamlessly access these libraries by using **Jython**. Similarly, C# programmers can use **IronPython** to access GUI construction features from the **.NET** framework.

For a comprehensive list of other GUI tools that are available to a Python developer, visit `http://wiki.python.org/moin/GuiProgramming`.

Tkinter in Python 2.x

In 2008, Guido van Rossum, the author of Python, forked the language into two branches—2.x and 3.x. This was done to clean up the language and make it more consistent.

Python 3.x broke backward compatibility with Python 2.x. For example, the print statement in Python 2.x was replaced by the `print()` function that would now take arguments as parameters.

We coded all the Tkinter programs in Python Version 3.x. However, in case you need to maintain or write new Tkinter programs in Python 2.x, the transition should not be very difficult.

The core functionality of Tkinter remains the same between 2.x and 3.x. The only significant change to Tkinter when moving from Python 2.x to Python 3.x involves changing the way the Tkinter modules are imported.

Tkinter has been renamed as `tkinter` in Python 3.x (capitalization has been removed).

Note that in 3.x, the `lib-tk` directory was renamed to `tkinter`. Inside this directory, the `Tkinter.py` file was renamed to `__init__.py`, thus making `tkinter` an importable module.

Accordingly, the biggest difference lies in the way you import the `tkinter` module into your current namespace:

```
import Tkinter  # for Python 2
import tkinter  # for Python 3
```

Furthermore, note the following changes.

Note how the Python 3 version is cleaner, more elegant, and more systematic in its naming conventions regarding the use of lowercase names for its modules:

Python 3	Python 2
`import tkinter.ttk    OR` `from tkinter import ttk`	`import ttk`
`import tkinter.messagebox`	`import tkMessageBox`
`import tkinter.colorchooser`	`import tkColorChooser`
`import tkinter.filedialog`	`import tkFileDialog`
`import tkinter.simpledialog`	`import tkSimpleDialog`
`import tkinter.commondialog`	`import tkCommonDialog`
`import tkinter.font`	`import tkFont`

import tkinter.scrolledtext	import ScrolledText
import tkinter.tix	import Tix

The following version will work for both cases:

```
try:
    import tkinter as tk
except ImportError:
    import Tkinter as tk

try:
    import tkinter.messagebox
except:
    import tkMessageBox
```

Summary

To conclude the book, let's summarize some of the key steps involved in designing an application. Depending on what you want to design, choose a suitable data structure to represent your needs logically. If required, combine primitive data structures to form complex structures such as, say, a list or a tuple of dictionaries. Create classes for objects that constitute your application. Add attributes that need to be manipulated and methods to manipulate these attributes. Manipulate attributes by using a different API provided by a rich set of Python-standard and external libraries.

We tried to build several applications in this book. Then, we had a look at an explanation for the code. However, when you try to explain a software development process in a sequential text, you sometimes mislead your readers by implying that the development of software programs is a linear process. This is hardly true.

Actual programming doesn't usually work this way. In fact, small- to medium-sized programs are normally written in an incremental trial-and-error process, where assumptions get changed and structures are modified throughout the course of application development.

Here is how you would develop a small- to a medium-sized application:

1. Start with a simple script.
2. Set a small achievable goal, implement it, and then think of adding the next feature to your program in an incremental fashion.
3. You may or may not introduce a class structure initially. If you are clear about the problem domain, you may introduce the class structure from the very beginning.
4. If you are not initially sure about the class structure, start with simple procedural code. As your program starts to grow, you will probably start getting a lot of global variables. It is here that you will start getting an idea of the structural dimensions of your program. It is now time to refactor and restructure your program to introduce a class structure.
5. Harden your program against unanticipated runtime failures and edge cases to make it ready for production use.

That concludes the book. If you have any suggestions or feedback, please leave us a comment. If you found this book helpful, please rate it online and help us spread the word.

QA section

Here are a few questions to reflect upon:

- How can we handle cross-platform differences in Tkinter?
- What are the advantages and limitations of using Tkinter?
- What are some of the common alternatives to Tkinter?
- What the various modes of validation in Tkinter?
- What is program profiling? How do we profile a program in Python?

Other Books You May Enjoy

If you enjoyed this book, you may be interested in these other books by Packt:

Learn QT 5
Nicholas Sherriff

ISBN: 978-1-78847-885-4

- Install and configure the Qt Framework and Qt Creator IDE
- Create a new multi-project solution from scratch and control every aspect of it with QMake
- Implement a rich user interface with QML
- Learn the fundamentals of QtTest and how to integrate unit testing
- Build self-aware data entities that can serialize themselves to and from JSON
- Manage data persistence with SQLite and CRUD operations
- Reach out to the internet and consume an RSS feed
- Produce application packages for distribution to other users

Qt 5 Projects
Marco Piccolino

ISBN: 978-1-78829-388-4

- Learn the basics of modern Qt application development
- Develop solid and maintainable applications with BDD, TDD, and Qt Test
- Master the latest UI technologies and know when to use them: Qt Quick, Controls 2, Qt 3D and Charts
- Build a desktop UI with Widgets and the Designer
- Translate your user interfaces with QTranslator and Linguist
- Get familiar with multimedia components to handle visual input and output
- Explore data manipulation and transfer: the model/view framework, JSON, Bluetooth, and network I/O
- Take advantage of existing web technologies and UI components with WebEngine

Leave a review - let other readers know what you think

Please share your thoughts on this book with others by leaving a review on the site that you bought it from. If you purchased the book from Amazon, please leave us an honest review on this book's Amazon page. This is vital so that other potential readers can see and use your unbiased opinion to make purchasing decisions, we can understand what our customers think about our products, and our authors can see your feedback on the title that they have worked with Packt to create. It will only take a few minutes of your time, but is valuable to other potential customers, our authors, and Packt. Thank you!

Index

W

WAV file 165
weather data
  references 328
Weather Reporter application
  creating 326, 328, 331
whole tone 241
Widget Construction Kit(WCK)
  reference link 194
widget data

formatting 370, 371
widget traversal 362, 363
window responsiveness
  about 267
  code, experimenting 268
WMA file 165
wxDesigner 392
wxFormBuilder 392
wxGlade 392
wxPython
  URL 392

Made in the USA
Monee, IL
10 June 2021